T0294060

THROUGH ADVERSITY

THROUGH ADVERSITY

THE STORY OF LIFE IN THE RFC AND RAF THROUGH THREE OPERATIONAL PILOTS

ALASTAIR GOODRUM

AMBERLEY

First published 2020

Amberley Publishing
The Hill, Stroud
Gloucestershire, GL5 4EP

www.amberley-books.com

Copyright © Alastair Goodrum, 2020

The right of Alastair Goodrum to be identified
as the Author of this work has been asserted
in accordance with the Copyrights, Designs
and Patents Act 1988.

ISBN 978 1 4456 9545 7 (hardback)
ISBN 978 1 4456 9546 4 (ebook)

British Library Cataloguing in Publication Data.
A catalogue record for this book is available
from the British Library.

Typesetting by Aura Technology and Software
Services, India. Printed in the UK.

CONTENTS

Part 1

THE PIONEER AVIATOR, 1912–1919

Major Leonard Dawes MID*, Legion of Honour (French),
RFC. Nos. 2, 15, 29 & 41 Squadrons

FLEDGLING PILOTS

As an intrepid young lieutenant in the embryo British flying service, Lt Leonard Dawes, Middlesex Regiment and Royal Flying Corps (RFC), caused quite a stir one day in 1913 when, at the controls of his BE 2a biplane, he unexpectedly dropped in near his Lincolnshire home for afternoon tea and a hot bath! It brought home (literally) the fragility of flight and we shall read more of that incident later.

Leonard was born on 20 July 1885, the third son of four to his parents Mr Edwin Dawes JP (Justice of the Peace) and Mrs Kate Dawes of Sutton House, Long Sutton, Lincolnshire, where Leonard lived until joining the Army in 1905. He attended the Royal Military Academy Sandhurst during that year. On completion of his training, he was posted to the Middlesex (Duke of Cambridge's Own) Regiment in which he rose to the rank of Captain (Capt) with the post of assistant adjutant of the regiment. It was, however, during 1912 that he decided the path of his future military career lay with the Army Air Battalion and he therefore took steps to learn to fly, in order to be able to apply for a transfer from his regiment to the new flying service. The story that follows relates how Leonard became one of the very first intrepid birdmen of the Royal Flying Corps and the 'home visit' mentioned above, being in part the result of an engine failure, serves to remind us just how fragile a career in aviation was in those far off days.

At this juncture it will be helpful to take a brief look at the organisation of flying training in Britain during this formative period since it will help to demonstrate how significant were the changes to the development of military flying in Britain that occurred from 1912.

Under the auspices of the Fédération Aéronautique Internationale (FAI) which from 1905 had governed aviation matters internationally, it was on 8 March 1910 that the Royal Aeronautical Club (RAeC) of the United Kingdom, as the officially recognised regulating body for aviation activity in the UK, began to issue certificates that formally recognised a person's satisfactory completion of a supervised practical flying test taken in Britain. This flying certificate – sometimes referred to as a 'ticket' – took the form of a pocket-sized fold of cloth-covered card containing the photograph of the holder, his sequential qualification number and his signature. The qualification test, observed from the ground by two experienced and certificated pilots, only required the barest evidence that the would-be pilot could take off, handle his aircraft in ideal conditions and return to earth – without killing himself, or anyone else! This required the would-be pilot to complete three separate flights around a 5-kilometre closed-circuit course. Each flight had to be ended with the engine switched off (what became known as a 'dead-stick' landing) either at, or just prior to, touch-down and the landing thus made was to be within 150 metres of a point previously announced by the candidate prior to take off.

The tests were subject to slight changes from time to time and, for example, between February 1911 and December 1913, the period in which Leonard Dawes took his test, the aviator's standard certification was slightly modified to include the following components:

1. Candidates must accomplish the three following tests:
   A. Two separate distance flights of at least five kilometres (3.1 miles) each, in a closed circular course, distance to be measured as set out below.
   B. One altitude flight, consisting of a minimum height of 50 metres (164 feet), which may form part of one of the two distance flights.
2. The course on which the aviator accomplishes tests 'A' must be marked by two posts situated not more than 500 metres (547 yards) apart.
3. After each turn round one of the posts, the aviator must reverse direction when going round the second post, so that the circuit will consist of an un-interrupted series of five figures-of-eight [i.e. no intermediate landings].
4. The distance flown shall be reckoned as if in a straight line from post to post.
5. The method of alighting [landing] for each of the flights shall be with the motor stopped at or before the moment of touching the ground and the aeroplane must come to a halt within the distance of 50 metres (164 feet) from a point

indicated previously by the candidate. The landing must be made under normal conditions and the officials must report the manner in which it was effected.

6. Each flight must be vouched for in writing by officials appointed by the RAeC. All tests to be under the control of and at places agreed to by the RAeC.

7. All flights to be made between sunrise and sunset and suitable notice to be given to the RAeC.

The test was amended again in January 1914 when the altitude element was increased to 100 metres and from which height the aeroplane was to be landed 'dead-stick', i.e., with the engine switched off. This altitude exercise had to be a separate, third, flight. As time passed and aeroplane and engine technology advanced, the military air services gradually introduced their own training organisations, methods and certification standards and from August 1916 onwards, military pilots in the UK were no longer required to obtain the RAeC certificate as a preliminary step.

In 1911 the RAeC introduced an 'advanced' but optional version of their certification test that included a long-distance cross-country flight (for example from Farnborough to Salisbury Plain and back) with official observers *en route*. This was brought in mainly to cover racing and public display events whose participants had to demonstrate they had a somewhat higher level of flying competence than the requirements of the standard certificate. As time passed, in an effort to give their certificate more substance and credibility, the flying qualification test thus became increasingly more demanding of both men and machines but when Leonard

Dawes learned to fly in 1912, the tests mentioned earlier were the rules by which he was examined.

Being in its infancy, initially many of the pilots joining the recently created RFC were products of courses run by civilian flying schools to RAeC standard. This situation applies to Leonard Dawes, who learned to fly at his own expense at the Bristol Aeroplane Company's school at Larkhill on Salisbury Plain while still serving in the army. To give some idea of the scale of flying training in the UK: in the four-and-a-half years from the commencement of the flying certification scheme to the outbreak of the war in August 1914, a total of 881 flying certificates were awarded by the RAeC. Of these, 492 were awarded to military personnel, of whom 352 were serving with the Army and 140 with the Royal Navy or Royal Marines. With all these certificates around it might suggest the RFC would be very well supplied with pilots – but this is not the case. It should be borne in mind that possession of a certificate indicated only a very basic level of flying ability and many soldiers did not seek transfers to the RFC. Even if they had done so, the air service was neither equipped with sufficient aeroplanes, instructors nor facilities to handle more than a very small intake at a time.

Flying training in the RFC was the role of the Central Flying School (CFS) at Upavon on Salisbury Plain and its key objective was *not* to produce pilots *per se*, but *professional war pilots*. To this end, the CFS began consecutive courses of four months duration and only managed to fit in five of these up to the outbreak of the First World War. Out of these five courses, some candidates were taken in for training from scratch (known as *ab initio*) and thus initially only progressed to basic

RAeC standard, while others – such as Leonard Dawes, who had already reached that standard – went through the more advanced War Pilot syllabus and emerged to be awarded with their RFC 'Wings'. Statistics about this important distinction are somewhat confusing, but there is an indication that by the start of the war only fifty-two pilots had been trained by CFS to Wings standard – and Leonard Dawes was one of these elite few. His story, therefore, provides us with a good example of the approach to military flying being taken at that time in the formative years of British aviation and in his own way, he can be seen as playing a small but valuable part in laying the foundation of military flying in Great Britain. It will also be useful now to take a look in a little more detail at how military aviation was evolving during the period when Leonard first became involved.

In 1910, Prime Minister Herbert Asquith asked the Imperial Defence Committee to examine the potential role of aviation, in military and naval terms, to Great Britain, with a view to proposing how to create an effective air force. The committee duly recommended that a British military air force should be formed but the government's penny-pinching and generally lacklustre attitude towards this relatively new phenomenon indicated it was, as yet, not entirely convinced that flying had any real military value. It was quite content to let private civilian effort and money – rather than taxpayer's – be spent on building aeroplanes and learning how to fly them. However, from early-1911, the Royal Navy (on 1 March) and the Army (on 1 April) by allocating ridiculously small amounts from their massive armament budgets had acknowledged that in view of the comparatively vast sums being allocated to aviation by rival

countries in Europe, some positive gesture should be made –
so they created their own quite separate flying organisations *viz*:
the Army's Air Battalion of the Royal Engineers and the Naval
Flying Section – the former with seven officers and the latter
with even less, just four officers!

The War Office then announced that serving army officers
wishing to take up a military flying career were free to have
themselves trained as pilots at civilian schools at their own
expense and that those who successfully obtained the RAeC
flying certificate would be granted the sum of £75 (equivalent
to about £8,500 in 2019) towards their expenses and receive
a posting to the Air Battalion. In the case of the Navy, its first
applicants not only had to foot the bill for their instruction
but must also be unmarried – which did rather point to
it being a perilous occupation. All this from the world's
wealthiest power!

Fortunately, it was not long before the rapid rate at which
France and Germany were spending money and making
progress on aviation matters brought the British War Office
and the government of the day to their senses. There was a
major rethink of aviation strategy and one outcome was a
Royal Warrant, issued on 13 April 1912 and implemented
from 13 May that year, which combined the whole of the
British military and naval aeronautical services into a new
autonomous entity called the Royal Flying Corps. In overall
command of the RFC was Brigadier General David Henderson
(later Lt Gen Sir David KCB KCVO DSO) who had obtained
his pilot licence in 1911 and was a leading figure on the
committee that helped to create the RFC. Henderson's key
role in the creation of a British air force is often unfairly

overshadowed by the attention paid to Hugh Trenchard. At its inception, the Corps comprised five sections:

1. Military Wing (directed by the War Office and commanded by Major Frederick Sykes). This component retained the title Royal Flying Corps (RFC) when the Naval Wing was subsequently hived off by the Royal Navy and named the Royal Naval Air Service (RNAS).

2. Naval Wing (directed by the Admiralty and commanded by Commander Charles Samson). This component evolved into the RNAS when the Royal Navy exerted pressure for more direct control in 1914.

3. Reserve: All Royal Naval Reserve (RNR) or Military Wing Reserve flyers must accept an obligation of service in any branch of the RFC in time of war. Those designated as on '1st Reserve' must complete not less than nine hours flying during each three-month period (quarter), including one cross-country flight of not less than one-hour duration. Also, to make one obligatory flight at an RFC or civilian flying school once per quarter. In return for this commitment a retainer of £50 per annum will be paid. Those flyers holding an RAeC certificate and designated as on '2nd Reserve' had no obligation to fly but should make themselves available for service in the RFC in time of war.

4. Central Flying School (CFS). The RFC's flying and ground training school, commanded by Captain Godfrey Paine RN. Formed out of the old Army Air Battalion based at Upavon on Salisbury Plain and operated as a joint Army and Navy facility.

5. Royal Aircraft Factory, Farnborough. Superintendent, Mr Mervyn Gorman. An aircraft design, build and repair facility.

It was clear that the supply of pilots was of prime importance in laying firm foundations for the RFC but it was also recognised that these airmen must be thoroughly trained, in a manner consistent with the potential demands on a national military aviation arm that was a tool of a government striding the world stage. This meant that pilots in the RFC should not merely be those who had managed to pass for their 'tickets' yet who may never have flown much beyond the boundaries of an aerodrome before or since. In other words, it became clear that possession of a 'ticket' did not mean the RFC would automatically consider a person could actually fly to its standards unless and until that person had undergone a programme of 'continuation' or 'advanced' training. The original outline plan for the RFC required that naval officers selected for service with the RFC would, in general – but not exclusively – undertake their basic flying training at the RFC Central Flying School (some flying tuition was conducted at RN Air Station Eastchurch).

In contrast, Army officers would, in general but also not exclusively, be required to take basic training at a civilian flying school before joining the Central Flying School. As the CFS expanded, this situation gradually changed, until the vast demands of the future war brought specialist service flying training schools into being. In these peacetime early days though, it was only upon satisfactory completion of their Central Flying School course that officers and other ranks from both services would either be (1) appointed for 'continuous service' with the RFC; (2) join the staff of CFS or (3) be placed on the RFC Reserve. The period of service for those officers who were appointed to continuous service or to the staff of CFS was initially a four-year engagement, with re-engagement on an annual basis thereafter.

Naturally the government did not wish to discourage civilian flying schools – not least because they were then the primary source of flying instruction for both civil and military personnel and composed a rapidly growing entrepreneurial activity in their own right – so it made a pragmatic arrangement with these schools and any person wishing to join the RFC as a pilot. This, in essence, was that any serving army or naval officer or a civilian wishing to take up a commission in the RFC should first learn the rudiments of flying at a civilian school, obtain an RAeC flying certificate there then, upon joining the RFC, in either the Military or Naval Wing, would attend the CFS to be taught and examined under a standardised ground and air programme: 'in order to maintain a universal standard of merit throughout all branches of the RFC.'

The Central Flying School was formed at Upavon on 12 May 1912 and officially opened on 19 June 1912. Its intended role was to provide, in a four-month course, ground instruction in theory of flight, aircraft and engine maintenance, meteorology, navigation, photography, and signalling, in addition, of course, to more flying tuition. After about a year though, the actual course structure had been slightly modified and the course duration reduced to roughly thirteen weeks, with an option of additional time for individuals if felt desirable, or indeed for the whole course if, for example, progress had been hampered by spells of poor weather.

In view of the staff numbers mentioned below, it was rather optimistically intended that by running three courses a year, 90 Army and 40 Navy pilots, plus a 'contingency' of 25 per cent, a total of around 165 service pupils – 50 per cent of whom would be non-commissioned – would pass through CFS annually.

There was also a provision for up to 15 civilian pilots (i.e. having an RAeC pilot licence but not already in the armed forces) to attend CFS in a type of 'direct entry' option. As previously mentioned, CFS's stated primary aim was not to produce aviators *per se*, but to turn out professional war pilots and having obtained their pilots certificate in order to qualify for the CFS course, these students were then taught to fly all the aeroplane types at the School and acquire skills in technical subjects.

First commandant of the School was Captain Godfrey Paine (RN) (later Rear Admiral/Air Vice Marshal (AVM) Sir Godfrey) and his staff comprised 5 flying instructor officers, 7 ground instructor officers and administrators; 54 non-commissioned for flying, technical and administration posts, plus other ranks and 20 civilians in assorted technical or labouring posts. The initial complement of 7 aircraft comprised 2 Avro, 2 Short, 1 Bristol, 1 Maurice Farman and 1 Henri Farman. It was on 17 August 1912 that 17 student pilots from the Army and Navy attended the first CFS course, being accommodated on and off the site in a rather makeshift manner and taking their ground instruction sessions in a hotchpotch of tents and buildings. Flying ability and ground training was assessed by various practical and theoretical examinations set at the end of the course.

Thus it was, with all its many fragilities, that the future of British military flying training was laid down, but the Central Flying School has gone on from these humble beginnings to acquire along the way a world-class reputation for excellence that has endured into the modern era. This, then, is the organisation into which Lt Leonard Dawes moved in 1912.

While remaining an officer in the Middlesex Regiment, Leonard Dawes had received his own first elementary flying instruction at the civilian Bristol School, which was also located on the wilds of Salisbury Plain. Forsaking his Army uniform for a period in 'mufti', in late April he presented himself at the civilian school. As indicated above, in the four-and-a-half years leading up to the start of the First World War, of the 881 RAeC certificates issued, 492 were awarded to officers and airmen of the Army and Navy and 389 to civilian pilots. Of those 881 pilots, 664 were trained at 28 civilian flying training schools with the 2 Bristol Schools accounting for a total of 309 (Brooklands: 182 and Salisbury Plain: 127). The Bristol School therefore accounted for the largest number of pilots trained and could justifiably regard itself as the leading civilian flying training establishment of its day. A further 153 pilots were trained *ab initio* at CFS on Salisbury Plain and the balance of 64 is believed to include those who acquired training on a squadron or overseas.

Monday morning, 29 April, dawned calm and bright and in the early light, Monsieur (Mons) Henri Jullerot, the chief instructor of the Bristol Company Flying School and one of the best-known French pilots of the day, began the week's work by twice taking up Lt Pickles in Boxkite 55. This was followed by Mr Bendall taking Mr Lindsay Campbell up for a couple of lessons. The Italian pupil, Lt Antonini, had reached solo standard and was sent off for a cross-country flight to Salisbury and back, in the Bristol Monoplane, with his countryman Lt Ercole as passenger. Other pupils – Jennings, Smith-Barry and Lt Wyness-Stuart – practised solo on the tractor biplanes and polished up their ground-taxying skills, while Capt (later Lt Col) Robert Harry Lucas Cordner of the Royal Army Medical Corps went up in No. 43 for his first solo.

After a briefing about the course, dealing with paperwork and being shown around the School, Leonard had the opportunity to watch intently some of the exciting flying activity on this typically busy day.

Leonard's big moment came the next day, Tuesday 30 April 1912, when he was taken up for his first flight by Mr Charles Howard Pixton, one of the Bristol School instructors, in a Bristol Boxkite bearing the maker's serial, either 43 or 55 – both of these two-seaters were in use at the School at this time. This first flight could not be followed up because the wind increased and put paid to any further instructional flights that morning. However, the wind dropped a little during the afternoon so that Capt Raymond Hamilton-Grace and Lt Allan Hartree could make solo flights in No. 55. The wind also died down sufficiently for Leonard Dawes and a number of fellow pupils – Mr Campbell and Lts Walls, Pickles and Bertie Fisher (later Lieutenant General Sir Bertie, KCB CMG DSO) – in turn to receive flying instruction, this time in a Bristol-Prier two-seat monoplane, from Mons Jullerot.

Henri Marie Jullerot was in charge of the Bristol flying schools at Larkhill and Brooklands for four years and can rightly be regarded, therefore, as being responsible for training more pre-First World War pilots than anyone else. Upon the outbreak of war, he returned to France to enlist in the French air service but came back to England to be commissioned into the Royal Naval Volunteer Reserve (RNVR) in May 1915. Despite his undoubted skill as a pilot, at first he undertook work as an air observer before finally being selected as a pilot and posted to the RNAS in 1916, with which he spent the rest of the war as a ground instructor.

On Wednesday 1 May, Pixton separately took up Lt Pickles and an Australian civilian pupil Mr Charles Lindsay Campbell in Boxkite 55. When they had finished, Leonard Dawes and the Italian Lt Rinaldi also underwent dual instruction with another Bristol School instructor, Mr William Bendall, (an unfortunate name for a flying instructor to be blessed with?) on the same machine. Capt Hamilton-Grace managed two solo flights on No. 55. On this day, too, Lt Allan Hartree (later Major, MC) of the Royal Field Artillery, made a great leap when, after a mere two previous solo flights, took his flying test in front of RAeC observers Lts Conner and Reynolds. Hartree passed 'with flying colours' having done some fine figures-of-eight; climbed to almost 1,000 feet and rounding it all off with a very slick engine-off landing to earn himself Certificate No. 214.

Next day, Thursday 2 May, in the morning flying was again out of the question due to the strength of the wind but it gradually died down during the afternoon and by evening was calm enough to allow some pupils to go up again. Jullerot took up Mr Lindsay Campbell (who lost his life in an aero accident later that year) in one of the School's Bristol Monoplanes while Howard Pixton gave instruction to Lts Dawes and Pickles and a new pupil, Major Lionel Boyd Moss, in another Monoplane.

Friday 3 May was the best day of that week for flying. Mons Jullerot went up first with Major Moss, then Mr Pixton went up with Lt Pickles and Mr Campbell. Much of the day was given to those pupils who had already gone solo, with Lt Ercole Ercole (Italian Army – and yes, he had both names) flying a Bristol-Prier Monoplane; Lt Hall and Mr Montague Jennings each went up solo in what was described as a 'tractor biplane', which is believed to refer to the Bristol-Gordon England (GE) design;

Lt Athole Wyness-Stuart also went up, first in a tractor biplane then off again in one of the Monoplanes. Capt Raymond Sheffield Hamilton-Grace flew solo in Boxkite 55 and was reported as reaching the dizzying altitude of 800 feet over the nearby Cavalry Barracks. Awarded his certificate, No. 327, on 15 October 1912, Hamilton-Grace returned to his regiment, 13th Hussars, in which he served with distinction during the First World War. Promoted to Major he was killed in action with his regiment on the Western Front on 4 August 1915.

Flying went on into that evening, with Mr Pixton taking up Lt Pickles and Mr Campbell. Mr Campbell managed another trip with Mr Bendall in Bristol Biplane Type T, '42' (a two-seater with some similarity to the Maurice Farman S7 Longhorn design) and the latter also took up Leonard Dawes later, in the same aircraft. That balmy evening also saw Jullerot going up in a Bristol Monoplane to give Major Moss some tuition. More flights were made by the solo pupils; Mr Jennings and Lt Hall in single-seaters and Mr Robert Smith-Barry, who reached no less than 1,000 feet altitude and did 'a clever *vol-plane* [gliding/engine-off] landing.' Smith-Barry later served in the RFC and in 1916 achieved lasting fame by devising what became known as the 'Gosport' system of standardised flying training for the RFC, which became so successful that it was adopted by air forces across the world.

Lt Ashton was airborne for about 10 minutes in a Bristol Monoplane, reaching a height of 450 feet before he landed. Lt Ercole, also in a Bristol Monoplane ventured out over the local countryside and landed back safely before a good day's flying was brought to a close with Lt Wyness-Stuart going up solo for a short flight to end the day's proceedings (Wyness-Stuart died in an air crash on 6 September 1912). Saturday 4 May started off foggy but it cleared sufficiently enough to allow Mr Bendall to take Leonard Dawes up for some tuition before the weather closed in again and stopped any further work. It was Tuesday 7 May before Leonard was able to have more tuition with Mr Pixton and he was fortunate to do so because the wind was described as 'tricky' and when they landed flying was scrubbed for the rest of that day.

Despite Salisbury Plain being wide open to gusty wind conditions (most people in the new air service, for example, never really understood why on earth someone chose to locate the CFS in the middle of Salisbury Plain, one of the most windy and inhospitable places in that part of the country) that frequently inhibited the continuity of training, by 8 May Leonard Dawes had progressed well enough to make his landmark first solo flight, believed to be on Boxkite 55 – indeed he made two solo flights that same day. Next day Mr Pixton took up Lts Dawes and Pickles and Major Moss for some more dual instruction but there was no more flying until the next Saturday due to bad weather.

There is no record of any flying by Leonard during the following week but after putting in some more solo practice in the days leading up to 29 May, the great day finally came for him on Thursday 30 May 1912. Under the beady eyes of his two examiners, Capt Eustace Loraine and Lt Fielding of the RFC, Leonard successfully completed the solo tests for his certificate on Bristol Boxkite 55, in the process known as 'receiving his ticket'. He was awarded Royal Aero Club aviator's certificate number 228, dated 4 June 1912. Just one month later, on 5 July, there was a tragic reminder of just what Leonard Dawes and his fellow aviators were letting themselves in for when one of his examiners, the experienced Capt Loraine, was killed in the RFC's first fatal air crash.

Of Leonard Dawes' activities between receiving his RAeC certificate to fly in June 1912 and his transfer from his regiment to the RFC when he joined 2 Squadron at the end of that year, there is little information. The latter unit was formed at (South) Farnborough – regarded as the home of British aviation – on 13 May 1912, and No. 2 proudly claims to be the first RFC squadron to fly aeroplanes. However, it is reasonable to assume that it took Leonard a little while to submit his formal application to the RFC and then to relinquish his regimental duties, but there is a good reference point, noted in 2 Squadron's records, when he is recorded as making a 15-minute dual flight with Lt Philip Herbert on Maurice Farman S7 Longhorn, RFC serial number 215, on 7 January 1913 at South Farnborough. Lt Philip Lee William Herbert (later Air Commodore (Air Cdre), CMG CBE) is known to have been serving with 2 Squadron at this date and the aircraft serial 215 is in the block of numbers allotted to 2 Squadron; so it is reasonable to presume that Leonard Dawes had joined the squadron possibly during December 1912. Other aircraft noted in use by 2 Squadron at South Farnborough at this time are: Breguet G3 biplane Nos.210 and 211 and Breguet L2 213.

It is also not unusual to find Leonard undergoing tuition with 2 Squadron rather than at CFS, since it is also recorded that because the new CFS training programme had taken quite some time to devise and implement and also suffered from limited accommodation – both in terms of course places and housing – the RFC authorised some elementary ground and air training to take place at Wing level, i.e. on the squadrons, to ease pressure on the embryo CFS. Squadrons were ordered to record the nature and extent of such training then, as vacancies became available, these airmen were sent to CFS to complete their training and take tests and examinations.

The first CFS course ran from 17 August to 19 December 1912, with just 17 students – although it was reported that there were well over 100 pilot recruits awaiting a place at CFS. There was a short gap before the next course began in order to allow aircraft to be overhauled and staff to take leave. For the reasons suggested above, Leonard Dawes did not attend the first course and the second course had not begun by the time he was posted to 2 Squadron – with whom he received some elementary tuition while presumably waiting for that second CFS course to commence. Contained within a report in *Flight* Magazine dated 25 January 1913 can be found evidence that the second course got under way on 17 January.

> A large number of pupils having finished their course at CFS ... another dozen naval officers were transferred from HMS *Acteon*, parent ship [actually a shore establishment or 'stone frigate'] of the RFC Naval Wing, to CFS on the 17th inst.

Leonard Dawes, having benefitted from the experienced members of 2 Squadron during January 1913, then found himself deprived of that facility by the War Office's decision to re-locate 2 Squadron from Farnborough to Montrose in Scotland. This resulted in the most experienced pilots and ground staff moving up north in February 1913 and as we shall see below, this seems to mark the point at which Leonard Dawes began his own obligatory period at CFS, as a member of its No. 2 course.

At this time, subjects covered in the CFS syllabus were: flying, general principles of mechanics relating to aeroplanes and engines, meteorology, observation from the air, navigation and steering by compass when flying, cross-country flights, signalling by all methods, and recognition of warships types. In addition, the construction, erection and rigging of aeroplanes was studied and the stripping, assembly and tuning of aero engines was taught. According to the RFC:

> The standard being aimed at – in addition to that of flying – is that an officer, upon completion of his course, should be capable in all respects to keep an aeroplane and its engine in thorough good order and condition.

The first firm indication that Leonard is actually at CFS – and indeed becoming a contemporary of future RFC and RAF high-ranking officers – comes in a report of its activities on 5 February 1913. On a typically busy – and windy – day, staff instructor Capt John Maitland Salmond (later Marshal of the RAF (MRAF), Sir John, GCB CMG CVO DSO*) made a check flight round the circuit in a dual-control Royal Aircraft Factory BE4, 417, then took up student Capt Alister MacDonnell for 32 minutes, followed by Leonard Dawes for 12 minutes in the same aircraft. Other aircraft noted at CFS at this time include an eclectic mix of: BE4 416; Short 'School' Biplane 401; Maurice Farman S7 Longhorn Nos.411, 418, 420; Avro 500 Type E, Nos. 404 and 406, confirming that the '400' series was initially allotted to aircraft allocated to the CFS. It is also interesting to note that Capt John Salmond was a member of the first CFS course and upon completion, he was retained as an instructor.

Another prominent person associated from the outset with the CFS was Major Hugh Montague Trenchard (RAeC certificate 270; later Marshal of the RAF Lord Trenchard and widely regarded as the 'Father of the RAF') who had been posted in as senior staff officer with responsibility for the preparation, conduct and marking of examinations. It was during his time in this administrative post that both he – and indeed Captain Paine the commandant – received further flying tuition on the second course in order to qualify for their RFC wings – but let's not forget that Hugh Trenchard was, of course, the man in charge of examinations!

From these examples and others below, it will be clear that CFS staff, even though in possession of RAeC certificates were, irrespective of rank and without exception or dispensation, required to undertake and complete satisfactorily their own CFS course as a compulsory condition of their posting to the School. It is worthy of note that the *London Gazette* later that year announced that both Salmond and Trenchard received promotions which indicated they were definitely on their way to the top echelons of the RAF. With effect from 31 May 1913, Capt John Salmond (King's Own Royal Lancaster Regiment), an instructor at CFS, was re-graded from flight commander to squadron commander; while with effect from 3 September 1913, Major Hugh Trenchard DSO (Royal Scots Fusiliers), relinquished the post of 'instructor' at CFS and was appointed assistant commandant of the CFS with the grade of squadron commander.

In mid-February three day's flying in a row were lost due to high winds but by afternoon on Friday the 21st, the wind abated sufficiently for CFS to put in some intensive flying before nightfall in an effort to make up lost time, particularly for those pilots who were anxious to increase their solo experience. Capt Fulton and Lts Francis G. Small, Cecil Marks and Henry de Grey Warter and Sub-Lt Hugh Alexander Littleton (RNVR; later DSO) flew some solo circuits and bumps in Avro 404 and 406, then Capt Salmond took up Leonard Dawes for an 11-minute dual flight in BE 417. More solo circuits of 10–20 minutes were made by Lt Arthur Soames and Sub-Lt Arthur Bigsworth (RNR). Maurice Farman aircraft Nos.403, 418 and 425 were variously flown solo for similar durations by Capts John Salmond and Frederick Tucker and Lt The Hon John Boyle (later Air Cdre), Sub-Lt Reginald Lennox George Marix (RNVR) (later AVM, CB DSO), Lt Arthur Longmore (RN) (later Air Chief Marshal (ACM) Sir Arthur), Lt Frederick William Bowhill (RN) and Lts Hugh Glanville and Edward Harvey. Lt Douglas Arthur Oliver (RN) made two flights of 20 and 9 minutes in Short 'School' biplane 401, while Lt Norman Roupell managed to stay aloft for a lengthy 40 minutes in Short biplane 402. Lt Bowhill made a distinguished career in the RFC/RAF during both world wars, retiring as ACM Sir Frederick GBE KCB CMG DSO*, while Douglas Oliver also made his own mark in the First World War as a Squadron Commander (Sqn Cdr) in charge of RNAS station Great Yarmouth, where he was awarded a DSO for gallantry in action.

Saturday, 22nd, saw a very busy flying programme, too, with nearly every CFS aircraft getting airborne during the morning. Capt Fulton took up Air Mechanic William Harrison as a passenger in Avro 404 to give him half-an-hour's gentle air experience. Lt Felton Vesey Holt (brevet 312; later AVM, CMG DSO) and Lts Marks and Warter used Avro 406 to practise circuits, then handed it over to Air Mechanic First Class Victor Colin Higginbottom who first took up Air Mechanic Harrison again and showed him some circuits and landings, after which Higginbottom gave 40 minutes dual tuition to Leading Seaman Marchant. Higginbottom, RAeC 317, transferred from the Royal Engineers to CFS, where he learned to fly in October 1912. He was retained as an instructor until joining 2 Squadron on active flying service when it went to France in 1914.

Capt Salmond gave instruction to Lt MacDonnell in BE 416 while Lt Desmond Arthur had a 15-minute flight in BE 417, which he managed to coax to the awesome height of 3,000 feet. Bigsworth went up for 10 minutes solo; Farman 418 was flown solo by Capt Tucker and then Lt Ernest Unwin; Farman 411 was used by Lt Longmore (RN) to give instruction to Air Mechanic 1st Class Joseph Charles McNamara (later 2/Lt; KIA 2 June 1917), Leading Seaman Philip Bateman (RN) and Sergeant (Sgt) Edward Street and after Capt Salmond made a couple of short test flights in Farman 425, Lts Eric Lewis Conran (RFC), Robert Peel Ross (RN; later Air Cdre, DSO AFC), James Kennedy (RN), Boyle, Marix, and Harvey (all RFC) made solo circuits. The Short Biplane 401 was used by Lts Oliver and Roupell each of whom made several circuits of up to half-an-hour duration. This extremely busy day was brought to a satisfactory close with the arrival from Farnborough of Major Eugene Gerrard, an instructor and 'C' Flight Commander at CFS, flying Short Tractor Biplane 423.

February over Salisbury Plain ended with strong winds that also brought March in like the proverbial lion and flying was scrubbed on many days. With a limited number of aeroplanes all being hotly pursued by everyone in order to get their flying hours up, Leonard Dawes had to wait several days before his turn came again. On Wednesday 26 February 1913 the wind had died down sufficiently prompting an intense flying training day to get the course programme back on track.

Lt Warter twice took up Avro 404; Lts Littleton, Small, Holt and Marks all made solo circuits lasting up to half-an-hour each. Major Fulton gave some dual tuition to Lts Rathbone and Read in Avro 406 before both airmen flew solo circuits. Air Mechanic Higginbottom was again giving dual tuition to Leading Seaman Marchant. Capt Salmond checked out BE 416, then Lts Soames, Burroughs and Arthur each took it up for yet more circuits. Then came Leonard Dawes' turn when he was airborne for 20 minutes dual with Capt Salmond. This was followed by Lieutenant Colonel (Lt Col) Henry Cook (an instructor and deputy commandant of CFS) and Lts Bigsworth, Soames, Burroughs and MacDonnell each flying BE 417 while Lt Longmore gave tuition to Captain G. W. Vivian (RN) and Leading Seaman Bateman on Maurice Farman 411. Sergeant William Stafford managed to complete five solo 'rollers' in his 40 minute spell in Farman 403 after which Capt Ernest Lithgow (a medical man, late of the RAMC and father of M. J. 'Mike' Lithgow, the renowned post-Second World War test pilot), Lts Kennedy, R. P. Ross and Assistant Paymaster John Lidderdale (RN) (the administrative secretary of CFS) and Air Mechanic Reginald Collis each went up for short flights on the same aircraft.

Farman 428 was also well used, first by Capt Salmond to give instruction to Lts Soames, Arthur and Vernon then for solo flights by Lts Smith-Barry and Burroughs. Finally, Major Gerrard took up Capt MacDonnell for a circuit in Short Biplane 401 and when they landed Lt Oliver flew it solo for 15 minutes to bring the busy day to a close.

In ideal flying weather, the next day, Thursday 27th, was almost as busy but Leonard Dawes had to wait until Friday 28th before he could get airborne again. BE 416 was kept busy with Capt MacDonnell taking it up solo for several full-stop circuits and landings, followed by Lt Burroughs who was aloft for 15 minutes. Capt Salmond then took over to give Leonard Dawes and Lt Thompson half-an-hour's dual instruction each. Salmond's next two instructional flights were one of 45 minutes with Major Trenchard and a little later, 30 minutes with Captain Paine. Several long-duration flights of about an hour each were made on M Farman 411 and 425 and many more, shorter, circuits were completed before the day's programme closed. Flying training continued on Saturday but high winds caused the abandonment of any flying on Monday 3 March. After this date Leonard's name does not appear in any more CFS diary reports, all of which tend to detail only flying activity and indicate he may have spent the remainder of the course on ground school activities and his final examinations.

It was confirmed in a government White Paper published in August 1913 that CFS course duration had been reduced to thirteen weeks (from four to three months). This would tie up with the date for the completion of the second CFS course being on or about 17 April 1913, since it was announced in the *London Gazette* that Lt Leonard Dawes – and several other pilots noted above at CFS with him – was appointed as a 'flying officer' and officially seconded from the Army to the RFC with effect from that date. He was now entitled to wear the coveted RFC pilot badge – he had earned his 'wings' and his posting to 2 Squadron was confirmed.

MONTROSE MANOEUVRES

The scene now moves to Montrose. Situated on the east coast of Scotland, just to the north of the Tay estuary, Montrose airfield – a large piece of ground at Upper Dysart Farm – was the daunting and remote destination for 2 Squadron, as it moved from Farnborough in what was the RFC's first major re-deployment exercise. The reason for Montrose being selected as an airfield base was that it was well-placed to offer aerial defence to the major Royal Navy installations at Rosyth to the south, where the Home Fleet battlecruisers were based, and Cromarty to the north, where escort destroyers for the fleet were based. These were thought to represent juicy targets for the already growing German Zeppelin force in time of war. The squadron commander, Major Charles Burke, considered the Upper Dysart site, about 3 miles south of Montrose, was less than satisfactory and took steps to relocate the squadron to Broomfield Farm, about 1 mile north of the town.

Hangars were erected at Broomfield in December 1913 and the squadron moved in during January 1914. Charles James

Burke (seconded from Royal Irish Regiment) was promoted to Major upon appointment as officer commanding 2 Squadron on 13 May 1912 and should not be confused with the similarly named Captain John Harold Whitworth Becke (seconded from Sherwood Foresters), who served as a flight commander under Major Burke before also being appointed officer commanding 2 on 2 June 1915. Surname similarities are a constant pitfall for a researcher, as we shall see later with Leonard Dawes, too.

With its main aeroplane equipment being the Royal Aircraft Factory BE 2a, it was hoped to fly the first aeroplanes north from Farnborough during mid-January 1913 but bad weather prevented long-distance flights. The refurbishment of Panmure Barracks that were to provide accommodation for personnel was not yet completed either. All was ready early next month though and in the first stage of this deployment, five airmen began the 450-mile air journey to Montrose (Dysart) on Thursday 13 February. These were: Capts John Becke (BE 2a), Charles Longcroft (BE 2a) and George Dawes and Lts Francis Waldron and Philip Herbert (the latter three each in a Maurice Farman S7 Longhorn biplane). Even now, all did not go according to plan due to some adverse weather. The first stop should have been at Towcester but due to running into fog, three pilots were obliged to land at Reading while the other two turned back to Farnborough. A second attempt was made on Monday 17th. This time Becke set out from Farnborough and made it to Towcester. Waldron also set off from Farnborough landed at Port Meadow, Oxford and Longcroft, who took off from Reading also made it as far as Oxford. George Dawes flew to Banbury and Philip Herbert managed to each Moreton-in-Marsh, both men starting from Reading.

These were not great leaps and so, with a few mishaps *en route*, it took nine flying days spread over a thirteen-day period for all five aircraft to make the transit to the landing ground at Upper Dysart, which was achieved on 26 February. Shortly after that date they were joined by non-commissioned and other officer pilots, ground crew and administrative staff who travelled north in a road convoy from Farnborough. The pilots were most anxious to become familiar with the surrounding countryside and by the second week of April they were all making regular reconnaissance flights over eastern Scotland. For example, the Caledonian railway line about 30 miles from Montrose, was being re-sleepered and the pilots used this to practise aerial observation of the work from various altitudes.

During May 1913 three BE 2a aeroplanes were collected from the Royal Aircraft Factory in Farnborough and flown north to Montrose (Dysart) but shortly after arrival, due to a poor-quality repair by the factory, one of these broke up in the air and crashed, killing its pilot and giving the squadron its first casualty. Lt Desmond Arthur was detailed to fly a practice reconnaissance flight from Dysart to the Lunan Bay area on 27 May. In the vicinity of Lunan railway station, the wing of his BE 2a, 205, was seen to crumple up and the aeroplane dived to the ground killing the pilot. It was later alleged that the structural failure was due to a poor repair made prior to BE 2a, 205, being flown to Scotland from Farnborough. Desmond Arthur was on the same CFS course as Leonard Dawes.

Again, there is an excellent reference point confirming Leonard's presence with 2 Squadron. He and many of the squadron members mentioned earlier can be placed there by means of a group photograph, taken, it is believed, at Panmure

Barracks in Montrose town in August 1913. In order to establish a clarity that is often overlooked, it is very important to point out here that 'our' Lt Leonard (L.) Dawes should in no way be confused with Capt George William Patrick (G. W. P.) Dawes. They were not related to each other but, rather confusingly, did indeed serve simultaneously in 2 Squadron.

There is further evidence of Leonard being based at Montrose by way of an interesting little social sidelight. On 3 July 1913, representing the RFC and led by Capt Frederick Tucker, 2 Squadron from Montrose fielded a mixed-ranks cricket team in a friendly match against Strathmore Cricket Club, held on the latter's magnificent ground in Forfar. Leonard was in the squadron team – he and Tucker had joined the squadron at the same time – and the local newspaper records him scoring 2 runs for his side. Strathmore CC batted first and made 73 runs with the RFC's bowler named Currier taking a creditable 5 wickets for 15. The RFC side, however, was no match for Strathmore's 'professional', a demon bowler named Page who took 5 wickets for just 8 runs, being backed up by his amateur colleague, J. A. Grant who took 5 for 27, the pair of them polishing off the airmen for a total of 50 runs and winning the game by a comfortable margin.

There were always aeroplane mishaps and unserviceability issues throughout the RFC and during mid-1913, for example, there were only about 4 aircraft at Montrose (Dysart) fit to fly at any one time. This figure represented just under half the number on the squadron's actual strength – a situation replicated throughout the RFC at that time – which was itself way below the 12 aircraft with 6 in reserve that the government had originally promised for each of 7 squadrons when the RFC was created. Apathy and under-funding, it seems, are not just modern ailments!

Conversely, Capt Charles Alexander Holcombe Longcroft (later AVM Sir Charles KCB CMG DSO AFC) who had been sent down to Farnborough to collect another new aircraft made, upon his return flight to Montrose (Dysart), a magnificent long-distance flight that spoke well of the reliability of the BE 2a. Setting off on 19 August with Lt Col Frederick Hugh Sykes (later AVM the Rt. Hon. Sir Frederick PC GCSI GCIE GBE KCB CMG MP) commandant of the RFC (Military Wing) as passenger, Charles Longcroft flew non-stop from Aldershot to Alnmouth, Northumberland at an average altitude of 1,500 feet, in 5½ hours. Having stopped for 2 hours to refuel and take a break, he pressed on to Montrose which he reached 2 hours later. Taking-off at 9.40 a.m., he had spent a total of 7 hours 40 minutes in the air and covered a total of 530 miles at an average speed of 70 mph. At that time, it was the longest recorded British flight made by a pilot with one passenger.

The world body governing the regulation of non-military aeronautics, the Fédération Aéronautique Internationale (FAI), founded in 1905, had recently decided to recognise cross-country distance records, irrespective of whether they were made in civil or military aeroplanes. To qualify for such a record, it was stipulated that the aeroplane must indeed carry a human passenger and not just an equivalent weight in ballast. Thus, Capt Longcroft's flight leg from Aldershot to Alnmouth, 287 miles non-stop, was validated by the FAI and RAeC as a British record. Charles Longcroft further secured his place in the annals of long-distance flying on 22 November 1913 when, in BE 2a, 218, specially modified with a 54-gallon fuel tank faired into the front cockpit, successfully completed a solo flight from Montrose to Farnborough, then on to Portsmouth before returning to Farnborough. This was all non-stop; a distance of 455 miles made in 7 hours and 20 minutes. It won him the accolade of the most meritorious flight of 1913 and led to him becoming the first of a long line of famous winners of the RAeC Britannia Trophy.

Further new horizons beckoned for Leonard Dawes when, on 27 August 1913, he was one of seven pilots from 2 Squadron making up the very first overseas deployment of the RFC from Montrose to Limerick in Ireland. Flying at 65 mph at 3,000 feet altitude he made a successful crossing of the Irish Sea in his BE 2a aeroplane, landing first at Dundalk where, watched by a crowd of 3,000 people – for whom it was the first ever sight of an aeroplane – he took off next morning for Rathbane, the final destination and location of the Army exercises in which 2 Squadron was to provide the air component for each of the two opposing forces. According to the *Irish Times*; in challenging flying conditions:

> The airmen of both sides were constantly in flight. The amount of information the observers in these machines were able to convey to their respective generals either directly or by means of messages dropped from dizzy heights to units of the force was most valuable. All the while the machines went steadily and fortunately without accident to their intrepid pilots and observers.

Some idea of the way in which the hazardous nature of flying in those days was viewed can be gained from the fact that it was also noted that Royal Army Medical Corps personnel attended all anticipated landings!

This large-scale exercise took place during September 1913 and required seven pilots to fly their aircraft from Montrose, via Stranraer and across the North Channel of the Irish Sea, to Dundalk and thence to Limerick. Six BE 2a aircraft: 217 (Capt Becke, 'A' Flight commander), 218 (Capt Longcroft, 'B' Flight commander), 222 (Capt F. St G. Tucker), 225 (Lt Leonard Dawes), 272 (Lt A. C. H. MacLean) and 273 (Lt F. F. Waldron) and one Maurice Farman S7 Longhorn (207), were detailed for the detachment. Farman 207, flown by Capt George Dawes with his mechanic Sgt Finlay Traylor left Montrose on 26 August and a further four aircraft left on the 27th. These latter included Longcroft, MacLean and Leonard Dawes, who was forced to land at Inverkeithing with a broken petrol feed pipe. This was rectified and Leonard arrived at Stranraer the next day (28th). Capt Frederick Tucker also force landed but damaged his machine too badly to continue and took no further part in the detachment to Ireland. Capt Becke left Montrose on 30 August and finally Lt Waldron set out on 1 September. All six aircraft reached Stranraer by the 1st and all except Lt MacLean, who was delayed until the next day with a damaged propeller shaft, set off on the crossing to Ireland that same afternoon.

Leonard Dawes flew BE 2a, 225, uneventfully as far as Dundalk where, having brought the town's first sight of an aeroplane, he stayed overnight. When interviewed by the local press, Leonard said that after making the crossing over the sea at about 65 mph he kept to the coastline, flying at 4,000 feet, until he came to Carlingford Mountains. There he circled, losing height to 200 feet while he crossed Dundalk Bay to land at the Royal Field Artillery Barracks near the town of Dundalk. Next day, suitably refreshed and watched by a rapturous crowd of 3,000 people, he took off for the final destination of Rathbane, Limerick, where the six remaining aircraft would be based for the duration of the army manoeuvres. These would involve 20,000 ground troops and encompass the counties of Limerick, Kilkenny and Tipperary. As historian Guy Warner explains:

> In these war games, aircraft were allocated to the two opposing 'armies.' The minimum flying altitude allowed was 3,000 feet and to ensure this rule was observed, a barograph was installed in each aircraft and inspected by the umpires. Flight at lower altitudes was not allowed for reconnaissance purposes because the aircraft were deemed vulnerable to ground fire. The 'battle' that was staged on September 16th saw the airmen of both sides constantly in flight. The amount of information the observers in these machines were able to convey to their respective generals either directly or by means of messages dropped from dizzying heights was most valuable. All the while the machines went steadily and fortunately without any accident to their intrepid pilots and observers, in challenging conditions.

With Leonard Dawes still flying 225, five BE 2s and the Maurice Farman, departed Limerick on September 23rd and having lost one (believed to be 273) in a mishap *en route*, after a couple of days waiting for good weather at Newcastle, County Down, four aircraft re-crossed the North Channel in poor visibility, during which all of the pilots became lost for a time, but eventually returned safely to Montrose on 26 September. Guy Warner explained:

The visit of 2 Squadron to Ireland may be regarded as a highly important dress rehearsal for the operational deployment of the RFC to France less than a year later. This was a very noteworthy feat for those early days; crossing the stretch of sea twice in rudimentary flying machines, with only a top speed of between 50 and 70 mph, was not for the faint-hearted. Useful field experience had been gained and it was also a considerable technical achievement for the pilots, mechanics and riggers – the aircraft flew an average of 2,000 miles during the period.

Mishaps during the Irish interlude and normal operations at Montrose (Dysart) had depleted the squadron's aircraft inventory somewhat so five pilots were ordered to travel south by rail to collect an aeroplane each from the Royal Aircraft Factory at Farnborough, then fly their way independently back to Montrose. Capts John Becke, Archibald MacLean and George Todd set out from Farnborough first, to be followed a few days later by Lts Leonard Dawes and Lawrence. Lieutenant Dawes picked up aeroplane BE 2a, 267, on Thursday 20 October 1913 and headed northwards. Aeroplane 267 was previously on charge to 3 Squadron in March 1913 but had been wrecked a month later. Now, having been repaired by the Royal Aircraft Factory, it was reallocated to 2 Squadron – hopefully with a better-quality repair than the earlier one made to 205.

Leonard headed north flying against a stiff wind and in the vicinity of Wisbech it became clear he would soon have to land as his petrol was almost exhausted. Peering into the slipstream he spotted a suitable-looking grass field alongside a prominent water course and set the aircraft down safely. The field belonged to Mr T. W. Maxey and was located in Tydd Fen near the North Level Drain. Making his way to the nearest farm house Leonard enquired about the availability of petrol and oil but although there was a small amount at the farm it was quite insufficient to continue his flight so, with the aeroplane guarded by two local policemen, Lt Dawes stayed near the field overnight while further fuel supplies were brought to him.

Word of the arrival of this wonderful flying machine naturally spread like wildfire and despite this being a sparsely populated area, a large crowd gathered to see him set off for Montrose at 9.00 a.m. next day aiming, he said, to reach Berwick-on-Tweed by nightfall. It was not to be, though, as fog had come down and delayed his departure until noon. When the fog cleared, Dawes swung the prop, climbed aboard and took off. In recognition of the crowd – and indeed his own parents Mr and Mrs Edwin Dawes who had motored over from Long Sutton in their car just to see his departure – he made a circuit of the field at 600 feet before climbing away and disappearing into the distance at about 2,000 feet.

By 12.45 p.m. he was nearing his home town of Long Sutton and less than five minutes after the clatter of his engine was heard and the aeroplane seen to be descending near the railway station, the town market place was absolutely empty. Everyone – townsfolk, traders, shop assistants and solicitors alike – rushed headlong to see their local hero. '[they] joined in the human stream until it gave one the impression of a cinematograph chase rather than real, live Long Sutton!' reported the local paper.

One of those tempted from his work-place was twenty-year-old Charles Albert Caley who wrote:

I experienced a wonderful spectacle, an aeroplane flying about 500 feet high had come from the Sutton Bridge direction and went on to land somewhere near Station Road. I naturally went over the fields which would take me the shortest way to the place where it had landed. When I got there it had been roped off and there was already a crowd around. Apparently, it was a Lieutenant Dawes, whose parents lived at Long Sutton. Anyhow, the children were all paraded down to the field to see it in the afternoon and then were given a treat the following morning by seeing him circle the church before going off. I imagine I must have arrived back late to the shop the previous day, but it was a real thrill as this was the first aeroplane I had ever seen.

Lt Dawes had landed in Mr H. M. Proctor's field where the machine was quickly surrounded by a couple of hundred people. Again he called upon the services of the local constabulary to rope off and guard this wonder of the age, while he was driven to his old home by the churchyard to indulge in a bath and a spot of lunch. Just before 3.00 p.m., suitably refreshed, he returned to his aircraft to find the crowd not only swelled by the arrival of many more people but with excited schoolchildren lined up in rows – no doubt absolutely delighted to see this flying machine and to have escaped a dreary classroom in equal measure! Several contemporary photographs of this event exist and one of the inquisitive lads pictured was still alive in the 1980s and able to identify himself. Then a fourteen-year-old ironmonger's errand boy, Mr Ben Gee vividly remembered the day he 'sneaked off to gawp at Lt Dawes' wonderful machine.' Then, as the *Spalding Free Press* put it:

As the man of the moment wrapped himself in thick warm waterproofs, nothing could repress a cheer, led by an elderly lady who waved her umbrella from her carriage. He then started his 70 hp Renault engine himself and climbed into his seat.

While the adoring crowd watched its brave Lieutenant fly away northwards, someone cried out 'He's down again!' Just a couple of miles from his departure point the 70 hp Renault engine clattered to an abrupt stop and Leonard Dawes was forced to land in a field on Mr Arthur Holborne's Manor House farm, near Gedney railway station. Diagnosing the problem as a faulty magneto, Dawes covered the engine with a tarpaulin and leaving the aeroplane in the charge of the village bobby, went into the village to send a telegram to Army HQ for a mechanic to come and carry out repairs. In the meantime, what better place to stay than at his parent's home just down the road in Long Sutton, where he was again entertained to a meal, a bath and a comfortable bed. In his absence, it was the turn of almost the entire population of Gedney to take this rare opportunity to admire his aerial steed.

Lt Dawes' brief sojourn in the Fens came to an end on the Saturday morning when, after a quick local air test (including flying round the spire of the church next to the family home in Long Sutton), he took to the sky at 11.00 a.m., heading towards Lincoln, York and thence for Scotland. Reported as making overnight stops in north Yorkshire (he came down

on Scarborough racecourse due to another engine failure)
and Berwick, eventually he reached Montrose, having flown
a distance of about 450 miles, almost a week after leaving
Farnborough.

Metal hangars at the new airfield at Montrose (Broomfield)
were completed in December 1913 and the squadron moved
into its new home in January 1914. Long-distance flights had
now become quite normal fare for the pilots of 2 Squadron –
but of course this was inevitable due to the remote location of
the airfield at Montrose. The majority of the 'action' was bound
to take place in the south of England thus involving 2 Squadron
in long flights in order to participate. It should be noted that
while a flight of 450 miles these days is regarded as 'nothing',
in those days that distance was of world record dimensions –
the *world* non-stop record in July 1913, for example, stood at
just 487 miles.

It was in May 1914 that Leonard Dawes and his fellow
pilots again began the long haul south, this time to attend the
RFC Military Wing Concentration (Camp) at Netheravon on
Salisbury Plain. The squadron aircraft would be away from
base for about a month and with the smell of war in the air,
one of the primary purposes of this mass move was to iron
out the logistics of moving an entire flying unit rapidly over
a large distance with all its support organisations. It was also
necessary to maintain good communications between the air
and ground echelons so that repairs could be effected *en route*
as required. The whole squadron's air and ground crews made
the trek south and in order for the air and ground components
to remain in close company, the move was made in a series of
relatively short legs of about 100 miles or less. If no ground

echelon had been involved, the aeroplanes could have flown this distance in about two 'hops'. Overnight stops on this occasion were made at Edinburgh, Berwick, Blyth, West Hartlepool (Seaton Carew beach), York (Knavesmire racecourse), Lincoln (Boothby Graffoe, outbound and Nettleham Hall, return), Northampton (Chapel Brampton) and Oxford.

Ten BE 2a aircraft, each carrying its pilot and an airman fitter, flew out of Montrose (Broomfield) on Monday 11 May 1914 accompanied a cavalcade of thirty-four assorted support vehicles wending its way south on the ground. Both echelons spent the night at Edinburgh. Next day, Tuesday 12th, both parties left Edinburgh and met up at Berwick for an overnight stay. Off again on Wednesday 13th, the next rendezvous was at Blythe. Thursday 14th saw both groups meeting up at West Hartlepool, where the aeroplanes used the firm beach at Seaton Carew as a landing ground. All went well until Friday 15th when the air echelon ran into a thick fog bank *en route* from Seaton to York. Thick fog disrupted the planned landing at York. Following the route of the Darlington-to-York road, Leonard Dawes and his fitter rather foolishly – and contrary to orders – pressed on when he flew into the fog and in almost zero visibility was eventually forced to make a hasty, but safe, landing at Brompton near Northallerton.

Six aircraft managed to reach the landing ground on York racecourse while three others made forced landings in the surrounding area, with some suffering damage as a result. Sadly, one of these three aircraft, BE 2a 331 with Lieutenant John (aka Jack) Empson and his fitter Air Mechanic First Class (AM1) Reginald George Cudmore on board, crashed between Hutton Bonville and Danby Wiske in north Yorkshire. The aeroplane was completely wrecked and both men were killed. When the fog cleared, all the serviceable aeroplanes were gathered together on the racecourse and Major Burke called a halt for the weekend, while the damaged aircraft were assessed and repairs carried out to one machine. In the meantime, two pilots were sent back to Montrose by rail while the squadron waited at York for them to return with replacement aeroplanes. This all took time and the squadron was not ready to move off again until dawn on Friday 22 May, for the next leg to Lincoln.

Great excitement was felt throughout Boothby Graffoe, a small village overlooking the River Witham Valley a few miles to the south of Lincoln. The previous afternoon some tents had been erected in a large grass field belonging to Mr Charles Marfleet (owner and resident of Boothby Hall) adjacent to the Grantham to Lincoln railway line (closed in 1965), by a group of military men and rumour spread like wildfire that aeroplanes were due to land there around 7.00 a.m. on the 22nd.

However, fog had again descended over parts of Yorkshire, delaying departure until well into the afternoon. In the destination village, patience was rewarded when, just after 6.00 p.m., a BE 2 landed in the field. At 6.25 p.m., Lt Leonard Dawes was the second of eight BE 2s to arrive at the landing ground near Boothby Hall. The field was marked with a large white cross laid out on the ground which, according to the pilots, was easily visible from the air. Leonard was quickly followed in by the rest of the squadron and within 45 minutes, they had all landed safely. The pilot group comprised: Major Charles Burke; Captains George Todd, Francis 'Ferdy' Waldron and George Dawes and Lieutenants Leonard Dawes, Hubert Harvey-Kelly, Edward Corballis and Rutter Barry Martyn. For reasons that are not known, Lt Reginald Rodwell set out from Montrose, flying '272' with the original ten, but crashed in Yorkshire – fortunately without injury to himself or his mechanic – and seems to have completed his journey to Netheravon with the ground party. It also appears that he did not participate in the return air journey to Montrose after the Concentration, but his place was taken by Lt Maurice Noel.

Later that evening the ground convoy of between thirty and forty assorted vehicles carrying heavy equipment such as lathes and drilling machines as well as a plethora of smaller tools and 140 airmen to wield them, all shepherded by motorcycle riders, arrived at the rendezvous. The next day's intended departure was yet again delayed, this time by a thick, low overcast sky left by the heavy rain and thunderstorms of the previous night. With no improvement in the weather that day, the whole squadron remained encamped at Boothby Graffoe over the weekend.

Monday morning, 25 May dawned fine and clear, allowing all eight aeroplanes to take off for Northampton before 6.00 a.m. Their route took them south towards Grantham, where they were seen passing overhead Caythorpe and then over Grantham around 6.30 a.m., followed by the ground convoy motoring through Grantham between 8.00 a.m. and 9. 00 a.m. Flying at 3,000 feet, the aeroplanes covered the distance of 60 miles in an hour but the weather was cold and snow showers were even encountered *en route*. The landing ground was at Chapel Brampton, about 4 miles north of Northampton and when the ground convoy reached the field, Major Burke announced that the stop would be for a few days to allow servicing of the aircraft and in particular, time for representatives of the squadron to travel to attend the funerals of Lieutenant John

Empson taking place at Blacktoft near Goole and Air Mechanic First Class George Cudmore in Manchester.

On Friday 29 May they went on to Oxford, which was reached without further incident and finally to Netheravon which was reached on 30 May, the whole transfer having taken not far short of three weeks. 2 Squadron was encamped at Ox Farm, Choulston near Netheravon, on a site adjacent to barracks and hangar facilities that eventually became the permanent base for Nos. 3 and 4 Squadrons. 2 Squadron remained at the camp area for the whole of June, working with the other three operational RFC squadrons, and into July when, on Monday 13 July, the whole process was reversed for the return journey to Montrose. Amidst a plethora of visits by British and foreign dignitaries, on 26 June the Squadron was inspected by the Prime Minister Mr H. H. Asquith who took time to speak to all the pilots. The idea of the Concentration was to test logistics, ground transport, fitters, riggers and organisation and, not least, the pilots, in all aspects of operating an Air Force, in a series of exercises simulating anticipated operational situations in time of war.

In the light of experience from the journey south, a slightly different itinerary was taken for the trip north. The ground echelon set off a day early to make the first camp at Lincoln. Nine aircraft, including that flown by Leonard Dawes, set off from Netheravon on 13 July, refuelling at Northampton with seven of them, including Leonard, managing to make the overnight stop at Nettleham Hall, north of Lincoln. At 8.00 a.m. next day, the 14th, these seven set off for Scarborough Racecourse which was reached – by six aircraft – about an hour later. Engine trouble had accounted for the other three aircraft at various locations along the route. Leonard Dawes was still among the leading group but he and the squadron was obliged to wait at Scarborough in poor weather conditions until the weather improved and the wayward three aircraft finally arrived, before they all moved out on 18 July. The remainder of the flight back to Montrose, via Newcastle, appears to have been completed without further incident. The ground support transport column arrived at Montrose on the 19th followed by the aeroplanes on the 20th.

Just prior to the departure of the squadron from Montrose for the journey south to the Netheravon Concentration, a formal photograph of the pilots involved was taken outside the

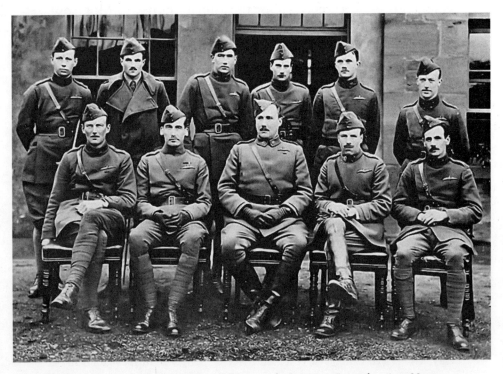

Flying officers of No. 2 Squadron RFC, outside Panmure Barracks, near Montrose Aerodrome, in 1914. Seated from left: Capt George Todd; Capt George Dawes; Major Charles Burke, Officer Commanding; Lt Francis Waldron; Lt Leonard Dawes. Standing, from left: Lt Hubert Harvey-Kelly; Lt John Empson; Lt Edward Corballis; Lt Maurice Noel; Lt Reginald Rodwell; Lt Rutter Barry Martyn.

officer's mess. It included Lt Leonard Dawes and ten colleagues and although most of them turn up from time to time in this narrative, it will be useful to learn a little more about their military careers to discover what sort of men could be found among Leonard's contemporaries as the founding members of the Royal Flying Corps. Four of these eleven airmen would not survive the First World War.

Major Charles James Burke was Officer Commanding (OC) 2 Squadron. An Irishman, born in 1882, he joined the Royal Dublin Fusiliers as a 'ranker', serving and seeing action in the South African (Boer) Wars between 1899 and 1902, during which he was commissioned. Returning to England he was posted to the Royal Irish Regiment, in which he served in West Africa reaching the rank of captain by 1909. Back in England again, he chose to learn to fly at a school in France where he qualified for his internationally recognised Aero-Clube de France certificate No. 260 on 4 October 1910. Next he transferred to the Air Battalion of the Royal Engineers and continued to fly some of the very earliest military aeroplanes – suffering at least one crash in the process. With the establishment of the RFC in May 1912, Burke was promoted to major and appointed OC No. 2 Squadron and his involvement in its preparations for war and deployment to France in 1914 can be found in more detail below. Once the squadron was operational in France, he moved to command No. 2 Wing at St Omer (Nos. 5 & 6 Squadrons) and for his services to the RFC in the field, he was awarded a DSO. With his wealth of knowledge and experience, Major Burke was brought back to England, initially to assist with recruitment for the RFC, then to be appointed commandant of the Central Flying School in 1916. His career took a U-turn when his old army regiment suffered severe losses among its officers and Major Burke was persuaded to re-join the Royal Irish Regiment. Serving in action in France, he was posted to command 1st Battalion East Lancashire Regiment with whom this gallant man was killed in action on 9 April 1917, on the first day of the Battle of Arras.

Captain George Eardley Todd was born in 1881 and commissioned into the Welsh Regiment as a Lieutenant in 1903. He served in the army until he got the flying 'bug' and learned to fly at the Bristol School at Brooklands, qualifying for RAeC certificate No. 385 on 7 January 1913. After a period of military flying training he was promoted to captain in August 1913 and posted to 2 Squadron, becoming a flight commander in May 1914. Todd went to France with the squadron but was posted as major in command of No. 4 Squadron in September 1915, then as OC 46 Squadron in April 1916. Major Todd served in the Salonika/Macedonia campaign during 1917 and 1918, after which he appears to have taken part in Britain's involvement in the South Russian campaign of 1919 as a lieutenant colonel in command of 16 Wing RAF, which he took over command from Lt Col George Dawes in June 1918. This seems to be confirmed by his award of an OBE in 1919 and the Order of the White Eagle, by the Serbian Government also in 1919. Lt Col Todd died in 1939 and is buried in Norfolk.

Born in Dublin in 1880, **Captain George William Patrick Dawes** was another professional soldier turned aviator, who fought in the South African Wars, during which he was commissioned in the Royal Berkshire Regiment. Undertaking flying training – with an inevitable mishap included – at a civilian club at Dunstall Park, Wolverhampton, at his own expense, it is no understatement to say that George Dawes was among the very first in England to qualify as a pilot – borne out by his RAeC certificate being No. 17 and dated 26 July 1910 – and became the first British Army officer to learn to fly. His service with 2 Squadron is well documented and after going with it to France as a flight commander, in March 1915 he was posted as major in command of 11 Squadron, remaining until December that year when he returned to England. In September 1916, now a lieutenant colonel, George Dawes was posted to the Macedonia/Salonika front and placed in command of No. 16 Wing, which he eventually handed over to George Todd when posted to No 90 Wing in France. He returned to Home Establishment in England in October 1918, being awarded a DSO, an AFC, being mentioned in despatches (MID) no less than seven times and receiving a Greek Order of the Redeemer and the Serbian Order of the White Eagle. During the Second World War, George Dawes served again in the RAF as a wing commander (Wg Cdr) in command of No. 2 Medical Rehabilitation Centre, a hospital for injured Bomber Command aircrew and for his work there he was awarded an MBE. He died in Nottingham in 1960.

Among the better-known junior officers of 2 Squadron is **Lt Hubert Dunsterville Harvey-Kelly**, RAeC certificate No. 501, dated 30 May 1913. Born in Devon in 1881 he was a Sandhurst-trained soldier, commissioned into the Royal Irish Regiment in 1910. With an appetite for adventure he decided his future lay with the new science of aviation and having qualified as a pilot he transferred to the RFC in August 1913. After his military flying course Harvey-Kelly was posted to 2 Squadron.

His operational flying brought the award of a DSO in February 1915 and in May he was promoted to captain and posted as a flight commander to 3 Squadron, which was equipped with the French-designed Morane-Saulnier Parasol LA single-seat fighter. In January 1916 he took command of 3 Squadron. Major Harvey-Kelly was noted for his good humour in the squadron and aggressive tactics in battle – frequently crossing swords with Manfred von Richthofen's squadron. January 1917 saw him posted to command 19 Squadron, equipped with the French SPAD S VII fighter. Major Hubert Harvey-Kelly became a victim of the infamous 'Bloody April' when he was shot down in A6681 by the German ace Kurt Wolff during an engagement with the 'Red Baron's' squadron, near Arras on 29 April 1917. Kurt Wolff claimed thirty-three aerial victories before being killed in action himself, shot down on 15 September 1917 at the age of twenty-two.

Old Etonian, **Lt John Empson,** was born in Yokefleet, in the East Riding of Yorkshire in 1891. After attending Eton school he joined the army, being commissioned as a second lieutenant into the Royal Fusiliers in 1911. He, too, decided his future lay with the RFC and learned to fly at the civilian Bristol School at Brooklands, being awarded his RAeC certificate No. 387 on 7 January 1913. Shortly afterwards, he transferred to the RFC and was posted to 2 Squadron later that year. It was during the epic deployment of the squadron from Montrose to Upavon for the RFC Concentration manoeuvres that disaster struck John Empson who, with his mechanic Air Mechanic Reginald George Cudmore, died when their BE 2a, 331, crashed in fog at Church Lane Farm, Hutton Bonville, near Northallerton, on 15 May 1914.

Lt Edward Roux Littledale Corballis, born in 1890, was educated at Stonyhurst College in Blackburn, Lancashire, before entering Sandhurst to pursue an army career in the Royal Dublin Fusiliers. During 1912 he took flying lessons at the civilian Vickers School at Brooklands Aerodrome and qualified for his RAeC certificate No. 378 on 21 December 1912. Posted to 2 Squadron, Edward Corballis went to France with the squadron, where he was promoted captain and a flight commander by the end of 1914. Like some of his colleagues, he was posted back to England to form new squadrons and Corballis was the first OC 65 Squadron when it formed at Wyton on 1 August 1916; handing over command when it mobilised a month later. He appears to have moved into administration at some point, being listed as an equipment officer in late-1916 and awarded a *Légion d'Honneur* in May 1917. When, in January 1918 he was awarded a DSO, he had reached the rank of lieutenant colonel. In August 1919 Edward Corballis was awarded a permanent commission as a Major in the post-war RAF and resigned his latent commission in his old army regiment in order to continue his RAF career. Under the new RAF rank structure, he became a squadron leader (Sqn Ldr) in April 1920 and commanded 55 Squadron from November 1923 to September 1925 when it was stationed in Iraq. Between May and July 1927 Squadron Leader Edward Corballis was posted to 22 Squadron at Martlesham Heath; advanced to the rank of wing commander and received an OBE. Around this time, he may have left the RAF. Married in 1915, Edward Corballis divorced and remarried in 1936, moving to reside in New York where his second wife died in 1961. He remarried in 1963 and moved to Florida, where he died in 1967, aged seventy-six.

Born in 1888 in Mauritius, **Maurice Waldegrave Noel's** family returned to Herefordshire in 1891. Maurice was commissioned into the King's (Liverpool) Regiment and learned to fly on the Caudron biplanes of the Ewen School at Hendon, gaining his RAeC Certificate No. 416 on 18 February 1913. Noel then transferred to the RFC to undertake his military flying training before joining No. 2 Squadron in early 1914. He flew to France with the squadron when it was mobilised for war and was soon flying reconnaissance patrols over enemy territory. In the vicinity of Maffle on 22 August 1914, while piloting a BE 2 with Sgt Major David Samuel Jillings as observer, they came under enemy rifle fire from the ground and Jillings was wounded in the thigh. Noel was mentioned in despatches in October 1914. Then his experience was drawn on to help form 15 Squadron at Farnborough in March 1915. Promoted to Captain in June he saw the squadron established on operations in France and was posted back to England to pass on more of his experience at 12 Reserve Squadron, a training unit based at Thetford. Promoted to major on 3 January 1917, Maurice Noel was posted to command 79 Squadron on 4 August 1917 and took the squadron of Sopwith Dolphin aircraft to France in February 1918 where it specialised in ground attack operations. Maurice Noel claimed one enemy aircraft destroyed on 20 May 1918 in Dolphin C4131 and remained with the squadron until June 1918. Posted back to Home Command at Montrose air station, he was awarded an Air Force Cross (AFC) in 1919. He served in an administrative post during the Second World War and died in 1958.

Lt Reginald Mandeville Rodwell was born in South Africa in 1890 and in 1909 passed through the Royal Military

Academy at Woolwich to join the 1st West Yorkshire Regiment. He transferred to the RFC in 1913, having qualified for RAeC Certificate No. 362 on 12 November 1912 at the Bristol School at Brooklands. Completing his military flying at CFS, in 1913 was posted to 2 Squadron, went to France where he remained until early 1915 when he fell ill and returned to England. Recovered by 3 May 1915 he was promoted to captain and posted to No. 1 Reserve Training Squadron, Farnborough, as a flight commander. From there in September 1915 he was promoted to major and tasked with forming 19 Squadron with Royal Aircraft Factory RE7 aircraft at Castle Bromwich. When the squadron moved to Filton, the poor-performance RE7s were replaced by BE12s and then Rodwell took the unit to France, where it took part in the Somme air campaign. In March 1917 he was posted to 43 Reserve Squadron at Ternhill. In May 1917 Rodwell advanced to the rank of temporary lieutenant colonel, based at Castle Bromwich in command of the three airfields of No. 25 (Training) Wing. He was awarded an AFC on 2 June 1919 and transferred back to his old army regiment in 1920. Rising through the ranks, by 1942 he was Brigadier Rodwell AFC, employed as military commander of the Galillee district of Palestine. He died in 1974.

Born in 1887, **Lt Rutter Barry Martyn** transferred from the Wiltshire Regiment to the RFC in January 1913 having gained his flying certificate No. 1032 from the Aero-Clube de France. As the result of a letter to the RAeC from its counterpart in France on his behalf, Barry Martyn's French certificate was accredited by the RAeC on 21 September 1912. He subsequently joined 2 Squadron at Montrose and went to war with the squadron. Martyn was recalled to CFS as an instructor in November 1914 and was then posted to a training squadron in April 1915. He was posted to 22 Squadron flying Royal Aircraft Factory FE2bs in France in September 1915, then took command when its previous Commanding Officer (CO) Capt Lord Lucas was killed in action on 3 November 1916, until January 1917. He was awarded a Russian Order of the Cross of St Anne in April 1916 which was upgraded to the status of Knight in October and received the Military Cross (MC) in January 1917. Posted to command No. 14 Wing in France in January 1917, then No. 29 and later No. 21 Training Wings back in England, Martyn ended up as a major/temporary lieutenant colonel in 1918. After a posting to 10 Training Squadron at Thetford in 1919, followed by a few months as commandant of a repatriation camp, Barry Martyn returned to his old army regiment in 1920. However, he joined the Royal Air Force Volunteer Reserve (RAFVR) in 1939 as a pilot officer (Plt Off) serving in an administrative and special duties branch during the Second World War.

The final member of the photo group (apart from Leonard Dawes) is **Lt Francis Ferdinand Waldron,** known as 'Ferdy' to his friends. Born in Kildare, Ireland in 1887, in 1907 Ferdy was commissioned into the 19th (Queen Alexandra's Royal) Hussars, which suited his keen interest in horses and allowed him to play polo for the regiment and occasionally ride at National Hunt meetings. It was always suggested that a horseman made a good pilot and Ferdy indeed succeeded in learning to fly, gaining RAeC Certificate No. 260 with the Bristol School at Brooklands on 27 July 1912. Transferring to the RFC, he trained at CFS and joined 2 Squadron on 27 January 1913. A flight commander by January 1914, Ferdy went to France with the squadron in

August but was posted to CFS as a flying instructor from March to September 1915, then he went to 1 Reserve Squadron. He had a short posting as OC 4 Squadron in France in September 1915, returned to England, then to 40 Squadron in April 1916 and quickly went on to become OC 60 Squadron when it formed at Gosport in May 1916. He took 60 Squadron into operations for the Somme campaign and it was during the battle on 3 July 1916 that he was killed while flying Morane Bullet 'A175' in action against a much larger German formation, near Épinoy. Ferdy Waldron was twice mentioned in despatches and is buried in the Commonwealth War Graves Commission Cemetery at Écoust-St Mein, near Arras.

1.3

FLYING TO WAR

The possibility of war had been discussed openly during the
Concentration meeting but with its accumulated experiences
of long-distance movement, 2 Squadron would be as prepared
as any when the need came to relocate across the Channel.
Britain declared war on Germany on 4 August 1914 and
the RFC Expeditionary Force was mobilised for deployment
to France shortly afterwards. During the week before war
was declared, personnel were re-called from leave and in
2 Squadron preparations were made to vacate Montrose. On
3 August, the squadron's air component flew south, initially
heading to Farnborough. Bad weather dogged this journey
and by nightfall the squadron's aircraft were spread out from
the Scottish Lowlands to the North Midlands, as pilots coped
with difficult flying conditions each in their own way. Leonard
Dawes reached Berwick in company with Lt Rodwell, whose
aircraft undercarriage was damaged on landing. The next day
Leonard reached Farnborough with Capt Ferdy Waldron but a
combination of high wind, engine failures and mishaps meant

the other members of the squadron limped in over the next few days, with some pilots even arriving by train. The squadron air component then flew out to Dover airfield (at St Margaret at Cliffe, overlooking Dover Castle) on the 10th and 11th, where it joined 3 Squadron on the crowded airfield.

Mobilisation plans envisaged making available 48 'operational' aircraft; 12 from each of 4 Squadrons (Nos. 2, 3, 4 and 5), each squadron having 3 Flights of 4 aircraft. A further 50 per cent (24) spare aircraft were held by a unit made up of spare pilots, aircraft and equipment known as an 'Aircraft Park', making a grand total of 72 aircraft. All 12 aircraft in 2 Squadron's complement were of the BE 2a type; 3 Squadron comprised 7 Bleriot, 4 Henri Farman and 1 Bleriot Parasol; 4 Squadron comprised 12 BE 2a type; 5 Squadron comprised 8 Henri Farman, 3 Avro and 1 BE8a and all these aircraft flew across the Channel to France. The Aircraft Park gathered together 6 BE 2a, 3 Henri Farman and 2 BE8a aircraft for the Force, while the remaining 4 Sopwith Tabloid aircraft were to be sent to France in crates. However, when the time came for the Expeditionary Force to depart for France, for technical and logistical reasons and mishaps – including some aircrew fatalities – it was reduced to 54 aircraft. Furthermore, due to lack of space at Dover airfield, 28 aeroplanes left that airfield on 13 August but 15 flew out from Eastchurch airfield on the same day. These were followed by 11 more departing from Dover on 15 August.

The overseas flying deployment began around 6.25 a.m. on the 13th, with aeroplanes taking off at 5-minute intervals, led by 2 Squadron, bound for Amiens in France. Leonard Dawes was in 'C' Flight of 2 Squadron and while some aircraft carried two men – mostly a mechanic as the passenger – he set off solo from Dover in '372' just after seven o'clock that morning. Personnel from Headquarters staff, together with squadron pilots not allocated to ferrying an aircraft, plus ground personnel, vehicles and equipment all travelled to France by sea and thence by train to Maubeuge.

Pilots were ordered to circle Dover after take-off in order to reach an altitude of 3,000 feet and then maintain that altitude on course for Amiens, via Boulogne; then go down the coast to the Somme estuary, and then follow the river inland to Amiens. If engine failure occurred over the Channel at that height, it would give pilots at least a chance to glide to safety onto the French coast. The privilege of being the first to land at Amiens at 8.20 a.m. is generally acknowledged to have fallen to Lt Hubert Dunsterville Harvey-Kelly who, with Air Mechanic Second-class F. Harris aboard, made the trip from Dover in 1h 50m in BE 2a '471'. Harvey-Kelly's notoriety was more widely established by this flight because it had been expected that the CO, Major Burke, having taken off first for Amiens, would lead the squadron and thus take the accolade of being the first RFC pilot to land in France in the First World War. It was not to be, though. Lt Harvey-Kelly, second away, made good time over the Channel; took a shortcut from the planned route, and pipped his CO to the post. Needless to say, Major Burke was not amused!

Having reached Amiens, the squadron stayed for three days before moving on to the squadron operating base at Maubeuge, where four RFC squadrons – Nos. 2, 3, 4 and 5 – were co-located. 2 Squadron's ground personnel with all their equipment and vehicles had been loaded on to railway transport for their journey from Montrose to Glasgow. At this port, everything was loaded aboard SS *Dogra* which set sail for Boulogne in France where, after disembarkation, the ground support was reunited with the squadron air component at Maubeuge, about 20 miles south of the town of Mons, close to the France/Belgium border.

The operational role of RFC aeroplanes and crews was to perform reconnaissance of enemy dispositions 'beyond the horizon' for the benefit of the British and French Armies on the ground. Despite fog descending on 19 August, 4 Squadron managed to put a couple of aircraft into the air but reconnaissance operations began in earnest on 20 August with sorties over the Nivelles, Halle, Wavre sector, continuing over and behind enemy lines almost daily thereafter.

Leonard Dawes himself was soon in action. Yet again fog delayed the start of operations on the 21st, but just after lunch on 22 August, the first enemy aeroplane to be spotted by the British flew sedately over Maubeuge airfield at an altitude of about 4,000 feet. A lookout on the field believed it to be a German aeroplane and his alarm call caused a mad scramble among all the squadrons to get into the air and chase it away. Grabbing their rifles, then running helter-skelter for their BE 2s, Major Charles Longcroft of 2 Squadron was first away, with Captain George Dawes who was armed with a rifle as his passenger. They were followed up by Lt Leonard Dawes with the CO of 2, Major Charles Burke, as his armed passenger. Lt Louis Strange from 5 Squadron fired up what was known as the 'gun machine' (probably a Henri Farman equipped with a Lewis machine gun) and he, too, joined the chase with Lt Penn-Gaskell in the front seat. However, the weight of the machine gun and its mounting bracket inhibited their aircraft from climbing above 3,500 feet and it was left well behind the pack. Major Longcroft was the only one to gain on the enemy aircraft, which was thought to be an Albatros type – probably a reconnaissance model 'B' – but it was now flying at 5,000 feet and when it dodged behind a cloud it was lost to sight and the chase was abandoned. But it was quite an exciting start to the air war in Europe!

It was 2 Squadron, however, that was obliged to retreat on 23 August, this time from its airfield at Maubeuge, which was imminently in danger of being over-run by the German Army. Trying to keep ahead of the advancing German army and moving to a new airfield almost every two or three days, the squadron nevertheless kept up its valuable reconnaissance patrols, supplying vital information to the Army about enemy dispositions during this critical period.

Leonard and his fellow RFC aircrew acquitted themselves well during August 1914 – and not least in the eyes of the French Army, too. On several reconnaissance flights he – or at least his observer – exchanged small arms fire with enemy aeroplanes and he was one of a number aircrew praised collectively by Field Marshal Sir John French in his despatch to the Secretary of State for War on 7 September 1914:

When the news of the retirement of the French and the heavy German threat on my front reached me, I endeavoured to confirm it by aeroplane reconnaissance; and as a result of this I determined to effect a retirement to the Maubeuge position.

I wish particularly to bring to your Lordship's notice the admirable work done by the Royal Flying Corps... their skill, energy and perseverance have been beyond all praise. They have furnished me with the most complete and accurate information which has been of incalculable value to the conduct of operations. Fired at constantly by friend and foe and not hesitating to fly in every kind of weather, they have remained undaunted throughout. Further, by actually fighting in the air, they have succeeded in destroying five of the enemy's machines.

In a further despatch, dated 8 October, the C-In-C reporting on the subsequent Battle of the Aisne, also wrote:

Sir David Henderson and the Royal Flying Corps under his command have again proved their incalculable value. Great strides have been made in the development of the use of aircraft in the tactical sphere by establishing effective communication between aircraft and units in action.

As a result of his flying during the period that covered the retreat from Mons to the battles of Le Cateau, St Quentin, the Marne and the Aisne, Leonard Dawes received a British Mention In Despatches (MID) for his contribution – as indeed did a number of his colleagues in 2 Squadron. In addition, the French government also awarded Leonard a *Croix de Chevalier de la Légion d'Honneur* medal, one of several listed in the *London Gazette* of 3 November 1914 under the heading: 'The President of the French Republic has bestowed the Decoration of the Legion of Honour ... with the approval of His Majesty the King, for gallantry during the operations between 21st and 30th August, 1914.' The medal was presented to Leonard in the field by General Henderson.

It was aerial reconnaissance – that crucial ability to see beyond the horizon – by these airmen of the RFC that spotted and most crucially reported German General Alexander von Kluck's 'left-wheel' manoeuvre which threatened the exposed flank of the French Army and enabled the French to make an effective counter-attack.

2 Squadron was back in action again on 25 August. Three BE 2s, including that flown by Leonard Dawes, chased an enemy aeroplane which was harried by rifle and pistol fire from the RFC crews and pressurised by some very close flying – indeed, sufficient to force it to land. Lts Hubert Harvey-Kelly and William Henry Charles Mansfield landed alongside it and continued the chase on the ground, running after the enemy crew who beat a hasty retreat into a nearby wood. Harvey-Kelly and Mansfield gave up the foot race and set fire to the enemy machine, then took off again to resume their patrol.

This is believed to be the first time an enemy aeroplane was forced down in action. Although at this very early stage of air fighting the RFC crews were generally armed with pistols and rifles, some of the more enterprising among them found (unofficial) ways of carrying a machine gun aloft. The weight of a machine gun, its mounting and ammunition, though, severely limited the speed and altitude of the aeroplane involved. In addition, hand grenades were carried to drop on the heads of enemy ground troops if the opportunity arose. It is also quite clear, however, that one of the basic concepts of battlefield reconnaissance and support was emerging during these engagements: i.e. that in addition to providing your own forces with information, aggression was necessary to deny that same facility to your opponent.

On his return to England during December 1914, Leonard spent some well-earned leave at his parent's house in Long Sutton. His arrival at the local railway station in the evening of Thursday 3 December was greeted by a large crowd of townspeople who treated him as befitted their local hero. Stepping from the train he was greeted by his father and numerous local dignitaries. They insisted he should be conveyed to his home in a Brougham carriage and enthusiasm ran so high that the pair of horses was removed from the carriage and it was hauled through the lanes to his home by many strong hands. His progress was applauded all along the route and accompanied by renderings of 'It's a Long Way to Tipperary' and other rousing and patriotic songs.

On reaching his father's house he was implored to make a speech; he duly obliged with great thanks and the ecstatic crowd then dispersed, well satisfied with their very own hero. Later Leonard described to a newspaper reporter one engagement he had with a German Etrich Taube aeroplane. Flying with an observer on board, Leonard came up behind the Taube and flew towards it, his observer firing his rifle and revolver at it as they approached. The Taube turned round and dived about 500 feet then its crew started to fire back at them with a revolver. Leonard spiralled down after the German with his observer firing more shots at it. Then the Taube flew off towards the river Rhine [sic] and Leonard flew back to the British lines.

He added that the Germans used to send over a large number of aeroplanes but of late there had not been so many. Zeppelins, he said, had not done anything yet, although he was of the opinion that they would be of use owing to the weight [of bombs] they could carry. Many times he had been over the German lines and on nearly every flight, he came across a German aeroplane. The battles in the air were generally between just two machines. He said whenever he crossed into enemy territory, he had had many bullets through his machine but neither he nor his observer had ever been hit.

It was not all reconnaissance flights and another important part of his duties was to drop bombs on the enemy. He had dropped bombs on enemy trenches, railway crossings, bivouacs and similar important strategic points – but never on towns – except to destroy petrol tanks or camps belonging to the Germans; he did not believe in attacking defenceless civilians. He urged the press to encourage young men to join the Flying Corps. The service needed all the new recruits it could muster to go into training ready for the spring when he was sure some very serious fighting would probably take place.

Fighting a series of delaying engagements in its retreat southwards, the Allied armies finally made their stand along the River Marne. The weather was ideally suited to aerial reconnaissance operations, which undoubtedly played a part in turning the German tide. Indeed, it might be said that the success of the Allied counter-attack from the Marne owed something to the aerial intelligence gathered by the RFC about the weaknesses in the German Army dispositions. The much-vaunted German plan of attack – known as the Schlieffen Plan – was in disarray and the resolve of the man who had placed so much faith in it being the route to quick victory, Chief of the German General Staff, General von Moltke, was broken.

It was during the period that followed that the ground forces came to recognise and accept the value of aerial observation – often referred to as the value of being able see 'beyond the horizon'. The mobile war had identified a need for speedy intelligence of enemy movements but as the opposing armies reached an *impasse* that evolved into less-mobile trench warfare, intelligence was still required to try to assess what the enemy was 'cooking up' behind his more static lines. The only way to accomplish that was by aerial observation. Thus, for the purpose of mapping and observation, the RFC sought out the dispositions of enemy airfields, encampments, supply dumps and his use of road and railway communications behind the lines. Furthermore, it also employed aerial photography to map trenches but found an important new role in spotting enemy artillery and ranging for the Allied artillery's response. The age of aerial support of the battlefield was born.

During the second week of September 1914, the good weather finally broke and severe storms in northern France not only curtailed reconnaissance work but also caused damage to many RFC aircraft. By the 12th, operational strength was reduced to just ten machines. In this very early, fluid tactical situation – flitting from one airfield to another almost every few days – hangars were not available and servicing aircraft in the field, out in the open, caused headaches for the hard-pressed ground crews. In the great gale, 2 Squadron saw its BE 2s bucking like frightened animals against picket lines and weights; some were ripped up and machines could be seen being tossed across the airfield like toys, resulting in several being reduced to matchwood. These aircraft had been in action almost continuously since arriving in France and those that were left operational were themselves somewhat unreliable.

This fragility was brought home to Leonard Dawes rather forcibly on 12 September. That day the squadron had moved from Coulommiers (to which it had moved on 9 September) to yet another new airfield, located this time at Fère-en-Tardenois, a village between Soissons and Rheims. The Battle of the Aisne (12–15 September) was in full swing and Leonard was tasked to fly a visual reconnaissance patrol over the Saint Quentin area, behind enemy lines. At this early stage of the war the RFC suffered from a shortage of specialist air observers – trained or otherwise – so his (un-authorised) observer for this flight was one of his fellow pilots, Lt Wilfred Rhodes Freeman (later ACM Sir Wilfred GCB DSO MC; who became Vice-Chief of the Air Staff during the Second World War) and they were about to have a very narrow escape.

Flying between Soissons and Laon, as they approached the village of Anizy-le-Château, the engine of the BE 2a, 384, began misfiring rather badly – unconfirmed reports suggest the aeroplane might have been hit by enemy small-arms fire from the ground – and with the airframe shaking, Leonard Dawes turned for home. The aeroplane began vibrating so violently that he feared its tail might break off and when the engine finally packed up, Leonard was forced to land while still 8 miles behind enemy lines. He made a passable dead-stick landing in a grass field but at least they were able to walk away from it. It was clear there was no point in trying to repair the engine because the aeroplane had rolled into the edge of a wood, slightly damaging its wings and propeller. They found the undercarriage, too, was broken beyond repair, so it would not be possible to take off again anyway. Alarmingly, small groups of enemy troops were spotted all around – some as close as a couple of hundred yards away – and the pilots were keen to get away from the area as quickly as possible.

Unhurt, the pair grabbed a packet of biscuits and some tubes of meat paste from the cockpit and ran off into the cover of the wood where they hid undiscovered for an hour or more while German infantry and cavalry, who had obviously heard and seen the aeroplane descending, scoured the countryside for them. As night fell, dodging more enemy patrols and encampments, Dawes and Freeman gradually made their way towards the River Aisne, about 8 miles away, which they reached at 3.00 a.m., then hid beneath some bushes to snatch a few hours' sleep until daybreak. To their horror, 3 hours later the roar of heavy gunfire roused them. They were right in front – but fortunately out of sight – of a German howitzer battery! It was lobbing shells onto the British, whose own artillery was merrily lobbing shells back over the river. German cavalry could also be seen moving between their gun emplacements, so it was no time to make a move yet.

When darkness fell again, evading more cavalry patrols they pressed on to quieter part of the river, swam across and having dried their clothes in an abandoned house, walked back to the British lines unscathed after two days absence. Soldiers from the 3rd Cavalry Brigade gave them some food and they hitched a ride on a supply wagon that carried them further away from the battle.

Re-joining their squadron on 14 September, having been posted 'missing', Dawes and Freeman were feeling rather pleased with themselves and their escape from the clutches of the Hun. They were soon brought down to earth with another bump! Rather than congratulating them for their escape their squadron commander, Major Burke, berated them most roundly for disregarding his explicit order that on no occasion should two pilots fly in the same aeroplane together. It was quite enough to run the risk of losing one valuable pilot, let alone two at the same time!

2 Squadron flew many more recce sorties in the run-up to the first battle of Ypres, which began on 19 October, then flew almost non-stop in support of the British 1st Corps during the course of the battle. On 24 November – after occupying no less than fourteen airfields since Maubeuge – the squadron moved to Merville airfield, where it was to remain for about seven months. It was during this hurried move that Leonard's namesake, Capt George W. P. Dawes was promoted to Major and given command of the squadron. In March 1915 George Dawes was posted away from the squadron and was succeeded by Major Tom Ince Webb-Bowen (later AVM Sir Tom KCB CMG) and around this time the squadron role changed to that of tactical bombing of enemy road and rail targets. It was on one particular operation by 2 Squadron in April 1915 that Lt William Rhodes-Moorhouse lost his life and posthumously received the VC for his bravery in action; the first VC awarded to an airman.

The Battle of Aubers began on 9 May 1915 and the pilots of 2 Squadron carried out yet another type of operation known as a 'contact patrol'. With the fluid situation in the ground warfare campaign, British army commanders had great difficulty in knowing where the various elements of their troops were at any given time and enemy gun barrages often cut telephone lines or made it impossible for couriers to move around. An experiment was devised that involved forward infantry units laying large strips of white cloth in front of their positions. These strips were visible to RFC aeroplane crews who then used the recently introduced rudimentary airborne wireless/telegraphy (W/T) sets to inform commanders of army units, with whom they were co-operating, of their troop dispositions and movements. It was this airborne diversity; aerial photographic and visual reconnaissance, wireless telegraphy and tactical bombing that turned 2 (Army Co-operation (AC)) Squadron into the premier army co-operation squadron that exists today.

Promoted to captain on 9 September 1914, Leonard Dawes commanded 2 Squadron's 'C' Flight while it was still based at Merville airfield. According to the diary of a certain Capt Smith, serving with the squadron at that time, he wrote:

Sat May 22nd [1915]: have re-joined the squadron at Merville, posted to 'C' Flight – machine BE 2c 1659. There are a number of changes since I was last here – Lt Moorhouse has been killed, Lt Jackson wounded, Capt Freeman sick. Capt Dawes is 'C' Flight commander – a very good fellow.

Smith also records that Dawes relinquished his position on 20 June and this coincides with him being posted to 15 Squadron in England during June 1915.

15 Squadron was formed at Farnborough in March 1915, moving a short time later to Hounslow then Swingate Down airfield near Dover in preparation for deployment to France. It was still in training mode when Leonard Dawes joined it at Dover, taking over command – albeit only temporarily – from Capt Philip Bennet Joubert de la Ferté (later ACM Sir Philip KCB CMG DSO). The squadron was equipped with the ubiquitous BE 2 (C-model) with which, of course, Dawes was very familiar and its role in France would be as a

reconnaissance unit and this too was a field in which Leonard had gained valuable experience from the outset of the war. It was Leonard's job to help prepare the squadron for its move to France before handing over command to a new CO, Major Edgar Rainey Ludlow-Hewitt (later ACM Sir Edgar GCB GBE CMG DSO MC; AOC Bomber Command from 1937) in September 1915. He duly completed his task but due to the need for more training it was December before the squadron finally went to France – under yet another CO, Major Henry Le Marchant Brock (later Air Cdre CB DSO).

Having established his leadership qualities, Leonard was now advanced to the rank of major and ordered to proceed to Gosport Aerodrome to oversee the creation of 29 (Fighter) Squadron in the post of acting squadron commander with effect from 7 November 1915. 29 Squadron was formed around the nucleus of a Flight drawn from 23 Squadron and initially was equipped with a ragbag of aircraft types such as the Avro, BE 2, Caudron and Martinsyde. Leonard was confirmed as squadron commander on 12 January 1916 and ordered to bring the squadron to operational readiness with the new Airco DH 2 fighter and take the unit into battle in France. Duly equipped, No. 29 would become only the third single-seat fighter squadron to be sent to France thus far.

Ten DH 2s left Gosport airfield on 25 March 1916 to make the cross-country flight to Dover, *en route* to St Omer airfield in France. Two more DH 2s, which had been detached to Hendon airfield some weeks earlier, also took off for France and arrived at St Omer without incident. The first ten, however, were not so lucky. During the flight to Dover a snowstorm was encountered and no less than six of them had to force land with the result that four aircraft were wrecked and two pilots injured. The remaining four aircraft reached Dover safely from where, having refuelled, they set off for France – but even one of these ditched in the Channel and yet another was written off while landing at St Omer. Six aircraft written off on the first day – not an auspicious start! Things became even worse by the time the squadron's strength was re-built to the required twelve aircraft since, during this process no less than fourteen DH 2s in total had been wrecked or seriously damaged – and on top of that, all the ground crew caught measles and had to be quarantined at Rouen!

The serviceable aircraft, now numbering just four machines, were moved on to the squadron's operational airfield at Abeele, near Ypres, while the main body stayed at St Omer to receive yet more replacement DH 2s from England. It was not until 10 April that the number of serviceable aircraft was finally restored to twelve and No. 29 was declared fully operational again. On 15 April 1916 the main body of the squadron left St Omer bound for Abeele.

In the meantime, the DH 2s based at Abeele had already been in action against the enemy. On 2 April, 2/Lt Graham Shurmur Bush fought the squadron's first air combat in a DH 2 when he engaged a German two-seater over the Ypres sector. The outcome was inconclusive but the DH 2's propeller was holed by a bullet as the enemy broke off the engagement. Another youthful, new – but aggressive – member of the squadron was soldier-turned-pilot, old-Etonian Lt Henry Segrave, who took on an enemy two-seater on 1 May. He gave it a burst from his machine gun and this prompted the German pilot to force-land in a field near Gheluvelt. Lt Segrave believed he had wounded one or other of the crew and claimed one enemy aircraft 'driven down'. Henry Segrave brought down several more enemy aircraft before being so badly shot-up himself that his injuries put an end to his combat flying career. He was to gain everlasting fame, however, as the holder of the world land and water speed records during the 1920s and was knighted for his achievements in that field.

By the end of May 1916 there had been many combat encounters with enemy aircraft and as a result Leonard Dawes was ordered to expand the squadron's establishment to twenty pilots and eighteen aircraft – of which two aircraft would be the new Royal Aircraft Factory FE 8 fighter in its first operational role – in preparation for the forthcoming Somme offensive. Having completed all these tasks successfully, Leonard Dawes handed over command of 29 Squadron to Major Eric Lewis Conran MC – with whom Leonard had trained while at CFS back in 1913 – and returned to England.

At this point in his flying career Leonard's organisational ability seems to have been recognised and it was noted on his service record, under the section 'Special Qualifications', that: '[Leonard Dawes has] seven years Regular Army service, including two years as assistant adjutant. Since joining the RFC ... a very thorough knowledge of the working of the RFC since its formation in 1912. [He] has flown all older types of machine and a few later types.' Now his experience was going to take him in a new direction.

Leonard's next posting took him to Wyton airfield on 26 May 1916 as temporary commander of 46 Squadron. Designated as a reconnaissance squadron it was to be equipped with Nieuport 12 aircraft but while these were in the course of being delivered, the squadron used BE 2s, so Leonard's knowledge of this particular aircraft was put to good use once more. In July 1916 Leonard handed over the reins to Major Philip Babington (later AM Sir Philip KCB MC AFC) and was off to his next posting.

New squadrons were being created at quite a pace now and Major Leonard Dawes' next posting was to 27 Reserve Squadron (27 RS) at Gosport where it was to form the nucleus of the new 41 Squadron. Its initial equipment was a mixture of Vickers FB 5 Gunbus and Airco DH 2 single-seat fighters, both the latter type and the airfield being familiar to Leonard. His task was to knock the new squadron into shape in preparation for its deployment into the shooting war in France. When another posting loomed, he handed over command to Major Joseph Herbert Arthur Landon DSO who, now it was fully re-equipped with the FE 8, took the squadron off to war on 15 October 1916.

Although Leonard already had experience of command, because of the demands of the service he had never found the time to attend a formal squadron commander's course – or perhaps he always managed to dodge going on one! Officialdom finally caught up with him and this omission was rectified on 11 March 1917 when he was posted onto a squadron commander course for a month. Back from his course, he was sent north to 68 Training Squadron (68 TS) at its new home on Bramham Moor (Tadcaster). It seems likely that he was responsible for overseeing the move and getting the training unit settled into its new home. In November 1917 he was himself on the move yet again, this time to 18 Training Squadron (18 TS) at Montrose. In a way this posting brought Leonard full circle in his Air Force career since it was to Montrose that he had been posted in his early days with 2 Squadron.

But the Service was not done with Leonard yet. On that momentous date of 1 April 1918, when the Royal Air Force (RAF) officially came into existence, Leonard was posted out to 2 Training Depot Station at Gullane. Training Depot Stations (TDS) were created as a progression from the Training Station (TS) structure, which had in turn grown from the Reserve Squadron structure. Usually three individually numbered TS units were re-designated as 'A, B or C Flights' of a new TDS. On 15 April 1918, 2 TDS re-formed in this manner and moved to West Fenton airfield, about 20 miles east of Edinburgh in East Lothian, where flying training was carried out using such diverse aeroplanes as the Avro 504, Royal Aircraft Factory SE 5a, Sopwith Pup and Sopwith Camel. Apart from a temporary attachment back at Montrose between November 1918 and January 1919, Leonard Dawes remained at West Fenton until 2 TDS was disbanded in November 1919 at which point he helped close down the airfield – now re-named Gullane – and place it on a care and maintenance basis. His war was over and on 6 December 1919 Leonard applied to be discharged from his former Army Regiment – from which, technically, he was only seconded to the RFC/RAF – and the Royal Air Force.

Thus Leonard Dawes quietly returned to civilian life and it is believed he eventually found his way back to his home in rural Long Sutton, where he is thought to have become involved with the management of the family wines and spirits business for a few years. There is, however, some evidence that he moved to live in Kent for the remainder of his life. An entry in a telephone directory dated 1923/24 mentions: 'Major Leonard Dawes,

Cars for Hire; Barn Elms, Margate.' A further item in the shape of an entry in Kelly's Directory for Thanet (Kent) in 1929 records in that year that a Major Leonard Dawes was a private resident living at 3 St James Mansions, Northdean Road, Cliftonville, Margate. In the telephone directory of 1933 he is listed as resident in Rosemary Avenue, Broadstairs. Unfortunately, he faded from the limelight at that point and his subsequent life history is not known.

The wine and spirits business in Long Sutton appears to have retained the family name in various formats – such as Duval & Dawes – until it was acquired by Peatling & Cawdron, then Thomas Peatling Ltd in the late 20th century, when the Dawes name finally disappeared, although the original shop in Long Sutton was still there in 2019. Leonard is believed to have died in 1962 and this is supported by an entry in the *London Gazette* dated 3 August 1962 in which the death of a Leonard Dawes of 4 Gloucester Avenue, Margate, Kent, on 10 January 1962 is recorded. The note also states that he was a retired Major, aged 76 and that claims on his estate should be directed to a Margate solicitor. The two addresses above are very close together; 4 Gloucester Avenue being just off Northdean Road and Rosemary Avenue is in that general locality, too.

In the twenty-first century, though, his RFC legacy is still very much with us, since most of the squadrons with which Leonard Dawes was associated are still (in 2019) in existence and a couple are even based in his native Lincolnshire. 2 (AC) Squadron is currently based at RAF Lossiemouth in Scotland and is equipped with the BAe Typhoon FGR4 for its Northern Quick Reaction Alert (QRA) role. No. 15 Squadron was disbanded in 2017, having flown the Tornado GR4, which is about to be retired from RAF service. In the light of the arrival into RAF service of the new Lockheed F-35, it seems possible that this squadron may be re-formed in the not-too-distant future with the new aircraft. 29 Squadron is still going strong and operates the BAe Typhoon FGR4 jet fighter from RAF Coningsby in Lincolnshire. 41 Squadron is also based at Coningsby where it operates the Typhoon FGR4 in the role of development and evaluation of operational tactics for front line Typhoon squadrons. These operational squadrons exist within that Royal Air Force which Leonard Dawes helped to establish more than a century ago.

Part 2

THE FIGHTER PILOT, 1925–1942

Group Captain Philip Reginald 'Dickie' Barwell DFC

Gp Capt Philip Reginald 'Dickie' Barwell relaxing in the summer sun at RAF Biggin Hill, 1942. (Courtesy John Barwell).

2.1

ON SILVER WINGS

In the fog of the Second World War it only took the blink of an eye for one of the RAF's rising stars to be plucked from the sky by a cruel twist of fate. Born in Knowle, near Solihull, Warwickshire in 1907, Philip Reginald Barwell was destined to pursue a distinguished RAF flying career that would see him acquire great skill as a pilot; become a respected leader of men in battle and yet lose his life in a tragic accident. Philip Barwell's parents Reginald and Alice moved their family in 1913 to a house named 'Chiltern' in the village of Clare, between Haverhill and Sudbury, Suffolk. There, Philip's father – desirous of a complete change of lifestyle – tried his hand at farming, having previously been employed in a metal factoring business in the Midlands. In the same year, Philip's younger brother Eric was born and it transpired that Eric would also have a long and distinguished flying career. When war came in 1914, Reginald enlisted as an ambulance driver and was later commissioned as a Lieutenant into the 2/5 Battalion of the Suffolk Regiment. By this time the family rented a house at 31 Hartington Grove in Cambridge, which seems to account for Philip being educated at Perse School in that city between September 1917 and Easter 1919.

By July of 1919, now safely returned from the war Philip's father, always interested in horticulture and keen to set up his own business, bought a house and some land in the village of Swavesey, on the edge of the Cambridgeshire fens about 10 miles north of the city and went into poultry farming, however, it was not the long-term success he had hoped for. Determined to provide his sons with a good education, Philip – followed later by his two younger brothers Eric and John – was sent to Wellingborough public school which he attended as a boarder from, it is believed, late 1919 until 1925 when he made the transition from schoolboy to budding fighter pilot in September of that year. While at Wellingborough, he was a keen sportsman and fine athlete showing promise, too, as a hockey, tennis and squash player and there were early signs of him 'having a good eye' when he became captain of the school rifle-shooting team. He also joined the school Officer Training Corps (OTC), which provided him with his first taste of military discipline.

Philip entered the Royal Air Force on a Short-Service Commission as a pilot under training, joining 19 Squadron at RAF Duxford where, in the custom of the time, he received his flying training on the squadron itself. Short-Service Commission officers were one of the cornerstones of the Chief of the Air Staff, ACM Sir Hugh Trenchard's plan for a slim, efficient and cost-effective force and they were to be the basis of his trained reserve of airmen. In January 1924 the Air Ministry publicly announced that:

400 officers are required for flying duty for the RAF Short-Service Commission scheme, which enables young men to join

[the RAF] for a limited number of years with the possibility of a permanent commission at the end.

This is what prompted Philip Barwell to see his future with the RAF and his application was successful. Perhaps flying was 'in the blood', since it is known that three of his cousins flew and died over the Western Front during the First World War.

Throughout his subsequent service in the Royal Air Force, Philip Barwell became universally known as 'Dickie' and although no one – not even his family – can remember quite how or when he acquired that soubriquet, the nickname stayed with him throughout his life. Indeed, as his son John recalled:

> the 'R' in his initials stood for 'Reginald' not 'Richard' but my mother could not abide that name and so did nothing to dispel any belief that 'Dickie' was so called because of his middle name!

Dickie's flying career began on 1 September 1925 when he took to the sky as a member of 19 Squadron for his first flight in the front seat of an Avro 504K, H5244, flown by Flying Officer (Fg Off) Gray. On the question of flying training, at this period in the early stages of Trenchard's plan for the development of the RAF, it should be noted that the recently established Royal Air Force College (RAFC) Cranwell acquired the responsibility for training 'career' officers, while the Central Flying School would find a new lease of life as the 'trainer of the trainers', i.e., it would specialise in the training of military flying instructors. The most noticeable aspect of Dickie's flying training therefore is that, as one of the new breed of Short Service Commission entrants, he was taught on the squadron by the squadron pilots.

In the days and weeks that followed, in a variety of 504Ks, including F8760 and E3525, he underwent a programme of classroom and flying exercises that taught him the usual basic skills: theory of flight; straight and level; climbs and descents; turns; take-offs and landings; spins and recovery and so on. His flying ability was tested at regular intervals and on 31 October the squadron commander, First World War ace Sqn Ldr Hubert William Godfrey Jones MC (later AFC and also known as H. W. G. Penderel), twice put him through his paces and seemed satisfied with his progress. On 2 November there came two more flights in which he practised landings with each of his regular instructors, Sgts Kemp and Miller. Then, at nine o'clock on the morning of 3 November, Dickie went up with Sgt Kemp in Avro 504K, E3575, for 40 minutes of 'circuits and bumps' followed immediately by a 20-minute check flight with Flight Lieutenant (Flt Lt) West.

After landing and taxying back to Duxford's apron, West jumped out and with the engine ticking over, patted him on the shoulder and shouted to Dickie to do a circuit on his own. Five minutes later, the circuit completed, he was safely back on the ground. After 11 hours and 10 minutes of dual instruction, Dickie had gone solo for the first time. Expressing his satisfaction, West told Dickie to take her up again for another half-an-hour on his own. There then followed many days of practice, practice, practice – mostly solo but occasionally dual instruction when he needed to be shown the finer points of flying, before going off and trying them out himself. Side slips into landings, practice forced landings and minor aerobatics were soon appearing in his log book and he probably really enjoyed looping Avro 504 E3575 for half-an-hour on 9 November, going off to lunch then looping it for another half-hour in the afternoon!

At this time 19 Squadron was equipped with the Gloster Grebe and with his tuition coming along nicely, Dickie had a foretaste of this nippy little fighter when Fg Off Clayton took him up for 10 minutes in a two-seat, dual-control Grebe III DC, J7528, on 16 November and again on the 18th. The Grebe entered service in October 1923 and when the two-seat version arrived, for the first time the RAF had a dual-control trainer fast enough to give trainee pilots some experience of the handling qualities of the single-seat version they might eventually fly.

Almost a month passed before Dickie got his hands on a Grebe again. During that time, he continually practised alone in the trusty Avro 504; yet more circuits and bumps, side-slips, stall turns, forced landings and – perhaps more enjoyably – half-rolls and loops. Then, on 10, 14 and 15 December, Sgt Kemp took him up in J7528 and J7532 to demonstrate and practise various manoeuvres in the Grebe III. These were now crucial days for Dickie's progress. After lunch on 17 December, Fg Off Wilkinson checked him out in J7528 for half-an-hour, followed by 10 minutes with Sqn Ldr Jones who, satisfied with what he found, jumped out and told him to do a circuit on his own. Ten minutes later Dickie was down again – he had gone solo in the Gloster Grebe. In the days preceding that Christmas he put in more solo flights in Grebes J7372, J7387 and J7592, with another dual test under the watchful eye of the CO, Sqn Ldr Jones, before spreading his wings with a 2-hour cross-country flight from Duxford to Martlesham Heath and back in Grebe J7392. After no doubt an enjoyable Christmas, Dickie bashed round the circuit three times on 28th before ending the year with another cross-country to Martlesham Heath and back on 31 December, which brought his total flying hours for that year up to 64 – including 10 hours solo in the Grebe.

With 30 more hours hard practice in the Grebe over the next two months, Dickie Barwell was beginning to gain competence and confidence in the air and in March 1926 nearly all his flying time was spent on solo cross-country flights, navigating to places such as Biggin Hill, Northolt and Kenley airfields. There was no let-up in practising all aspects of flying in a fighter and he was subject to regular tests by the senior squadron pilots to keep an eye on his progress.

Now it was time to learn to take his place in the squadron. On 16 April he took part in what he described as a 'formation circular tour', in which he flew J7524 in company with others in the squadron, from Duxford to Digby then Cranwell then Spittalgate (Grantham) and back to Duxford. This took 2 hours and was repeated on 20th – with Dickie in J7390 – by flying at 2,000 feet from Duxford to Kenley, Hawkinge and back to Duxford in about 2½ hours. Longer duration trips were becoming the norm now with practice flights and climbs to 15,000 feet, for example, lasting up to an hour or more.

Through the summer of 1926, Dickie's solo hours in the Grebe steadily built up and, during June, included much practice at formation flying in preparation for the annual Hendon Air Pageant. Later in the month the squadron, including Dickie in J7375, flew down to Hendon on several days to put their evolutions into shape over the airfield until the CO was satisfied. Then Dickie's big moment came in the afternoon of 3 July when, to quote his log book, he and the squadron performed 'group evolutions at pageant'. These group evolutions involved two fighter Wings each of three squadrons, each of which flew nine aircraft – 54 aircraft in all –wheeling about the Hendon sky in front of HM King George V, HM The Queen, and the King and Queen of Spain.

As July and August progressed so did Dickie's training; becoming ever more ambitious with stalls off the top of loops, slow rolls, flick rolls and plenty of sorties simply described as 'stunts', mixed in with cross-country and map-reading exercises and cloud (blind) flying. Then another huge milestone arrived. On 28 August 1926, with a total of 190 hours to his name, Plt Off Dickie Barwell was awarded his 'wings' flying badge.

By January 1927 Dickie had mastered the Gloster Grebe and now with 286 hours under his belt, his training could be considered complete. On 3 January his CO graded him as 'Above Average' on this type. He was now considered to have great potential as a fighter pilot and was an asset to the squadron. That is not to say he was complacent, for his log book records that it was practice, practice, practice with longer and more complex cross-countries, formations and battle-climbs and in July 1927, he and the squadron again put in days of practice for that year's Hendon Pageant at which he flew Grebe J7568. In the second-half of that July he and the squadron went off to Sutton Bridge Armament Practice Camp for the annual air gunnery training, using live ammunition and bombs. Sutton Bridge and its associated range on Holbeach marshes had opened for the first time in September 1926 and shut down between October '26 and March 1927, so it had hardly gained any momentum yet in the process of effective range utilisation – although that was to change very rapidly in the years to come.

No opportunity, however, was lost to keep up flying standards and the squadron CO, instead of having spare pilots just hanging around waiting for their turn over the firing range, sent them off on yet more cross-country exercises – to Henlow, Bircham Newton and Northolt for example – and it was similar fare when they returned to Duxford. The squadron returned minus one Grebe. This was due to its pilot, Fg Off William Andrews crashing on to The Wash marshes while firing at a ground target. Fortunately, he escaped with his life but the Grebe, J7580, was a wreck, the second accident to occur on the range since it opened and a precursor of hundreds over the next eighty years.

In 1927 the Air Officer Comanding-in-Chief (AOC-in-C) Air Defence of Great Britain, Air Marshal (AM) Sir Robert Brooke-Popham presented a trophy to be awarded to the single-seat fighter pilot achieving the highest marks in a competition to be held annually at Sutton Bridge Armament Camp. Competitors were selected from the top scorers in each squadron that attended Summer Practice Camp during the year, and the best two from each squadron attended the competition held at the close of the air gunnery 'season', usually around the end of September just before the range closed for winter. It seems that Dickie Barwell was already displaying some prowess at air gunnery as his log book records that he flew to Sutton Bridge on 29 September 1927 and flew two sorties over the range for this competition the next day. In this its inaugural year, fifteen fighter squadrons, including No. 19 and Dickie, sent competitors and the trophy was won by Flt Lt Harold Charles Calvey from 23 Squadron – who sadly died in an air accident the following year.

By September 1927 Plt Off Barwell was considered competent enough himself to undertake some instruction of new pilots. The first evidence of this comes on 12 September when he took two pupils: Aircraftman First Class (AC1) Lennon and Flight Sergeant (Flt Sgt) Ortway, up in Avro 504 J8362 and during October it became one of his main duties that he had to fit in around enhancing his own flying skills in the Grebe. Once or twice a week, he flew up to six trips a day, usually putting in at least one flight for himself in a Grebe followed taking several pupils aloft in an Avro 504. On 7 October, for example, he practised cloud flying for over an hour in Grebe J7601 then during the rest of the day took up AC1 Lennon, Leading Aircraftman (LAC) Lott, LAC Cleland and Plt Off Tiete in Avro J8362 to give them dual instruction. On other occasions he was employed to test the progress of these pupils. It is interesting to find that LAC Ralph Cleland, having qualified as a fighter pilot with 19 Squadron, was posted to 29 Squadron and as a sergeant pilot, won the Brooke-Popham trophy in the 1930 competition.

All the time, though, Dickie was constantly practising and honing his own flying ability on cross-country flights over the Midlands, doing cloud flying, formations, aerobatics and on 28 February 1928 even tried his hand in a Hawker Woodcock fighter that he took to the dizzy height of 17,000 feet for a weather check.

In the spring of 1928, still at RAF Duxford, 19 Squadron re-equipped with the Armstrong Whitworth Siskin IIIA fighter and Dickie, now promoted to flying officer and in command of 'B' Flight, was soon logging sorties regularly in J8889, J8892 and J8382. For most of May 1928 he flew to and from RAF North Weald to practise for the annual Hendon Pageant but took time out on the 24th to fly down to Sutton's Farm, Chelmsford, to watch the Sir Phillip Sassoon Cup Race fly past. This was a 100-mile race for a single entrant from any of the RAF fighter squadrons, taking a circular route from Northolt via Duxford, Halton and back to Northolt. There were time handicaps for the different fighters competing and this year nine squadrons entered with Fg Off Alexander Hutchinson Montgomery from 32 Squadron, Kenley, winning the trophy at a speed of 156 mph. The pilot from 19 Squadron, flying a Grebe, was placed seventh out of the nine entrants.

Practising for the Hendon Pageant continued apace throughout June, culminating in Dickie taking part in the 1928 Pageant itself on 30 June in front of a crowd of 150,000 spectators. 19 Squadron's 'act' was to show-off in formation and put on a dive-bombing display on some dummy tanks.

On 1 October 1928 the 778 hours in Dickie Barwell's log book provides evidence of his rapid development as a fighter pilot. Furthermore, the new squadron commander, Sqn Ldr Maxwell Henry Coote, graded his flying ability on the Avro, Grebe and Siskin as 'exceptional' in each case.

The beginning of 1929 found Fg Off Dickie Barwell being posted to 602 (B) City of Glasgow Squadron, an Auxiliary Squadron based at RAF Renfrew in Scotland with, it is believed, the appointment of adjutant. His 'types flown' list was starting grow and at this point it showed he had handled: Avro 504, Gloster Grebe, Armstrong Whitworth Siskin IIIA, Bristol Fighter, Airco DH 9A, Gloster Gamecock, Hawker Woodcock and now, with 602 Squadron, the Fairey Fawn light bomber. In addition to flying various exercises in Fawns J7190, J7212, J7222 and J7770, for example, the squadron also had on charge several

Avro 504 trainers and it appears that Dickie's talents as an instructor were regularly employed taking budding new pilots into the air on dual training flights in both the Avro 504 and the Fawn, confirming that this practice of on-squadron training still continued. Being a Royal Auxiliary Air Force squadron, a high proportion of Dickie's pupils were civilians and are noted in his log book as 'Mr' among the many Aircraftman (AC) and Leading Aircraftman (LAC) pupils. This posting clearly indicates the recognition of Dickie's ability as an instructor and with another 'exceptional' rating on the Fawn from his CO, Sqn Ldr John Fullerton in July 1929, his forthcoming posting to the Central Flying School (CFS) will come as no surprise.

Meanwhile 602 was in the process of re-equipping with the Westland Wapiti and Dickie made his first flight in J9094 on 22 July 1929 and he continued to instruct in that aircraft until he was posted to the Central Flying School in the middle of August 1929. After a week's leave he moved to RAF Wittering, home of CFS, as a flight lieutenant and to undergo formal training as a military flying instructor. Just prior to his posting to CFS, in May 1929 Dickie found time to get married and he and his new wife Mary Elizabeth, the daughter of Dr Gray, a Peterborough GP, spent their honeymoon in the West Country in a caravan, which he towed around behind a two-seater Alvis.

Taking up his new post at Wittering, for the remainder of August he brushed up his aerobatics in the faithful Avro 504 and Gloster Grebe and even De Havilland (DH) Genet Moth J8816, one of a batch of six DH 60 Moths powered by an Armstrong Siddeley Genet 75 hp five-cylinder radial engine, specifically acquired by the CFS for aerobatics. Under the watchful eye of the CFS Chief Flying Instructor (CFI) – yet another First World War fighter ace – Sqn Ldr Alfred Whistler DSO DFC*, in the months between September 1929 and May 1930, Dickie Barwell renewed acquaintance with the Avro 504 (e.g. J8739), Grebe J7417, Siskin J7760, Bristol Fighter F4946, Gamecock J8089, DH 9A (Dual Control) J8474 and Armstrong Whitworth Atlas J8799, all while refining his knowledge of instructing, improving his flying technique and practising his 'patter' on other potential instructors. His flying skill was quickly earmarked for public display and during almost the whole of June 1930 he found himself practising highly innovative aerobatics in the delightful DH Genet Moth, for example J8816, in a team that would perform at the forthcoming Hendon Aerial Pageant.

Despite the undoubted talents of the CFS display team, disaster struck on Friday 13 June during one of its practice sessions. Part of the new routine was to fly upside down for quite a long time, in line astern. It was while trying out this section of the programme that Flt Lt Nigel Henry Neville Fletcher was killed. He stalled while flying inverted in DH60 Moth J8820, and crashed near Wittering. However, the pilots were all good professionals so the display routine was not changed and practice continued until the team went down to Hendon on 26th for a couple of days flying over the airfield, before doing the actual display on Saturday 28 June 1930. CFS sent five Genet Moths (Dickie flew K1215) and five of its best aerobatic display pilots to this pageant and because – apart from Dickie, who though a pupil was nevertheless regarded as one of them – these were the 'instructors of the instructors', and much was expected of them.

In its bumper Hendon Pageant issue of 4 July 1930, *Flight* magazine reported the CFS programme item thus.

Event 8 was looked forward to with great expectancy by those who take more than a superficial interest in service matters. The Central Flying School instructors are held in very high esteem wherever pilots foregather and it was rumoured that this year the five pilots selected to represent the CFS had really excelled themselves. Events proved that for once rumour had spoken truth. For sheer downright skill in actual piloting and for judgment of time and distance, these five must surely be unsurpassed. Led by First World War ace Flt Lt John Stanley Chick MC AFC (later Air Cdre) and with Flt Lt Dickie Barwell and Fg Offs Thomas Geoffrey Pike (later MRAF Sir Thomas GCB CBE DFC*), Pat Johnson (later AFC and colleague of Frank Whittle) and Percy MacGregor Watt piloting the other four machines, this Flight, mounted on Gipsy Moths [sic] showed a degree of precision, particularly in inverted 'mass' formation that would be extremely difficult to beat.

Whether they were in line astern, upside down, or 'going round the mulberry bush' still inverted, they kept their places with an accuracy which many a good pilot would take pride in. After the demonstration of inverted flying, the Flight did a loop in formation and then Chick inverted and, in this position, led his Flight along, the other four machines remaining the right way up. The formation, distance-keeping etc., were perfect and the Flight was justly applauded when it finished its display.

In common with many of his contemporaries in those inter-war years, Dickie felt he had much to gain by learning more about aero-engineering. Now coming up to five years in the service on his original short-service commission, in order to be awarded a permanent commission in the RAF, which he greatly desired since he saw it as his long-term career, he knew the Service required him to acquire a (non-flying) specialism. Dickie thus applied for a place on a two-year engineering course at the Home Aircraft Depot at RAF Henlow, for which he sat and passed an entrance exam. He left CFS on 31 July 1930 as a Qualified Flying Instructor (QFI) with a total of 1,255 flying hours to date and with yet another glowing 'exceptional' endorsement of his flying ability by the Commandant of the CFS, Group Captain (Gp Capt) John Eustace Arthur Baldwin DSO (later AVM Sir John, KBE CB).

Fresh from a spell of leave, at the end of August 1930 Acting Flt Lt Dickie Barwell reported for duty at the engineering instruction section of the Home Aircraft Depot, RAF Henlow. There he began an officers' engineering course that would occupy him until July 1932. Between the wars, it was highly beneficial for a General Duties (GD) officer to become qualified as an engineer if he wished to advance to the higher echelons of the Royal Air Force. There is, however, little information available about the syllabus he followed during that two-year course, but his flying log book shows that there was every facility to keep one's flying hours up, courtesy of the Air Depot practice flight. The Lynx-powered Avro 504N was much in evidence (e.g. K1041, K1047) but he also logged Grebe J7417, Bristol Bulldog K2210, and DH Moths K1868, K1869 and K1873, always managing to do about ten or so flying hours during most months of this posting.

The Moth seems to have become his favourite mount and in June 1932 he was again practising hard at formation aerobatics in this aeroplane ready for the Hendon Air Pageant. He records flying Moth K1870 in formation aerobatics 'at Hendon' during the week preceding the Pageant on the 25th but there is no indication that he actually took part on the day. However, his engineering course was coming to an end and his next posting in July 1932 was back to CFS at RAF Wittering, where, attached to 'E' Flight, he was a pupil on No. 21 Instrument Flying Course. Arising from his commitment to the engineering course and the service, Dickie was, with effect from 1 September 1929, awarded a permanent commission with the substantive rank of flight lieutenant.

In a paper to the RAF Historical Society, published in Journal 11: 1993, the renowned aviation historian and author John W. R. Taylor wrote of this period:

> The CFS moved to Wittering in 1926 with Avro 504s, Bristol Fighters and Sopwith Snipes [and] the next decade saw far more significant changes. Structures became all-metal with fabric covering. The Schneider Trophy seaplanes foreshadowed the clean metal monoplanes of the mid-thirties that would have retractable undercarriage, enclosed cockpits, flaps, closely cowled, in-line engines, blind flying panels and radios. The flying training programme did not lag behind. Between 20 October 1930 and the end of 1933, the CFS trained 329 pilots in the new technique of instrument flying and the RAF began to cease being a 'fine-weather' air force. For this purpose, Lynx-Avros were fitted with a hood that could be pulled over the rear cockpit. At the same time the instructor could pull strings to cover with blanking plates the ASI and compass in the rear cockpit. After that the pupil had no outside reference and had to keep straight and level with the aid of altimeter, turn indicator and fore-and-aft level. Bulldogs, Harts,

Siskins and other front-line types joined the Lynx-Avros at Wittering in the early thirties. At last, in 1932, the old Avro 504s gave way to Avros of a later all-metal generation – the Tutor.

Dickie did not fly the Avro Tutor during his course, logging almost all his time in the Avro 504 Lynx. One rather unusual instrument training aircraft in which he flew while at Wittering was Vickers Victoria K2344. This large, twin-engine, aircraft was, in CFS service, fitted out with two blind-flying positions inside its capacious fuselage. Two trainee 'pilot' positions were installed towards the front of the fuselage interior. At each of these stations was a blind-flying instrument panel suspended from the roof and a set of standard flying controls – control wheel, rudder pedals and throttle. There was no blackout arrangement but, being inside the fuselage, there were no windows and therefore no reference aids other than those on the instrument panel. The interior flying controls were linked to the main aircraft operating control system which, when a pupil was on instruments, he had control of the actual aeroplane itself. While one pupil took control, another could sit at the adjacent panel and observe what was going on through his set of instruments.

The idea of utilising such a large aircraft made it possible to take up several trainees and instructors at a time, with the latter being able to stand alongside the pupils to offer both instant tuition and advice and monitor their performance. On 24 July Dickie went up in K2344 and tried out turns, climbs and straight flying while seated at the trainee station, then on 27th he flew it up front as second pilot for a few take-offs and landings while other pupils in the back received instruction in cloud flying. In the first week of August his progress was finally assessed by a series of tests in the Lynx-Avro and having flown 22 hours during the course, he left Wittering in the second week of August 1932 as a Qualified Instrument Flying Instructor with a rating of 'above the average in instrument flying' together with his general flying once again noted as 'exceptional'.

Flt Lt Dickie Barwell's next posting would take him overseas for two years to the RAF Aircraft Depot at Hinaidi, near Baghdad in Iraq, with an effective start date of 4 October 1932.

Of the RAF's role in Iraq, Winston Churchill wrote in the late-1920s:

The maintenance of British aircraft in Iraq [also] enabled any part of the Middle East to be reinforced without trouble or expense and without any ostentatious movement of force.

Dickie's own role in Iraq was in a ground-based engineering capacity but by the time that posting was over, he had moved onto the staff of RAF Iraq Command. As always, though, Dickie was keen to keep up his flying hours and try to take trips in as many different types of aeroplane as possible. Arriving in Iraq at the end of September 1932, he soon made acquaintance with the Westland Wapiti, the RAF's workhorse aircraft in the Middle East in those days. Putting in a few local familiarisation flights at first, he then branched out in October and included a cross-country in Wapiti J9847, with a certain Cpl Bone in the back seat, from Hinaidi to Rutbah Wells in the Al Andar province of western Iraq, a flight of about 3 hours each way. Rutbah Wells was something of a crossroads in the desert, being a stop-over airstrip for the Imperial Airways route to India and a watering hole for travellers making the overland drive from Baghdad to Damascus in Syria. There is little of note over the next few months until, on 3 February 1933 he logged another cross-country trip from Hinaidi to Rutbah during which bad weather *en route* caused him to crash land J9847 at Landing Ground (LG) 3 with LAC Gibson on board. They must have been rescued by vehicles since there is no return air journey logged and the next day Dickie flew the same route and back again, carrying mail in K1401. Later that same month he flew K1401 while escorting the British Ambassador from Hinaidi to Amarah, on the Tigris River 50 miles south of Baghdad, and back again. He was posted to the engineering staff of HQ Iraq Command with effect from 1 June 1933.

When able to get airborne, Dickie made most of his flights in the ubiquitous Westland Wapiti but his logbook notes an occasional new type. He managed to scrounge a short flight in a Hawker Demon, K2842, on 4 October 1933 and put in half-an-hour of aerobatics over Hinaidi. Later that month Dickie did some air tests on a biplane torpedo bomber, Vickers Vildebeest Mk 1, S1714. He then, between 26 and 31 October, flew it and a crew of two on a lengthy cross-desert trip from Hinaidi to Amman and Abu Sueir to Aboukir where he stayed for three days before returning via Abu Sueir and Amman, to Hinaidi; it amounted to 17 hours flying time in total.

At some point around the beginning of November 1934, Dickie's wife Mary seems to have turned up in Iraq. The first mention of her presence comes on 8 November when Dickie took her up for 10 minutes in a civilian DH Puss Moth, G-ABBS, at Baghdad West airfield. It is not clear what the specific circumstances were that caused Mary to make the long trek out to Iraq, but there is certainly further evidence, from a later air journey he made, with his wife as passenger, in another civilian DH Gipsy Moth, G-ACXK. According to his log book this trip began on 16 November 1934, in several 3-hour hops starting from Baghdad via Rutbah, Amman and Gaza – where they stayed overnight – before flying on the next day to Almaza airfield in Cairo, where the couple appear to have spent a few days. Sight-seeing was certainly on the cards because Dickie recorded that he flew his wife around the Pyramids on the 21st. Curiously, though, he also noted that while the aeroplane was at Almaza, on three occasions he gave some dual flying instruction to Lady Lucy Hoare, wife of the British Air Minister, Sir Samuel Hoare. Quite how this came about is not too clear, but an examination of the history of the following two aircraft may provide a clue.

If we turn our attention first to a DH 80A Puss Moth, G-ABBS, we can establish a link. G-ABBS was sold to Lady Hoare in July 1934 and it was ferried during that month by Lady Hoare and Wg Cdr Ernest Howard-Williams from Alexandria to Baghdad West. From Baghdad it was flown on to Teheran by Flt Lt Hawkins. However, during that leg of its journey, Flt Lt Hawkins discovered some worrying fuel flow problems when the machine was flown at reasonably high altitude and he was instructed to take this unreliable machine back to Baghdad, where it was put up for sale. Since Dickie and Mary flew in G-ABBS on 8 November at Baghdad West it was clearly still in Iraq at that point.

Two days later, with Cpl Bridge in the passenger seat, Dickie did a 15-minute air test in a Gipsy Moth from Baghdad West to Hinaidi and back. Turning now to DH 60G III Moth Major, G-ACXK, it was registered on 18 August 1934 to Lady Lucy Hoare, c/o the British Legation in Teheran, Persia, and it was delivered by air to Teheran by Flt Lt Sidney Oliver Bufton (later AVM, CB DFC). Its next known address was in Bucharest, Romania, where it turned up in late 1934, coinciding with Lady Hoare's husband taking up the appointment of British Air Minister to Romania. It would seem, therefore, that Lady Hoare's new acquisition G-ACXK was moved – when her husband was 'posted' – from Teheran to Baghdad and then Flt Lt Dickie Barwell was co-opted to fly it from Baghdad to Cairo, from whence it found its way to Romania. Since all this seems to have coincided with the approximate date of Dickie's return to England, it may well have been a journey planned as an 'end of posting' holiday for his wife as well as himself and to have a pleasurable sea passage from Egypt back to England.

Dickie Barwell returned to England in late-1934 and on 7 January 1935 found himself back at RAF Wittering, posted to CFS, this time as a staff instructor and OC 'C' Flight. The family rented a house in the village of Upton, east of the A1 main road, not far from the airfield. As mentioned earlier, by this time RAF training had moved on and now indeed the standard trainer aircraft was the Avro Tutor, in which Dickie carried out much of his flying duties. Among the Tutors he logged time in are: K2513, K3292, K3293, K3294 and K3399 and he also took up one of the ground crew, LAC Butt, for 30 minutes of aerobatics in one of CFS two-seat Bristol Bulldog TMs, K3174.

It appears from entries in his logbook that Dickie was posted out to Egypt in February 1936 as a flying instructor at 4 Flying Training School (FTS) Abu Sueir. This posting included air testing pupil pilots in the Hawker Hart (e.g. K4900, K4908 and K4909) and lasted until December 1936 when he returned to England to take up a staff instructor post once more with CFS, which was now based at RAF Upavon. His family was also on the move again and they were now living in the village of Pewsey. Logging flights in the Hawker Hart (K6499), Hawker Audax (K5248), Avro Tutor (K4817) and Avro Anson (K6163), as usual he managed to get his hands on something a little different to throw around the sky – in this case a Hawker Fury K8239 on 1 December 1936 – but perhaps that was by way of a celebration, since his promotion to squadron leader came through on that date and with it another major change in the direction of his RAF career. Having made steady progress in the peacetime service he had established and demonstrated his flying, leadership and organisational qualities and was appointed Officer Commanding 46 (Fighter) Squadron with effect from 4 January 1937. Based at RAF Kenley, 46 Squadron was equipped with the Gloster Gauntlet II, the last of the open-cockpit era of RAF biplane fighters.

46 (F) Squadron was re-activated at Kenley on 3 September 1936 from 'B' Flight of 17 Squadron with three officers, three airman pilots and four Gauntlet II aircraft. For the remainder of that year new pilots and aircraft were arriving and practice flying times totalled about 70 hours for each month. This process continued into the new year, with Dickie also arriving on 3 January. By February the squadron was up to its full complement of aircraft but flying activity decreased due to the grass airfield becoming waterlogged and at times unserviceable. In March it was 46's turn to donate pilots and aircraft to start up another new squadron, this time 80 Squadron at Henlow.

From 31 March until 9 April Dickie, flying Gauntlet K7796, took seven pilots and aircraft down to RAF Hawkinge for an affiliation exercise with 2 (AC) Squadron. They practised set-piece fighter attacks (Nos. 1 to 5) and ground attacks and this bumped up the total flying hours by the squadron to almost 200 for the month.

On 23 June, Dickie flew to RAF Duxford with eight pilots to polish up their formation discipline ready for the Hendon Pageant and this was followed on 26th when, led by Dickie, nine of 46's Gauntlets took part in a mass flypast of fighters at the pageant. In August the annual RAF air exercises occupied the squadron between the 9th and 13th. 12 September brought the squadron to 3 Armament Training Camp at Sutton Bridge for its annual live gunnery practice camp, remaining there until 2 October.

Leading from the front, Dickie topped the squadron averages by scoring 231.5, while the second placed was the New Zealander, Plt Off Patrick Geraint Jameson (later Air Cdre, CB DSO DFC*), with 225.75. The rest of October was given over to the squadron's annual leave period, although it was recorded on 26 October that the squadron crest was approved by HM the King. This would have been of particular satisfaction to Dickie who, as we shall see below, had a hand in the design of the badge and came up with the squadron motto 'We rise to conquer'. Formal presentation of the heraldic version of the badge was made on 9 November by AVM Leslie Gossage DSO MC, AOC 11 Group, during his annual inspection of RAF Kenley.

With effect from 15 November 1937, 46 Squadron moved from RAF Kenley to RAF Digby in Lincolnshire where little of note happened during 1938; it was mainly a process of consolidation of the squadron as an efficient unit and flying was directed to practising this in the air. Dickie kept them all hard at it; air 'drill', battle climbs, Fighter Command attack numbers 1 to 6, formation, breaking formation, second target formation and he still enjoyed doing aerobatics. Furthermore, Dickie was a family man and his son John now provides us with a rare glimpse into their family life at Kenley and Digby:

I was six years old and my father, Dickie, had just turned thirty years of age when he was posted to Kenley on 3 January 1937. This was important because, to discourage the hasty marriage of its young officers, the RAF did not officially recognise the marriage of officers under that age and hence, previously, Dickie had not qualified for married quarters, nor even for a full marriage allowance of pay. Kenley was therefore my first experience of life on an RAF station.

Our quarters comprised a spacious first floor apartment in a big old building which was, I believe, the original officer's mess when Kenley was first established as an RFC station during the First World War. The present building that is designated as the officers' mess was built during the 1930s to the standard 1932 design. There was a well-maintained garden to one side of our building, with lawns and rose-beds and it was there that Dickie checked me out on my first bicycle.

I have very happy memories of Kenley and seem to remember that I had, by today's standards, quite extraordinary freedom as a six- or seven-year old. Dickie took me round the station to show me what was what, including the squadron offices and hangar and the inside of a Gauntlet's cockpit. The intricacies of helmets, oxygen masks (the Gauntlet had a service ceiling above 30,000 feet and was therefore equipped with an oxygen supply) microphones, earphones and parachutes were all explained to me and then I was largely left to myself. I seem to have recollections of being free to roam the station at will but, in reality, I am sure everyone knew who I was. Unknown to me I was probably being closely watched and never for a moment in danger. I even remember going in some fear and trepidation to the edge of the airfield itself to watch these beautiful little biplanes taxi out, take off and land (no runways in those days, just a big grass airfield). In the evening, when I told my father what I had been doing, his only reaction was to say that he had seen me, so that was all right!

A few words now about the squadron crest and motto. It appears that in its original First World War/RFC incarnation, 46 Squadron had no official or heraldic crest. When my father took command in January 1937, one of his first tasks was to attend to this. He was very keen to build camaraderie, morale and the squadron image and saw the possession of a crest as an important component of that process. In those days the allocation of insignia was very much an individual matter for the unit itself. The unit had to make its own application and submit its own ideas for the design of its crest to, I believe, the College of Heralds.

It so happened that my mother had a very sure artistic flair and accordingly Dickie delegated the design aspect to the person he thought best suited. I thus remember Mum becoming deeply involved in the details of design. I would like to think that she single-handedly designed the final version as approved by the College of Heralds, but that is probably an exaggeration.

Suffice to say that I believe 46 Squadron ended up with by far the most inspirational crest and motto that can be imagined for a front-line operational squadron and this alone should have guaranteed that the squadron standard was never again laid up!

I don't remember much about formal education. In those far-off pre-war days, we moved about quite a lot and every time we moved, I went to a new primary, kindergarten or dame school and had to start again with the Romans, so school didn't mean very much to me. I do remember that Dickie made a private arrangement with the station physical training instructor (PTI) to give me individual tuition in gymnastics and boxing. This must have done me some good because later, when I was sent to board at a preparatory school, I managed to win cups for PT and boxing. My father was a fine athlete and keen sportsman. His team game was hockey and I remember watching him play often and shouting 'hip-hooray' at what I thought were appropriate times; he also played tennis and was a keen squash player. Dickie was a keen shot, being accomplished both at target shooting with a rifle or game shooting with a shotgun.

Although my memories of Kenley are still vivid, we were not there for very long and went to RAF Digby when the squadron moved there, with its Gauntlets, on 15 November 1937. At Digby we were housed in a 'proper' Married Quarter on the 'patch' and outside the working area of the station. The house faced onto a large sports field in which I recall grew the most delicious wild mushrooms, which it was my job to gather. Our immediate neighbours were Sqn Ldr and Mrs Finch, who became 'Uncle Finco' and 'Auntie Doris' to me. Eric 'Finco' Finch was OC of 46 Squadron's companion squadron,

73 and I remember him as a kind and gentle soul, with a fund of conjuring tricks for entertaining small boys and adults alike.

Much entertaining went on at my home. There were frequent dinner parties and they always seemed, although fairly formal, to contrive to be quite noisy and boisterous as well – perhaps convivial is the right word. Squadron pilots were frequent visitors and I was always impressed by these, to a small boy, mighty men. My parents also had a great capacity for making close and lasting friendships among the local community. We were never insular or isolated. One important event occurred while we were at Digby – I ceased to be an only child when my brother Richard was born.

Again, I have no recollection of going to any school! Dad took pains always to make sure that I was well informed and knew what was going on. It was after the squadron had re-equipped with the Hurricane (February 1939) that I well remember him telling me about the deteriorating international affairs and the looming war. When things were quiet at the week-ends he would take me to visit the squadron offices and hangar, where I could climb in and out of aircraft. I remember him explaining that they were doing some experiments with the lining up and sighting of the guns on the Hurricanes and for this he had to borrow some of Mum's lipstick to put temporary marks on the aircraft windscreen. I think he must have been quite inventive.

On the outbreak of war, my parents thought that a front-line fighter airfield would be much too dangerous a place for young children, so my brother and I were dispatched to live with my father's parents in a Cambridgeshire village, along with two of my cousins – and at long last I had to go to school!

Following the Munich agreement in September 1938, the RAF hierarchy probably heaved a sigh of relief, then set about readying itself for the inevitable. Certainly there is evidence that the pace of large-scale air exercises increased dramatically during January 1939, with 46 Squadron moving temporarily to RAF Church Fenton and then RAF Woolsington to simulate the defence of the Humber area and Newcastle. Back at Digby, February however brought great excitement for the whole squadron. It was to be immediately re-equipped with the Hawker Hurricane and the job, begun on 6 February with great enthusiasm, was completed by 15 March; then it was back to air exercises once more – Dickie listed L1792, L1793, L1802, L1816, L8274 among the Hurricanes he flew – with detachments to RAF Usworth and later, RAF Abbotsinch for tactical exercises in the defence of the Forth and Clyde areas. Sandwiched among these exercises and deployments came the annual Empire Air Day on 20 May 1939, for which 46 sent sections of three Hurricanes to each of the shows at Hucknall, Doncaster, Tern Hill and Meir. Through the summer of 1939 yet more air exercises and detachments – to Acklington, Speke and Driffield – but by 24 August it was back at Digby and with the deterioration in the situation with Germany, Dickie Barwell was ordered to bring the squadron status to 'Available' followed by, on 1 September 1939, the order to mobilise the squadron onto a war footing.

2.2

HURRICANES AT WAR

At the outbreak of the Second World War, RAF station Digby in Lincolnshire was part of 12 Group. In October 1939 the station was home to 46 Squadron, equipped with Hurricanes, and 611 Squadron, operating the Supermarine Spitfire I – both providing daylight air cover for convoys passing the Lincolnshire coast and defence against bomber attacks overland between The Wash and the River Humber. 46 Squadron had its full complement of 21 Hawker Hurricane I aircraft and under Sqn Ldr Dickie Barwell's command there were 20 officers and 6 NCO pilots on strength at that date. September 1939 passed uneventfully with just routine flying exercises and minor adjustments to flying personnel. 611 was previously based at RAF Duxford but took over from 504 Squadron at Digby when the latter moved its Hurricanes to RAF Debden.

In late-October 1939 a government communiqué broadcast on the wireless announced to the listening public that enemy aircraft, searching for a convoy of merchant ships, had been engaged off the Lincolnshire coast in what was to be the first sustained air engagement of the Second World War. Background to the events that are now about to unfold is that information was received at HQ 12 Group on 20 October that two convoys of British ships, one heading north and the other south, were estimated to pass each other off the coast of the Group's 'F' Sector during the following day. This would be roughly between Spurn Head at the mouth of the Humber and The Wash. The build-up to the action and the disposition of RAF fighters became quite dynamic and the progress of events that led up to what became known as the Battle of Spurn Head are now examined in detail. The southbound convoy was FS24 comprising thirteen merchant ships which departed Methil, a port on the north bank of the Firth of Forth, on 20 October bound for Southend, where it arrived on 22 October.

Names of ships in convoy FS24.
Benlevers
British Valour
Corland
Fulham V
Hornchurch
Inver
Lolworth
Maja
Monarch
Perth
Scottish Musician
Sheaf Field
Sherwood

Escort vessels:

HMS *Broke*, anti-aircraft (AA) destroyer

HMS *Bittern*, sloop

HMS *Enchantress*, sloop

The northbound convoy was FN24, comprising eight merchant ships, departing Southend on 20 October bound for Methil, where it arrived on 22 October.

Names of ships in convoy FN24.

Barrister

Bassano

Birtley

Cairnross

Chatwood

Gitano

Kumasian

Rio Azul

Escort vessel:

HMS *Pelican*, struck an underwater obstacle shortly after departure and returned to port.

When convoy FN24 reached the vicinity of the Humber it was joined by HMS *Coventry*, an Anti-Aircraft (AA) light cruiser, which left Immingham on the 21st to support the convoy as it came under air attack. Two more AA light cruisers, HMS *Cairo* and HMS *Calcutta*, steamed out of Grimsby to add their weight to the defence and they continued to escort the convoy as far as Flamborough Head before returning to port.

Featuring prominently in the aerial part of the engagement is Sqn Ldr Phillip 'Dickie' Barwell who by now had amassed 2,600 flying hours – mostly on fighters – in the fifteen years he had been in the RAF and the events that unfold can be seen as an almost natural culmination for all his talents. In the confusion that unfolded, he was surely the right man, in the right place, at the right time and success put him on the ladder to higher command.

In anticipation of enemy air action against such a juicy convoy target, 46 Squadron (radio call-sign: 'Banter') was instructed to send the six Hurricanes of 'A' Flight on detachment to RAF North Coates Fitties shortly after dawn on the 21st, where it would be reinforced at 11.00 by 'A' Flight of 611 Squadron (radio call-sign: 'Conger'). Having been originally based at RAF Digby, 504 Squadron, equipped with Hurricanes was, since 10 October, part of 11 Group and based at RAF Debden in Essex. 504 now received orders to take-off at 11.00 on the 21st and fly up to RAF Digby to reinforce the two resident fighter squadrons there. Upon arrival at Digby, 504's aircraft (radio call-sign: 'Daring') were re-fuelled and also sent forward to North Coates where its 'Blue' and 'Red' sections were instructed to take off and patrol over the convoys. This was 504 Squadron's first war patrol but by the end of their allotted time over the convoy, they had seen no enemy aircraft and therefore returned to Digby. By the time they had landed and refuelled, the enemy had been engaged by other squadrons and 504, much to the disgust of its pilots, missed out on the action. 504 flew back to RAF Debden during the afternoon of 23 October.

611's 'A' Flight (Red section: Flt Lt Arthur Banham, Plt Off Douglas Watkins, Sgt Alfred Burt; Yellow section: Fg Off Sidney

Bazley, Plt Off Lancelot Mitchell, Sgt John Mather) was ordered from Digby to North Coates at 10.25 and were proud to record that the six aircraft were airborne in 3 mins 57 sec from receiving the call. Landing at North Coates they were placed on standby.

From 12.00 hours onwards on the 21st, further information arrived at RAF Digby Operations control (radio call-sign: 'Aurora') from Group HQ and the Observer Corps, that led Digby Ops to believe an enemy reconnaissance of the convoys was taking place. At 13.40 an unidentified enemy aircraft was reported flying west from Grimsby and 'Yellow' section of 504 Squadron was scrambled to patrol inland near Retford at 20,000 feet altitude but they too made no contact with enemy aircraft and returned to Digby. At 14.09 and 14.12 two enemy raids, 'X1' and 'X2', were plotted by Digby controllers and at 14.15, 'A' Flight of 611 Squadron and 'A' Flight of 46 Squadron were scrambled to patrol at 15,000 feet between North Coates and Mablethorpe. These two raids were plotted heading towards the convoys, which by this time were passing each other just north of Spurn Head and Group HQ now ordered the following disposition of our fighters in the air: 'A' Flight of 611 Squadron was to orbit Mablethorpe at 16,000 feet; meanwhile, 'B' Flight of 611 Squadron was to orbit North Coates at 7,000 feet and 'A' Flight of 46 Squadron to orbit North Coates at 5,000 feet.

The next incident came at 14.52 hours when another enemy raid, 'X4', was reported 30 miles south-east of the convoys and 'A' and 'B' Flights of 611 were ordered to intercept. These Flights sped off to intercept this new threat but encountering cloud it transpired that for all its efforts only one Spitfire from 611 actually made contact with raid 'X4'.

Apparently, all of 611 Spitfires had failed to receive any further radio telephony (RT) transmissions and thus were without 'vectors' (course instructions) at the crucial time. During the climb through cloud, 611's Sgt John Mather lost the formation and quite by accident at 14.40, this single Spitfire from 611 'Red' section, came across a pair of Spitfires from 72 Squadron (RAF Leconfield). Mather latched on to these two and around 14.57 the three of them sighted and attacked a gaggle of enemy aircraft, identified as Heinkel He115s, at about 9,000 feet. Sgt Mather thought he was 30 miles east of Spurn Head, while his two companions thought they were 15 and 20 miles east, respectively! Sgt Mather also reckoned there were ten or twelve enemy aircraft but the 72 Squadron chaps thought there were fourteen or fifteen aircraft.

Enthusiastically, Sgt Mather dived at a target on the flank of the enemy rear group, probably opening fire at far too great a range since he loosed-off all his ammunition (about 2,400 rounds) by the time he had zoomed in to 100 yards range and then found he had to break away sharply because he had also misjudged his approach speed. He didn't see if he had actually hit his target, either. The floatplane at which he had fired dived steeply away and was not seen again and Sgt Mather subsequently submitted a combat report claiming one enemy aircraft damaged.

The two Spitfire pilots – 'B' Flight's 'Green' section from 72 Squadron – Fg Off Thomas 'Jimmy' Elsdon (later Battle of Britain ace, DFC OBE) and Australian Fg Off Desmond Sheen (later Battle of Britain ace, DFC*) submitted combat reports upon their return to Leconfield. On this sortie Desmond Sheen was flying Spitfire K9959, code RN-J and –

becoming the first Australian pilot to fire his guns in anger in the Second World War – described his engagement thus:

Scrambled at 14.30. Fourteen enemy aircraft [E/A] intercepted over convoy and attacked while flying north and five miles east of convoy, fifteen miles SE Spurn Head. Enemy formation – leading five in 'vic' and three sections of three very loose and spread out, speed 160 mph. Rearmost three attempted to provide covering fire and went up and astern prior to attack. My section of two aircraft attacked these three, whereupon they split up and employed individual evasive tactics of steep turns, diving and climbing and throttling back. One EA abandoned evasive tactics and dived steeply apparently in trouble and attack broken off. Second EA seriously damaged and petrol tanks leaking badly. Observer obviously killed or badly injured. [It] proceeded east losing height and skidding after attack, broken off through lack of ammunition. Thought not possible [for EA] to reach home base. Main formation left convoy when attacked and made for home and seen later to be attacked by six fighters. EA camouflage: olive green and brown above with white underneath wings. Large black cross under wings. Armed: light gun mid upper fuselage. Front armament unknown.

Jimmy Elsdon's report was similar and he noted that the Spitfires attacked individually, since '[standard] Fighter Command attacks not being applicable due to evasive tactics'. The pilots claimed two 'possibles'.

At 14.30, having missed out on the action, 611 Squadron's 'Yellow' section was ordered to patrol North Coates at 7,000 feet, then landed there at 15.45 to re-fuel. By that time

Sgt Mather had also returned to the fold, landing back at North Coates to re-fuel and re-arm. Still airborne was 611's 'Red' section, one of which was now ordered to patrol seawards below the cloud base. Fifteen minutes later Plt Off Douglas Watkins (later BoB, DFC) from this section, intercepted an unidentified enemy aircraft 30 miles off Spurn Head. He managed to make one attack, closing in to just 25 yards, before it disappeared into the cloud cover and he lost sight of it. Watkins, too, landed at North Coates at 15.45 to re-fuel and re-arm.

While orders were being broadcast (unheard!) to 611 Squadron, yet more information came down the line from Group HQ to Digby control that nine German seaplanes – i.e. those of the original formation that had not engaged with the Spitfires – were flying due west and heading for the south-bound convoy. Now 'A' Flight of 46 Squadron, led by Dickie Barwell, was ordered to leave its orbit pattern and intercept this enemy formation. Simultaneously 'B' Flight of 46 Squadron was ordered up from Digby to back-up 'A' Flight by repositioning to North Coates.

Continuing their patrol, the six Hurricanes of 46's 'A' Flight Hurricanes were controlled by radio from Digby operations, which itself was still being bombarded by information coming in from ships, coastguards, radar stations and Group HQ. A mobile R/T van was located at North Coates to help relay some of the radio traffic as and when the aeroplanes flew out of range of the base transmitter but even so this was fraught with difficulty.

At 14.50, after various changes of course, Dickie Barwell was holding 'A' flight in formation at 5,000 feet altitude circling between Spurn Head and North Coates when its slice of the action began. At 14.55, their radios crackled out a new order: 'Twelve [sic] enemy floatplanes approaching convoy from the south-east at 1,000 feet. Intercept!' Spotting the ships 5 miles off Spurn Head, Sqn Ldr Barwell immediately led his formation to the east of them at full speed, losing altitude to 2,000 feet as he did so. Now he told his pilots to take up line abreast in search formation and keep their eyes peeled.

Back in RAF Digby control room, seven minutes later a faint 'Tally Ho!' was heard through the loudspeaker. The fighter pilots had spotted some German floatplanes 4 miles away to port and a couple of thousand feet higher. Ordering his pilots to close up, Barwell banked towards the enemy and gave chase. He had no difficulty in overtaking the slower enemy aircraft and soon manoeuvred his formation into a textbook attacking position behind, above and up-sun of his target.

Sqn Ldr Barwell could now see nine aircraft and identified them as twin-engine Heinkel He115 floatplane torpedo-bombers. He gave crisp commands: 'A Flight; aircraft line astern!' followed by 'Number 5 Attack!' and with that, telling the rest to pick out their own targets from the left, he dived on the extreme left-hand enemy aircraft. 'Number 5 attack' refers to one of the six standard attacks devised, before the war, for engaging enemy bombers.

Standard Fighter Command Attacks
1. From above cloud: a three-aircraft section against a single enemy aircraft.
2. From directly below: ditto
3. From dead astern: approach in pursuit or approach while turning.
4. From directly below: as in 2 but attacking several enemy aircraft.

5. From dead astern: attacking a large enemy formation.

6. From dead astern: an attack by a full squadron.

The squadron leader opened fire on his target at 400 yards range, firing several long bursts and closing to within 30 yards before he broke away. Opening fire at this range would, by the time the later Battles of France and Britain, be proven to be very ineffective but it has to be remembered that at the time of this particular engagement, it was Command policy to harmonise RAF fighter guns to focus at 400 yards – later this would be reduced to 250 yards – and these young tyros, though keen and in a state of high morale, had no experience of combat. Furthermore, the relatively successful use of a standard attack may have been counter-productive since on this occasion it could give the attackers a false sense of its effectiveness. As will be seen below, each enemy aircraft shot down took several passes by the RAF pilots and the expenditure of a lot of ammunition in the process.

Determined to hit hard while he had the chance, Dickie Barwell fired almost two-thirds of his ammunition at this aircraft – nearly 1,800 rounds! However, he had the satisfaction of seeing flames coming from the starboard engine before diving away under its tail. Turning back towards his target the squadron leader watched it crash-land on the surface of the sea, its starboard wing folding back as it did so. Meanwhile, Red 2, Plt Off Philip Frost, had picked out another Heinkel and his gunfire, too, drew flames from its port engine. In the melee that followed, Red 3, Flt Sgt Edward Shackley, also attacked the same target as Frost and they both saw it crash into the sea. So far, so good.

After the British fighters' first swoop, the enemy formation scattered in confusion and the Hurricanes broke away to make individual attacks. Then Sqn Ldr Barwell spotted a Heinkel diving away towards the south. He called for the flight to follow him and chased it, firing the remainder of his ammunition at a range of 300 yards but without any noticeable effect. This target continued to race off but was no match for the three Hurricanes of Plt Offs Bob Cowles and Richard Plummer who, together with Flt Sgt Ted Shackley, lined up, one after the other, to make firing passes at it. Now out of ammunition Sqn Ldr Barwell watched proceedings from above and could see his pilots were over-eager and firing from too great a range to be effective. He called over the radio for the last Hurricane to get in much closer. Pilot Officer Dick Plummer did so and after two passes the enemy aircraft crashed upside down into the eastern end of The Wash.

Meanwhile, Philip Frost and Plt Off Peter LeFevre had latched on to another Heinkel that was trying to make its escape by dodging in and out of cloud. After chasing it for some time, firing bursts each time it popped out of cloud, eventually the cloud cover ran out. A final concerted attack by the two Hurricanes, drove the Heinkel down onto the surface of The Wash, apparently intact but with both engines stopped. This one is possibly the aircraft that almost got away and its pilot may have restarted the engines, taken off again and limped towards Denmark before finally having to crash land in the middle of the North Sea.

Landing back at Digby at 15.35 there was good cause for celebration. Originally it was believed twelve or more Heinkels homed in on the convoys but the other fighter squadron at

Digby – the Spitfire-equipped 611 Squadron – drove some off. Nine Heinkels managed to break through to the convoy and it was these raiders that the Hurricanes of 46 Squadron's 'A' Flight engaged. The squadron had had its first taste of action; caught the enemy unawares; shot down four aircraft and put the rest to flight. Only two Hurricanes had felt the effect of any return fire and even that was limited to just four bullet grazes on the wings of one and one graze on the engine cowling of another. The 46 Squadron pilots and aircraft involved in the action that day were:

L1802	Sqn Ldr Philip 'Dickie' Barwell	Red 1	(1 + ¼ shared)
L1801	Plt Off Philip Frost	Red 2	(½ + ½ shared)
L1817	Flt Sgt Edward Shackley	Red 3	(½ + ¼ shared)
L1815	Plt Off Robert Cowles	Yellow 1	(¼ shared)
L1805	Plt Off Richard Plummer	Yellow 2	(¼ shared)
L1892	Plt Off Peter LeFevre	Yellow 3	(½ shared)

There was of course a review of everyone's actions that day. The main engagement by 46 Squadron took place between 15.06 and 15.08 at an estimated 30–35 miles due east of Withernsea. Among the criticisms to emerge was that R/T messages sent out by Operations were consistently spoken too rapidly and squadron call signs were frequently omitted, which caused some confusion. It also appeared that despite a number of separate raids being reported, in the end only one enemy formation was involved as far as the south-bound convoy was concerned and only about twelve enemy aircraft in total were involved. Post-war analysis of German aircraft losses relating to this engagement confirms the four claims made by 46 Squadron

as being the only actual victories. It appears therefore that the
'possible' and 'damaged' claims by Nos.72 and 611 Squadrons
were, at best, just 'damaged' and indeed Luftwaffe records
admit to three 'damaged' He115s as a result of this battle.

The enemy aircraft were Heinkel He115A and B model,
twin-engine, three-crew, multi-purpose sea (float) planes from
1/*Küstenfliegergruppe* 406 (1st *Staffel* of Coastal Aviation
Group 406; 1/Kfg 406) based at List on the island of Sylt.
Aircraft coded K6+EH (*werk nummer* 1876) crashed into the
sea and sank 5 miles east of Spurn Head. The bodies of its crew:
Lt Fritz Meyer, pilot; Oblt-zur-see Heinz Schlicht, observer, and
Uffz Bernhard Wessels, wireless operator, were washed ashore on
the Norfolk coast and buried in Happisburgh Church cemetery
on 2 November. Aircraft coded K6+DH (1882) crashed into the
sea off the eastern end of The Wash and its crew: Oblt-zur-see
Peinemann, Uffz Günther Pahnke and Uffz Hermann Einhaus
were all rescued and became Prisoners Of War (POW).

Aircraft coded K6+GH (1887) crash-landed and sank in
The Wash and its crew: Fw Rolf Findeisen (injured), pilot;
Oblt-zur-see Günther Reymann, observer, and Uffz Hans
Schultze were captured. A fourth aircraft, K6+YH (2093) was
badly damaged during the engagement. Its wireless operator
Uffz Helmuth Becker was killed and the observer Lt Gottfried
Lenz sustained bullet wounds in his right hand and leg during
the battle, but the pilot Uffz Peter Grossgart, after being forced
down into The Wash, managed to get the seaplane airborne
again and headed for the coast of Denmark. He struggled as far
as position 54.02N; 03.29E, 150 miles east of Spurn Head but
still 200 miles from the Danish coast, before spotting a ship and
attempting to land on the sea close to it.

On touching the water, one float broke off, the aeroplane cart-wheeled in a welter of spray, then sank, taking the body of Uffz Becker down with it – not, however, before the two survivors scrambled clear and were rescued by a boat from the ship, a Danish vessel from Odense named *Dagmar Clausen*. The two airmen told their rescuers that they were the only crew on the seaplane. Four days later the ship arrived in Korsør, a small port near Odense, where the airmen were handed over to the police. At this time Denmark was a neutral country but instead of interning the Germans, the government decided on 30 October to allow them to return to Germany.

Three other He115s from this unit were damaged by machine gun-fire during the engagement but were able to return to base. These were K6+EH which sustained 65 bullet strikes; K6+ZH with 35 hits and K6+XH with 5 hits. With the loss of four aircraft, 1 *Staffel* had to be re-organised; this was carried out the very next day when the remnant was re-designated as 1 *Staffel*, KuFlGr 506 – which carried the new fuselage unit code of S4.

German Naval Staff Operations Division recorded that in addition to ten (sic) Heinkel 115s, three Junkers Ju88s of the recently formed 1/KG30 based on Sylt also took part in the action and bombed one of the Royal Navy escort cruisers. It is interesting to note that not one of the RAF pilots involved mentioned seeing a Ju88 at any time during the engagement.

Dickie put in one more operational patrol from Digby, 90 minutes in Hurricane L1854 during the morning of 27 October, then he readied himself for his next posting to RAF Sutton Bridge as station commander. It was also around this time that an oil painting depicting the Battle of Spurn Point was commissioned, believed by the Air Ministry. The brilliant artist Lt Col Harold Wyllie OBE RSMA, was instructed to visit Dickie, question him thoroughly as to the events that took place on that momentous day then to paint a scene that would epitomise the battle. In modern times, two oil paintings of the air Battle of Spurn Point attributed to Harold Wyllie have been identified. One is owned by the RAF Museum but the whereabouts and ownership of the second is not known, although a very tiny image of it can be found on the 46 Squadron website.

As a consequence of this air battle HM King George VI visited RAF Digby on 2 November 1939 to congratulate 46 Squadron on protecting coastal shipping from enemy action and he spent 10 minutes talking to the pilots in their dispersal area. Officially, Sqn Ldr Dickie Barwell had by this date been posted to RAF Sutton Bridge but was still at Digby, where he was presented to the King and in turn, Dickie presented the new squadron commander, Sqn Ldr Kenneth Brian Boyd Cross (known as 'Bing'; later ACM Sir Kenneth, KCB CBE DSO DFC), to the King. On 28 November 1939 Sqn Ldr Barwell was awarded the Distinguished Flying Cross for his 'high standard of gallantry and leadership' during the October battle. Promoted to wing commander, his next task was to take command of RAF Sutton Bridge where he was to oversee the formation of three new fighter squadrons at the station.

Just after war was declared, RAF Sutton Bridge seemed to be drifting, somewhat, on the rising tide of hostilities; going through a period of abrupt re-adjustment – as no doubt was the rest of the war machine – until a new sense of purpose could be established. This new direction was not too long in coming for on 1 November 1939, Sutton Bridge was transferred from

Training Command to 12 Group Fighter Command and a few days later the newly promoted Wg Cdr Philip Barwell DFC took command of the station. His family, of course, were also on the move again and they took up residence in the East Lighthouse, a couple of miles downriver from the station on the east bank of the River Nene outfall. This building, not actually a lighthouse but built in the style of one, had been until just before the war the home of Peter Scott the naturalist and painter.

Postings to and from SHQ at Sutton Bridge were designed to create a station establishment to support the formation and operations of 264 Squadron, under the command of Sqn Ldr Stephen Haistwell Hardy and 266 Squadron under Sqn Ldr John William Arthur Hunnard. It was now up to the station commander, Wg Cdr Barwell, to see that these new squadrons were brought to operational readiness as rapidly and efficiently as possible. As we shall see, though, this was not going to be an easy task but he was the right man for the job.

264 Squadron officially came into existence on 1 November 1939 with the arrival at Sutton Bridge of Sqn Ldr Hardy. As yet, no aircraft were allocated to 264 but three Miles Magisters (known affectionately as 'Maggies'), N3857, N3867, N3868, were collected from RAF Hullavington to enable the new boys of both 264 and 266 to keep their hands in until their 'proper' aircraft turned up. Dickie Barwell also kept his flying hand in and made some local 'recce' flights in these Maggies during November.

Finding something to keep these aircraft-less fellows occupied was difficult, resulting in numerous sight-seeing visits to Sector Ops at RAF Wittering and further individual visits by squadron pilots to RAF Northolt to get the feel of a Defiant. This air experience was augmented by ground personnel being sent off to attend Boulton & Paul's Wolverhampton factory for a four-day Defiant servicing course. All in all, Sutton Bridge seemed to resemble no more than an 'hotel' for transient 264 Squadron personnel. However, this period of relative inactivity came to an end on 7 December 1939 when all air and ground elements of 264 left RAF Sutton Bridge bound for a new home at RAF Martlesham Heath, where, within days, Defiants began arriving from depots such as Brize Norton and Little Rissington. Ever eager to add a new type to his log book, Dickie Barwell flew over to Martlesham and went up for 20 minutes in one of the new Defiants.

Meanwhile, across the airfield, 266 Squadron, too, had been stirring since 30 October when it began the process of forming under the command of Sqn Ldr Hunnard. The established size of this proposed two-seater squadron, in manpower terms, was declared as 13 officers, of whom 11 were pilots and 204 airmen, of whom 10 were NCO pilots and 20 aircrew (air gunners). One of the most notable names to arrive at Sutton Bridge for flight commander duty with 266, was one of Dickie Barwell's old squadron colleagues, the diminutive Flt Lt Ian Richard 'Widge' Gleed (later Wg Cdr, DSO DFC) posted in from 46 Squadron, Digby. Experience and leadership were obviously the qualities most required to bring a squadron to an effective state quickly and it was for this reason that Gleed was selected for this job, together with another 'old hand' Flt Lt James Baird Coward (later AFC) formerly of 19 Squadron, Duxford.

Any aircraft, let alone a 'real' fighter, were hard to come by in those days of rapid expansion so 266 also had to settle for three Miles Magisters, collected from 10 MU Hullavington, on which to begin their work-up. With the arrival of the Maggies on 11 October, local flying got under way, while the Link Trainer was also put to good use. The inevitable stand-by activity, those visits to Sector Ops Wittering, still continued.

On 18 November word came down from on high that 266 Squadron was to be equipped with Fairey Battles instead of Blenheims as originally intended. At a guess, neither would have inspired these hopeful fighter 'tyros' but it seemed to point to an intention to turn 266 into a single-engine – most likely Spitfire – unit eventually, once the production lines moved into top gear. Accordingly, the squadron personnel establishment was quickly scaled down as the air gunners were shipped out to pastures new.

It was not until 4 December, however, that the first three Fairey Battle Is: L5348, L5350 and L5374, materialised at Sutton Bridge, flown in from 24 MU Ternhill by Hunnard, Gleed and Coward. Within a couple of days, training began with these three, which were joined shortly afterwards by a further batch comprising L5343, L5365 and P5244. A spell of fog, rain and low cloud hampered flying but soon the sky around Sutton Bridge echoed to the roar of six Battles doing everything from circuits and bumps to formation practice. The next day five more Battles (L5375, L5442, P5248, P5368 and P5369) were collected from 24 MU Ternhill by other squadron pilots: Plt Offs Wilkie, Williams and Bowen and Sgts Eade and Jones. Being December, the weather was a constant hazard and flying became subject to continual interruption. Although on 31 December the flying strength of 266 Squadron stood at 20 pilots and 15 Battles, the ground echelon was desperately short of servicing equipment for their charges. In fact, if it had not been for the co-operation of RAF Upwood, 266 might well have been grounded as most of its aircraft were due for 30-hour inspections. To overcome the difficulty, Battles were flown, one by one, to RAF Upwood for vital servicing and repair until the arrival of ground equipment – yet another bottleneck in the system.

Despite day after day of severe frost during January 1940, 266 pressed on with its task, even managing to raise the daily totals of hours flown compared to previous months. In the end it all seemed worthwhile for, on 10 January, Fighter Command ordered the squadron to be re-equipped with Spitfires 'forthwith'. With renewed vigour the pilots continued to practise in all weathers, severe frosts, ground fog, snow and even blizzard conditions until, finally on 19 January 1940, the great day arrived. The first three Spitfire Mk Is were flown to Sutton Bridge by Sqn Ldr Hunnard and his two flight commanders, with a fourth arriving a day later.

The weather, though, did not relent. More snow fell daily until in the last week of the month, with more than 6 inches lying on top of the already frost-hardened grass airfield and the temperature below zero, flying was abandoned. It was no better when February arrived either. A thaw set in and the rains came, turning the airfield into a quagmire. Not until 9 February was the grass surface sufficiently water-free for flying to re-commence and on this date training with the new Spitfires began. Dickie Barwell was at the front of the queue to get his hands on a Spitfire and he himself air tested N3175, 3092, 3120, 3175 and 3118 within the first week. Within days most of the Battles had been exchanged for Spitfires, the former being flown to or collected by other squadrons, such as 234 and 245.

By mid-February, 266 was up to strength with nineteen Spitfires on charge but on 18 February one of these, N3120 that Dickie had flown on 14th, was written off by Flt Lt Gleed in a spectacular manner.

Flt Lt Gleed was quite severely injured and spent several weeks in hospital. In spite of the setback of the loss of one of its flight commanders, 266 Squadron pressed on apace with war practice. Daily now the programme tested engine boost at rated altitude – fortunately without further mishap – formation flying, cross-country flights, cloud penetration, battle climbs, fighter attacks and rapid re-fuel and re-arm exercises. This intense activity culminated in Fighter Command's acceptance, on 26 February, of 266's readiness to join the fray. On 29 February the squadron moved out of Sutton Bridge for a new home at RAF Martlesham Heath.

In these opening months of the war, the third flying unit to find its feet under Dickie Barwell's watchful eye at RAF Sutton Bridge, was 254 Squadron. It was actually re-formed at RAF Stradishall but, in need of time to become effective, was relocated from that operational station to 'quieter pastures' at Sutton Bridge. Thus on 9 December 1939, 254 arrived with just nine Bristol Blenheim Mk Is, which were intended to be converted to Mk If night fighter standard. Only one of these was fitted out for dual control and all were sorely under-equipped, lacking such essentials as R/T, oxygen apparatus and guns. Pilot training, begun at Stradishall, now ground to a halt through a combination of lack of the afore-mentioned equipment plus an acute shortage of aeroplanes themselves.

HQ Fighter Command must have been equally exasperated for in mid-January 1940 it announced a change of heart.

254 was to be re-equipped with 'long-nosed' Blenheim Mk IV, '...for employment in trade defence'. This coincided with the return of ten RAFVR air gunners to the station from a gunnery course at RAF Evanton. The squadron diary lamented the fact that three months had elapsed since re-forming and it was still far from being declared operational. Blame was laid squarely on the appalling present equipment and that there seemed to be no chance of the squadron crews reaching effectiveness until the unit was fully equipped with the new aeroplanes.

Meanwhile, the Mk Is were still becoming unserviceable (u/s) through lack of spares or plain mishaps. 254 Squadron was being reduced inexorably to a standstill by this attrition rate and in fact never became operational at Sutton Bridge. On 27 January 1940 the luckless squadron was ordered to transfer to Coastal Command and move immediately to RAF Bircham Newton, where it did eventually receive its Mk IVs, maintaining an anti-shipping role for the rest of the war. During its stay at Sutton Bridge, Dickie had a few trips in a Blenheim before the squadron left for pastures new.

While all these new boys were striving to become operational under all sorts of trying conditions, the 'regular trade' of range firing practice continued to be provided by the Station. By early 1939 the Fairey Gordon target tugs had gone, being replaced by the Hawker Henley described earlier. Sutton Bridge Station Flight, comprising the Henley contingent – and known locally as the Henley Towing Flight (HTF) – was integrated with 254 Squadron when the latter arrived. Space was at a premium on the airfield now that there were three fighter units in the process of working-up. From 16 December 1939 therefore, the HTF – comprising Plt Off N. L. Banks,

Sgts R. F. Worsdell, M. U. Wilkin and J. M. Cockburn, with four Henley aeroplanes L3310, L3320, L3335 and L3375 – was attached to 254 Sqn for matters of maintenance and discipline. Naturally Wg Cdr Barwell made sure he put some air time in on the Henley (L3335).

It was now time for events at RAF Sutton Bridge to take another significant, historic, twist and for Dickie Barwell to oversee the arrival of a new training unit that would have a significant part to play in this fateful year. This latest change of direction allowed the station to retain its niche as a vital component of the process – begun before the war – which enabled the Royal Air Force to engage the enemy with growing confidence. On 3 March 1940 an advance party from 11 Group Pilot Pool arrived from far-off RAF St Athan in South Wales. This was the forerunner of what, one week later, became known as 6 Operational Training Unit, (6 OTU) which would remain at Sutton Bridge for the next two years – training Hurricane pilots for battle. Wg Cdr Barwell managed 3 hours in some of the OTU's Hurricane (L1895, L2011, N2356, N2616, N2617), Gladiator K8020 and Miles Mentor (L4400, L4404, L4420) aircraft, for visits to Group HQ at Hucknall and local air tests.

To cope with the rising tide of pupils, the inventory of 6 OTU was increased, serviceable aircraft gradually increasing over the next few months to 34 Hurricanes, 4 Harvards, 8 Masters, 4 Battles and 4 Mentors, plus an unknown quantity classed as temporarily unserviceable. In addition to a few remaining Fairey Battle Trainers, four Battle Target Tugs also appeared in the OTU inventory during July 1940. This seems to reflect the increased workload on Sutton Bridge Station Flight –

which operated the Henley Tugs primarily for 'visitors'. Dickie therefore re-organised things so that the Battle (TT) aircraft were operated by the OTU for its own purposes, which then allowed Station Flight to concentrate on providing a service for visiting operational units.

Similarly, the influx of so many aeroplanes caused another problem; how to accommodate upwards of fifty machines both for protection against the elements and for servicing purposes. To this end Wg Cdr Barwell had pressed for more hangarage and on 1 May work began to erect the first of two Bellman Hangars.

It did not escape the Station Commander's notice that, situated as it was, close to the east coast and within the potential invasion area, his airfield might attract hostile attention from the Luftwaffe. He surmised that the enemy might attempt to carry out attacks on the aerodrome either by dropping bombs or parachute troops. Under certain circumstances, they might arrive over or in the vicinity of the aerodrome without having been intercepted by fighter squadrons. Therefore, being a man of action, on 12 May Dickie drew up his Operational Order No. 1, the stated intention of which was: 'To provide from Station resources air opposition to an attack on this Station'. Wg Cdr Barwell ordered the OC 6 OTU to detail one section of three Hurricanes to be brought to readiness:

a) whenever air raid warning 'yellow' was received in daylight hours.
b) from half-an-hour before sunrise to half-an-hour after sunrise.
c) at other times as ordered by the Station Commander.

The readiness section, call sign 'Domino Green', must always be led by an instructor but the other members could be either pupils or instructors. Pilots were to be strapped in, ready for take-off with aircraft positioned on the leeward side of the airfield, fully armed and with starter batteries connected. As might be imagined, there was no shortage of volunteers!

Wary of trigger-happy ground defences and for the wellbeing of his men, Dickie Barwell also took care to warn the section to be particularly careful of how they returned to the airfield after a sortie. There was to be none of this high-spirited stuff – '... a wide circuit at 1,000–1,500 feet must be made, at a speed of 140 mph so that ground defences may have time to recognise friendly aircraft. Pilots must NOT approach at low altitude, high speed or by diving on the airfield.' It was made pretty clear that if they did so they risked getting their heads shot off by the ground defences!

2.3

SPITFIRES AND BIG WINGS

In mid-June 1940, Wg Cdr Barwell was posted to 12 Group HQ at Watnall (Nottinghamshire) and he rented a house in the village of Papplewick for the family. With Hucknall airfield nearby he was still able to keep his hours current since by having to visit all the stations in the Group, flying was the only effective way to accomplish this duty. He generally used a Miles Magister (L8249) or a Percival Proctor (P6191) but other light types appear in his log book, such as Percival Vega Gull (P5989), Miles M11 Whitney Straight (G-AERO [sic]) and Parnall Hendy Heck (K8853). This miscellany of aircraft was used to fly himself (with occasional passengers, including AVM Trafford Leigh-Mallory, AOC 12 Group) to airfields such as Digby, Wittering, Kirton Lindsey, Church Fenton, Duxford, Debden, Elmdon, Castle Bromwich and Coltishall. However, during his visits to these stations he quite frequently borrowed a Hurricane or Spitfire from the squadrons based there to keep his hand in on those types too.

During the period between 4 and 12 October 1940, Dickie attached himself to 242 Squadron, which had its base at RAF Coltishall. Sqn Ldr Douglas Bader was the squadron's CO at this time and known to be a vociferous proponent of the 'Big Wing' principle – where several squadrons were assembled in the air to co-operate as a single unit against an attacking force. Leigh-Mallory had allowed Bader to implement Big Wing operations, using Duxford airfield as the base for these and now Dickie Barwell took an opportunity to see for himself how this concept worked. It would also enable him to report back at first hand to his boss AVM Leigh-Mallory who, while encouraging Bader, had to account for his commitment to the Big Wing strategy to his own boss, Hugh Dowding.

On 4 October Dickie flew over from Hucknall to Coltishall in Proctor P6191, where he familiarised himself with one of 242's operational Hurricanes for an hour, doing some aerobatics and taking it up to 26,000 feet before landing and returning to Hucknall in the Proctor. On Saturday 5 October, he flew from Hucknall directly to Duxford in the same Proctor, early enough to do a 10-minute circuit before joining the rest of 242 Squadron, who had flown over as usual from Coltishall, to be at readiness. Then, with Wg Cdr Dickie Barwell flying Hurricane R4115 as Douglas Bader's wingman, 'Red 2', (Bader was in V7467) the squadron was scrambled as part of a Duxford Wing operation. The employment of this strategy would be expanded before too long but, at this stage of the air war, the Big Wing concept was essentially a No. 12 Group tactic that involved this daily, temporary transfer of at least three fighter squadrons from airfields in the Group's East Anglian area to a single airfield that was selected for its size and proximity to London – in this case: RAF Duxford.

This Wing 'show' was Dickie Barwell's first Battle of Britain operational sortie and on this occasion the Wing, comprising Nos. 242 (from Coltishall), 266 (from Wittering) 19 and 310 (from Duxford itself), took off at 11.15 and was ordered to orbit Duxford at 25,000 feet to await further instructions about joining that morning's action. The Wing flew round and round but, in the end, were not committed to the fray and so, just about an hour later, landed back at Duxford. The main reason for not being committed to battle seems to be that the three enemy raids that developed during the morning all headed to Kent and airfield targets south of London. These raids consisted of about 125 aircraft in total but they were made up of several small groups of about twenty-five to thirty fighters and fighter-bombers coming in at high level before dropping on to their targets.

At this late stage in the Battle, the Luftwaffe had changed tactics more towards mounting sweeps by fighters and fighter-bombers, rather than the earlier multiple mass formations of twin-engine bombers escorted by fighters. One outcome of the new tactic was that it produced more dog-fighting between the RAF – particularly Spitfires, which were employed because of the high altitudes – and the enemy fighters and fighter-bombers, but these raids also moved around much faster and did not last long. When carrying a bomb, enemy fighters' fuel consumption allowed them to loiter – after release – even less than before. This made it difficult to involve the distant Big Wing – which took at least 20–30 minutes to scramble and form up – effectively when the raids were south of London. It was also a fact that the Hurricane Mk I did not perform at its best above 20,000 feet, or, to quote Bader in conversation with his AOC, 'our Hurricanes fly soggily at 23,000 feet, so when are we going to get the new Hurricane II, sir?'

Later during the 5th, the Duxford Wing, with Dickie flying once more as 'Red 2' to Douglas Bader, was again scrambled and ordered to climb to 25,000 feet then make its way towards Kent to await 'trade'. Although somewhat closer to the action this time, still no enemy aircraft were seen and although aircraft from Luftflotte 3 flew across Kent and another enemy group attacked Southampton, the fierce action was dealt with by the Kent-based RAF squadrons. According to the RAF campaign diary the result for 5 October was: Enemy losses: 22 confirmed, 5 probable, 16 damaged; RAF losses: 9 aircraft and 2 pilots lost.

After the Wing returned to Duxford, Dickie flew back to Hucknall to update his boss Leigh-Mallory. There was no let up for Dickie and his log book shows that over the next few days he flew in the Proctor and Vega Gull to visit Leconfield, Church Fenton and Wittering. It was the following Saturday, 12 October, when Dickie next flew to Duxford to make his third and last operational Battle of Britain sortie. On this occasion, too, it was a Wing scramble to patrol Duxford at 18,000 feet but no action came its way and they landed 40 minutes later.

Raids that morning involved around one hundred enemy aircraft to the south of London followed, in the afternoon, by another hundred attacking targets in south-east Kent. That day's result was: Enemy: 11 confirmed, 11 probable, 7 damaged; RAF: 10 aircraft and 4 pilots lost. It was on 12 October that Hitler called off his invasion, at least for the time being and from that time the pressure from the Luftwaffe upon the RAF noticeably declined, too. Bader's 12 Group Wing still assembled at Duxford and patrolled around the capital once or twice a day but little action came its way and the tension in the air, like the presence of the enemy, declined. The outcome was that the daily gathering of 12 Group Wing's squadrons was simply no longer necessary; 242 Squadron therefore went back to normal readiness operations at Coltishall and the other squadrons were similarly occupied at their own respective stations.

The Battle of Britain arbitrarily – but officially – ended on 31 October 1940 and Wg Cdr Dickie Barwell, with his three operational sorties with 242 Squadron, had qualified to be awarded the subsequent and coveted Battle of Britain Clasp to his 1939–1945 Star. Sadly, he would never live to see either the announcement of the 39–45 Star on 8 July 1943 or the award of the Battle of Britain Clasp in 1945.

With the Battle of Britain effectively at an end, Wg Cdr Dickie Barwell was posted from Watnall to Headquarters Fighter Command (HQFC). His precise start date is not known, although it may have been in February 1941, nor are any details of his duties, but he remained at HQFC until 2 June 1941. By that time, his former boss AVM Trafford Leigh-Mallory was firmly in place as AOC 11 Group and had implemented Big Wing operations against the Luftwaffe over western France and the Low Countries. This strategy was endorsed by the chief of the air staff, Air Chief Marshal (ACM) Charles Portal, and by the new head of Fighter Command, Air Marshal (AM) William Sholto Douglas, so anyone who displayed keenness for that strategy would find favour with his commanders and this may account for Dickie's next posting. Meanwhile, his service at HQFC is evidenced by his flying total in May being solely related to a sort of round-Britain tour. He took off from RAF Chilbolton on 9 May in an unidentified Spitfire and proceeded to Heston. From there, on 11 May, he flew north to Drem then on to Inverness. The next day he flew back to Drem then Sherburn-in-Elmet and finally to Heston. Of course, in a Spitfire the whole trip took only 4 hours 30 minutes flying time!

With effect from 2 June 1941 Dickie was promoted to group captain and posted to take over command of RAF Biggin Hill and its Sector from Gp Capt Frank Soden DFC* – a prestigious appointment that would make him one of the youngest station commanders in the RAF at that time. RAF Fighter Command had gone over onto the offensive now, using Wing-based tactics and was always working out various ways of harassing the enemy over his own territory. Since Dickie's new appointment coincided with the implementation of this strategy, during his time at Biggin Hill he flew many combat sorties on 'Rhubarb', 'Circus', 'Sweep' and 'Rodeo' operations with the squadrons that made up the Biggin Hill Wing.

By way of explanation, a 'Rhubarb' was a low-level strike operation, usually by a small number – often just a pair – of fighters or fighter-bombers mounted in cloudy conditions against enemy ground targets in occupied territory. 'Circuses' were heavily fighter-escorted, daylight bombing attacks – by a nominal number of bombers – against short-range enemy targets, with the aim of enticing enemy fighters into an air battle. A 'Sweep' was a systematic operation, by fighters, fighter-bombers or bombers or a mixture of any of these, over a pre-determined area of enemy territory with the aim of trying to tempt enemy fighters into the air or catch unaware those that were already airborne. 'Rodeo' was the term for a sweep, usually at Wing-strength, carried out by fighters only. All these operations were limited by the range of the Spitfire to just inland from the coasts of north-west France and the Low Countries. It would be the RAF pilots who would now have to watch their fuel gauges when the fun started!

With Circus No. 1 being mounted on 10 January 1941, these Wing- and multi-Wing-scale operations were the basis of the RAF's 1941/42 air offensive. It developed into a battle of attrition for nearly two years and certainly the numerical outcome – and arguably the strategic outcome – of it was not in the RAF's favour. For Dickie Barwell, though, his own motivation was that he felt it was essential for him to see what the men under his command had to do and in his book that meant he had to fly with them – and no doubt he also savoured the prospect of combat operations. However, the weather up to the end of May 1941 had impeded this type of operation but June brought an improvement and cross-channel ops began in earnest, to such an extent that June and the first half of July saw some of the biggest air battles of the war. Biggin Hill Wing was in the thick of the action and its squadrons suffered losses of 62 pilots killed and 26 made POW during that year.

Shortly before Gp Capt Barwell's arrival, the squadrons began taking delivery of Spitfire Vb fighters, armed with two 20 mm cannon and four .303-inch machine guns (m/g) and it was not long before he had picked out one of these for his own use – W3365, coded PR-Y (PR was 609 Squadron's fuselage code) – in which he made regular flights to other stations in 11 Group as well as his several, self-authorised operational sorties.

When Dickie arrived at Biggin Hill, the post of Wing Commander (Flying) – also known as Wing Leader – was in the capable hands of the South African fighter ace, Wg Cdr Adolph

Gysbert Malan DSO DFC – known as 'Sailor'. It was his responsibility to ensure the operational efficiency of the squadrons under his control and to lead the Wing on offensive operations. Biggin Hill Wing at this time comprised Nos.74, 92 and 609 Squadrons and Dickie Barwell flew many of his 'ops' as No. 2 to both Malan and 609's CO, Sqn Ldr Michael Lister Robinson DFC.

For some reason, perhaps due to the sheer intensity of fighter operations at this time, his log book page for July 1941 lacks the clarity of other pages, with entries out of sequence, pencil additions and the 'details' column not filled in for the end of June and the first part of July. The book contains evidence of several different handwriting styles so perhaps settling in to his new post overwhelmed such mundane admin tasks, even if delegated. It was during July that Dickie is credited with shooting down one Messerschmitt Bf 109 and damaging another in a sortie on 11 July. His log book, however, records no flights at all between the 9th and the 12th and no (declared) operational sortie that month except a faint pencilled addition: 'Sweep, 1 hour', dated 23 July but with no details. One possible explanation is that higher command generally frowned upon senior officers, such as a Group Captain Station Commander, flying on operations and this might account for such flights not being properly recorded. On a number of occasions, Dickie had crossed swords with his Air Officer Commanding (AOC) 11 Group, AVM Trafford Leigh-Mallory, about him being far too valuable to lose by going on operations. Dickie always countered this by saying that in order to represent the views and actions of his Wing in high-level discussions, he needed to speak from experience.

While on the subject of group captains flying fighter operations, there were many good reasons why this practice was frowned upon, not least because of the value of such men concerned in terms of experience in leadership and organisational skill alone. The RAF could not afford to lose such charismatic and capable leaders. Naturally, though, these 'old' fighter hands saw it differently but sadly, for all their good intentions, there were dire consequences. Not to put too fine a point on it, they were indeed 'old' by the aircrew standards of the day – but they had the skills that come with age and that is why they were in the appointments they held. But, at thirty-five years of age – or more – their lack of practise and diminishing reaction times, ill-equipped them for the cauldron of fighter combat into which they bravely ventured. We shall hear more about Dickie Barwell who, as a group captain, flew such operations at the age of thirty-five, but he was not alone and there were a spate of incidents – including Dickie's – involving high-ranking officers during 1942.

In 1941, Kenley Sector, for example, was commanded by Group Captain Francis Victor Beamish DSO* DFC AFC who was thirty-eight years of age. A Battle of France and Battle of Britain veteran – with two air victories in the former and three in the latter to his name – he, like his contemporaries, continued to lead from the front, flying operational sorties over western France at the head of his Wing. That is until his luck ran out on 28 March 1942, by which time he had a total of ten confirmed air victories to his name. It was while flying a Rodeo operation with 485 Squadron, in Spitfire Vb, W3649, FV-B, that he was shot down and killed south of Calais, believed to be by Uffz Konrad von Jutrzenka flying a

Bf 109 of I/JG 26. At that time Beamish was the highest-ranked officer to be lost on fighter operations.

The same fate almost befell Beamish's replacement, Gp Capt Richard Llewellyn Roger Atcherley AFC. Richard Atcherley had been in the RAF since the mid-1920s and along the way earned a reputation as an exceptional pilot. Now appointed Station Commander of RAF Kenley he, too, was aged thirty-eight but had little combat-flying experience. Despite having no qualms about leading by example, he would be fortunate to escape with his life. Although he had flown a few sorties with Kenley Wing, he soon realised he was out of his depth flying on such operations and took to going off on his own – one might suggest this was an even greater risk – usually patrolling off the French coast while his Wing completed its particular task. Flying Spitfire Vb, BM235 during one of these Kenley Wing operations on 26 May 1942, Atcherley was jumped by three FW 190s and badly shot up. Cannon shell splinters wounded him in the left shoulder and arm and stripped the flesh from one finger. Shellfire stopped the engine and smoke began to fill the cockpit; the elevator controls were useless; his radio destroyed and when the hydraulics were hit, the undercarriage flopped down. Unable to control the Spitfire, it fell into a spin and he had to get out rapidly. It was with some difficulty he managed to bale out, parachuting into the English Channel where, having swum to and scrambled into his survival dinghy, he floated until rescued, half-drowned and suffering from exposure, by a Royal Navy minesweeper. Gp Capt Atcherley was extremely lucky to escape from his badly damaged aircraft and to be rescued by a British vessel. No doubt he had time to reflect upon his fate and reach the conclusion that he was indeed too old for this game!

An even more astonishing example of the perils of senior officers entering the fighter combat arena at this period of the war can be found in the story behind the loss of Group Captain Hugh Wolfe Corner AFC MD ChB MRCP on 25 April 1942. Between 1917 and 1919 Hugh Corner served as an officer in the British Army and saw action in France before entering the medical profession after the war. In 1925, while in general practice, he applied for a short service commission in the RAF, was accepted and after a number of medical posts in the UK and Middle East he went to RAFC Cranwell, where he qualified as a pilot. Further RAF medical postings continued up to the outbreak of the Second World War, at which point Hugh was appointed senior medical officer to No. 51 (Training) Group where his specialist work on raising the efficiency and morale of trainees brought him the award of an AFC. He was posted to HQ Fighter Command to apply his medical expertise to advising aircrew on how they might handle the stress and strain of combat operations and thus improve their effectiveness.

It was in this role that Hugh Corner felt he needed to fly alongside these airmen to experience what they were feeling – but this brought about his eventual demise. Mixing it with Bf 109s and FW 190s was no place for a forty-three-year-old man – even if he was a competent pilot and could fly a Spitfire. Visiting Kenley Wing, he volunteered for an operation on 25 April, flying with 602 Squadron, under the watchful eye of Battle of Britain ace Flt Lt James Harry (Ginger) Lacey DFM*. Circus 137 was flown in the afternoon of 25 April and involved Biggin Hill, Hornchurch and Kenley Wings flying escort to 36 Boston bombers, elements of which were detailed to attack several French coastal targets. Kenley Wing carried out a sweep towards Le Touquet, where it encountered a swarm of FW 190s. It is believed Gp Capt Corner was flying Spitfire Vb, BM187, as wingman to Ginger Lacey, who engaged and damaged two enemy aircraft. During the course of the dogfight, Hugh Corner's aircraft was hit and severely damaged. As it dived towards the waters of the Channel, the group captain was seen to exit the aircraft but was by then too low for his parachute to open. Despite a search being made by an ASR launch, his body was never found and he is remembered on the Runnymeade memorial to the missing.

Barwell's local flights and visits to other airfields in the south of England are listed in his logbook but these are generally of relatively short duration. However, there is a flight recorded on 21 June of 1 hour 40 minutes duration in Spitfire W3239 but with no details as to its nature. It seems possible, though, that this may have been Dickie's first foray onto ops with the Wing since, according to Wing reports, there was a return to ops on 21 June after a spell of bad weather. In fact, two separate operations were mounted that day and Sailor Malan led the second, Circus 17, to the Luftwaffe airfield at Desvres, in the late afternoon. There was plenty of action, with the Biggin Hill Wing mixing it with Bf 109s at altitudes up to 22,000 feet around Le Touquet and Boulogne. The duration of Dickie's flight would certainly be consistent with this operation. Dickie Barwell's first taste of continental action would, if nothing else, demonstrate how various things had changed since his first brush with the enemy less than two years ago.

Dickie's log book entry for 3 July has a similar look to it – a duration of 1h 25m in W3365 with no details. However, on this occasion Sailor Malan's own reports mention Dickie flying as his wingman. Circus 30 on 3 July 1941 saw Biggin Hill Wing acting as target support to a formation of Bristol Blenheims bombing Hazebrouck and Dickie flew as wingman to Malan. In the vicinity of St Omer, Malan took on a pair of Bf 109Fs; a dogfight developed and during the spirited manoeuvres that ensued Dickie managed to stick to Malan like the proverbial glue – even through his leader's spins! Malan claimed two 109s damaged on that op. The next day, 4 July, after lunch the Wing was briefed to fly top cover for the squadrons escorting Circus 32, an attack on Bethune, and Dickie was again flying as wingman to Malan, who was attached to 609 Squadron for this trip. When the Blenheims turned for home that was when the 109s pounced. They had been lurking nearby at around 20,000 feet and now dived past the Biggin Wing to try to reach the bombers. Sailor Malan latched on to one and fired enough to persuade it to break off its dive. Re-joining his Spitfires, he spotted two 109Es slowing down as they completed their initial dive and he and another Spitfire succeeded in shooting down one of the pair. As Malan broke away, another 109 drifted into view. Closing to 100 yards, he opened fire, it exploded into smoke and flames and went down. In the thick of the action, Dickie became separated from his leader but managed to re-join him in time for both men to find themselves lagging well behind their main formation and about to become a nice juicy target for twenty to thirty 109s. Gp Capt Barwell described this engagement in his combat report.

In the vicinity of Bethune while flying as No. 2 to Wg Cdr Malan, who was leading the Wing, we attacked some Bf 109Es.

As Wg Cdr Malan was engaging one 109, another passed beneath him and climbed away from us to our right. I turned for this enemy aircraft and got in a quarter deflection attack from underneath with about a two-second burst at the range of about 300 yards. The 109 emitted black smoke and petrol vapour and went into a dive. I lost sight of the E/A as I concentrated on re-forming into my position behind Wg Cdr Malan, but he confirmed that it was probably destroyed.

Shortly after this, while still in position as No. 2 to Wg Cdr Malan and while he was turning to port to attack another 109, I sighted a 109 almost behind us and slightly to starboard, diving and opening fire. I had no time to warn Wg Cdr Malan but turned towards this E/A, which then turned and dived away. I then found I had lost sight of Wg Cdr Malan and could see no other friendly aircraft. My height was then about 8,000 feet and I proceeded to weave my way home.

On the way back I was attacked on numerous occasions, firstly by single 109s and at one point by as many as five. All I was able to do was to turn very quickly towards the attacks just before they got within firing range and then open fire myself with a short burst. I saw no results from my fire except in one case, where I saw my bullets strike the E/A and a few small pieces break off. I had no time to watch for any further results.

Between Bethune and Gravelines, my height varied between 8,000 feet down to 5,000 feet. At one time, when I was rather hard pressed, I managed to hide in cloud for a short time. I saw no friendly aircraft until I was about five miles from Dover, when I had just been attacked for the final time from behind by a Bf 109.' (National Archives AIR 50/387).

6.6

ok6 666

666 6

Spitfires and Big Wings

Malan had further brushes with the enemy and finished the day with one destroyed, one shared destroyed and two damaged. Dickie emerged unscathed with one probable and one damaged.

In the midst of all this excitement, back on the ground Gp Capt Barwell had to pay attention to the efficient running of the station and because of Biggin Hill's status, it drew visits by many VIPs, all of course needing to be entertained by the station commander. No less a personage than Winston Churchill himself arrived on 7 July 1941, accompanied by newly knighted Air Marshal Sir William Sholto Douglas KCB MC DFC, AOC-in-C Fighter Command, so Dickie had to be on his toes that day. The Prime Minister spent much of his visit walking round in the glorious sunshine, speaking to pilots and ground crew and looking over the Spitfires as they were being readied for the next operation.

The 11th was also going to be a pretty hectic day for Dickie. In the morning, in his capacity as Station Commander, he had to greet and entertain the Prime Minister of New Zealand Mr Peter Fraser who was making an official visit to Biggin Hill. He was there not only to inspect the RAF's aeroplanes and meet some NZ pilots, but also to watch the Army put a selection of tanks and field guns through their paces. In the afternoon Dickie was off on ops again, this time on Circus 44 as wingman to Sqn Ldr Michael Robinson, CO of 609 Squadron who was leading the Wing on this show – a role he fulfilled on several occasions before being promoted to wing commander himself. It would be a hectic operation for 609, too, since only one of its pilots returned without having firing his guns. Biggin Hill Wing was briefed to go in as part of a diversion in front of the main bomber formation, covering a single Blenheim that was equipped with a special IFF (Identification; Friend or Foe) set emitting radio signals in an effort to draw off enemy fighters.

Crossing the coast near Dunkirk, Sqn Ldr Robinson saw a formation of nearly forty Bf 109s, in three groups, climbing near Cassel. Robinson ordered the Wing to turn onto a course that followed the coast but about 15 miles inland from it. With luck the Wing would converge on the enemy's track with a 1,000-feet height advantage. The first enemy group was allowed to pass by, then Flt Lt Paul Henry Mills Richey DFC led 609's Yellow section down on the second enemy group, while Sqn Ldr Robinson, with Dickie in tow, dived on the rear enemy group. Robinson caught one of a section of three Bf 109s from dead astern and with a short burst shot it down; the pilot being seen to bale out. Latching on to a second 109, Robinson followed that one in a steep dive from 27,000 feet down to 10,000 feet, firing ineffective bursts all the way. Dickie Barwell stuck with Robinson all the way down, too, and just as the latter's ammunition was about to run out, Dickie got a bead on the target at 200 yards range and let rip with a three-second burst from his own cannon and machine guns. The 109 turned into a ball of fire, the pilot baled out and its wings folded up as it plunged to the ground. Not only had he stuck with Michael Robinson in his dive, but Dickie had somehow also managed to put a burst into the third enemy aircraft on the way down. He was forced to break off that attack in order to keep his position clinging to Robinson's wing but that target fell away trailing black smoke.

Yellow section had also made a good 'bounce' on its targets and everyone in the squadron came home intact. It had been a good result for the Wing with 92 Squadron claiming two destroyed (but losing one pilot) while 609 Squadron claimed three destroyed, two probable and three damaged and no one was more pleased than Dickie Barwell who, in addition, claimed one destroyed and one damaged. For Dickie, this memorable day was still not yet over. When he landed at Biggin he had to spruce himself up to receive no less a person than Marshal of the RAF Lord Trenchard himself, to whom the day's successes were recounted and the participating pilots introduced at their dispersal areas.

As we have learned thus far, Dickie was an avid 'collector' of aeroplane types for his log book and he now found himself presented with what he hoped might be a unique opportunity to add a rare bird to his list. Dickie was always keen to test himself and his flying ability, but with the aim of self-improvement rather than self-aggrandisement. Furthermore, he always gave the impression that he believed this would help him to better understand the tools of his trade and thus to be able to pass on the lessons he had learned to those under his command. According to his log book, on 13 July Dickie flew over to Farnborough in W3365 where, accompanied by Michael Robinson, he was allowed to inspect the first Bf 109F-2, *werk nummer* 12764, to be brought down intact in England – although they realised it was in no state to fly and even if it was, they would never be allowed to do so. It had been flown by Hauptmann Rolf-Peter Pingel and crash-landed near Dover on 10 July after being hit by return fire from a Stirling bomber that he had rather unwisely followed a bit too closely across the Channel. Pingel was leader of I/JG26 and a noted 'ace' with twenty-eight air victories (including twenty-two in this war) from 550 combat sorties flown during the Spanish Civil War, the Battles of France and England and the current battles.

It was not until 23 July that Dickie Barwell managed to fit in another combat operation, which was Circus 60 to Mazingarbe, mounted during the evening. On this occasion Dickie led Yellow section of 609 Squadron, which was under the command of Flt Lt Paul Richey. Leaving one of his twelve aircraft behind with mechanical trouble, eleven Spitfires set off, but two more returned early with oxygen problems. That left nine. Before the squadron reached its objective, Dickie hand-signalled to Richey that his radio had packed up and that he, too, was returning to base. Unfortunately, the other three pilots of Yellow section misunderstood his intentions and much to Richey's consternation, all three broke away and followed Dickie home, leaving Richey to complete the operation with just five aircraft! His own radio was playing up but there was some compensation in that he bagged a Bf109 when his depleted force finally tangled with the enemy.

A significant event in Dickie Barwell's flying career occurred during the evening of 9 August 1941. While taking off to begin an offensive sweep operation from Biggin Hill, the engine of Spitfire W3365 cut out and in the subsequent crash-landing his back was badly injured. Although the Spitfire came down on its belly and did not disintegrate catastrophically, the fuselage cracked in half across the cockpit and the impact caused Dickie to fracture a couple of vertebrae in the lumbar region of his back.

There are differing accounts of how severe the injury was and some accounts suggest he was 'encased in plaster' for 'several months'. Dickie was indeed admitted to hospital immediately after the accident but was discharged on 22 August.

He resumed his administrative duties but the discomfort from his injury caused him to return to hospital on 11 September. His son John, however, recalled that his father, with his torso now heavily 'strapped up', 'resumed his duties in a matter of days', having been discharged again on 15 September. He continued to run the station but it is believed he did not regain sufficient mobility for safe flying for some time. Indeed, his log book shows that he flew a total of just 15 hours between 1 August 1941 and 1 January 1942, however, he was determined to renew his flying with the squadrons in his sector and was certainly back in the air flying local practice sorties, visiting other stations and joining in a few practice Wing sweeps during January 1942. It is quite certain Dickie Barwell would never have allowed himself to fly where there was the possibility of engagement with the enemy when, by doing so, he might pose a risk to his fellow pilots.

During the time Barwell was incapacitated, Michael Robinson, who had been in continuous action since the Battle of Britain, was promoted to Wing Commander and took over as Wing Leader from Sailor Malan at the end of July 1941. Robinson was then rested in late September and this also applied to Malan, who had been flying combat operations day in, day out, for two years and was just about 'burned out' by the constant pressure of planning, leading and fighting. Malan was taken off operations and sent to the USA with a small group of RAF fighter pilots on a public relations tour. Michael Robinson had a spell as Station Commander of RAF Manston and then as an aide to the RAF Inspector-General, before returning to operations in January 1942 as Tangmere Wing Leader. Wg Cdr Robinson was lost in action on 10 April 1942.

Biggin Hill Wing Leaders – Wg Cdr (Flying). 1941–1942.

March 1941 to July 1941	Adolph Gysbert Malan DSO* DFC*.
August 1941 to September 1941	Michael Lister Robinson DFC
September 1941 to 17 December 1941	James Rankin DSO* DFC*
December 1941 to 28 January 1942	Robert Roland Stanford Tuck DSO DFC** (POW)
February 1942 to April 1942	Cedric Audley Masterman DFC OBE
April 1942 to July 1942	James Rankin DSO* DFC*
July 1942 to September 1942	Eric Hugh Thomas DSO DFC*.

The sheer scale of this aggressive campaign and its potential effect on all the participants can be judged from some bare statistics for 1941. It is widely accepted that the RAF 'kill' claims were grossly overstated – and largely unverifiable – and many versions of such statistics have been published over the years. In one version, for example, it was stated that in the forty-six Circus operations mounted during six weeks of June/July 1941 the RAF actually lost 123 fighter pilots killed, missing or POW. During that same period the RAF claimed 320 enemy aircraft were shot down – a figure that was greater than the actual quantity of fighters on the Luftwaffe books in France at that time!

From March 1942, now using Spitfire Vb, AB806, Dickie's participation in operations becomes quite frequent again and appears to be fully recorded – at least in his logbook, if nowhere else. He flew some practice sweeps with the Wing on 27 January but it was 3 March before he made his first sortie again over occupied France, when the Biggin Hill Wing was ordered up as a 'feint' operation over the area between Berck Plage and Hardelot, a sortie lasting 1 hour 15 minutes. As the list below shows, Dickie flew many operations while still finding time to intersperse them with flights to all the airfields around his sector: Gravesend, Hawkinge, Lympne and West Malling. As an enthusiast of Wing-sized ops, his was an energetic schedule keeping in touch with the component squadron and wing leaders, always maintaining a highly visible presence and leading by example, sometimes flying ops two or three times in a day. Interspersed with frequent flying visits to airfields on his 'patch' and to many further afield, he was certainly no armchair warrior! Dickie's participation during 1942 was as follows:

14 March	1h 25m	Circus 115	Escort Bostons to Le Havre.
4 April	1h 40m	Circus 119	High cover, Bostons to St Omer.
14 April	1h 35m	Sweep	Le Touquet, Desvres, St Inglevert.
16 April	50m	Circus 126	Escort 8 Bostons to Dunkirk.
17 April	1h 25m	Circus 129	Escort Bostons to Calais.
19 April	1h 10m		Offensive patrol over Guines.
24 April	2h 0m	Sweep	Diversion, Ambleteuse, St Omer, Calais.
27 April	1h 15m	Rodeo 111	Gravelines, St Omer, Boulogne.

28 April	1h 10m	Circus 144	Rear support, Bostons to St Omer.
30 April	1h 45m	Circus 148	Diversion op over Le Havre.
30 April	55m	Rodeo 7	Sweep, Ambleteuse to Gris Nez.
30 April	1h 20m		Operation at night – no detail.
1 May	1h 40m		Wing sweep to Le Havre.
4 May	1h 30m	Circus 153	High cover, Bostons to Le Havre.
24 May		Offensive Wing Patrol	Gris Nez area; one 109F damaged.
27 May		Rodeo	Dieppe area; one Bf 109F probable shared.
30 May	1h 30m	Rodeo 60	Fécamps area.
31 May	1h 20m	Rodeo 63	Dieppe.
2 June	1h 25m	Circus 182	Rear support to Bostons; Dieppe.
6 June	1h 10m	Circus 189	Diversion sweep, Berck to Dieppe.
8 June	1h 25m		Diversionary sweep to Flushing.
22 June	1h 15m	Feint Rodeo	Hardelot to Le Touquet.
26 June	1h 25m	Circus 194	Support Wing in Abbeville area.
29 June	1h 25m	Circus 195	High cover to Bostons: Hazebrouck.

Circus 119 on 4 April, Easter Sunday, is typical of these massive operations that give a flavour of just what sort of combat flying pressure Dickie (and, of course, everyone else involved) was putting himself under. There were twelve Bostons and four Wellingtons to be escorted to attack the rail yard at St Omer and to lure the Luftwaffe into combat. As the bombers turned over Aire onto the target run, the Luftwaffe duly obliged. Over forty Focke-Wulf FW 190s took the bait and a mass of dogfights followed. The outcome also followed the usual pattern, with the Luftwaffe downing fifteen (confirmed) Spitfires for the actual loss of two or three of their own. Eight RAF pilots were killed; two escaped safely and five were made POW. In this Channel theatre of operations, during March 1942 the RAF lost twenty-seven pilots to the Luftwaffe's seven pilots.

On 14 April Dickie was part of a sweep by the Biggin Wing which itself was part of a seven-Wing operation over the Pas de Calais area – a force of around 260 fighters. At least four of the Wings saw action in which each side lost three or four aircraft. A diversionary sweep on 24 April was cover for Circus 132, a raid by twelve Bostons on Vlissingen, a small port in the Scheldt estuary. Hornchurch and Kenley Wings were engaged first but they were operating well to the north of Biggin Hill Wing, which was engaged by FW 190s from I *Gruppe* of JG26, scrambled from Arques, near St Omer, around 14.30. Biggin Wing lost three Spitfires quite quickly, without scoring itself. Dickie was airborne again on Rodeo 111, a three-Wing operation on 27 April that brought no action for the Biggin Wing.

Several other large-scale Circus operations were mounted that day, bringing RAF losses of sixteen Spitfires, one Hurricane and two Bostons, for nil losses to the Luftwaffe. During Circus

144 on 28 April just six Boston light bombers were covered by
no less than sixteen RAF squadrons in six Wing formations –
about 200 Spitfires in all. Dickie and the Biggin Hill Wing were
providing rear support when they were intercepted by FW 190s
of III *Gruppe* JG26 near Calais and lost two Spitfires in the
engagement. Dickie was airborne again for Circus 148, a late
evening raid on Abbeville. Three Luftwaffe *Gruppen* attacked
the RAF force south of the Somme estuary with considerable
success. Seven Spitfires were shot down to crash-land on the
coast and in the sea just off the estuary. During this engagement
the Luftwaffe lost two Bf 109s and one pilot. During April,
ninety-five RAF pilots were lost compared to the Luftwaffe's
thirteen. It was pretty one-sided.

A Rodeo to Le Havre in the late afternoon of 1 May aimed to
draw off the Luftwaffe from a Circus planned for that evening.
JG26 was tempted by this and intercepted the Biggin Hill Wing
but it turned out to be an inconclusive engagement for both
sides and Dickie returned unscathed.

For the Biggin Hill Wing, take-off on Circus 153 on 4 May
was at 09.45 and it was an escort job for six Bostons that were
detailed to attack the power station at Le Havre. For a change,
it turned out to be a reasonably successful trip for the Wing,
led by Wg Cdr Jamie Rankin at the head of 72 Squadron.
Four Bf 109s and an FW 190 were claimed destroyed. Flying
in Spitfire AB806 with 72 Squadron, as 'Red 2' and wingman
to Jamie Rankin, Dickie also had success that day. His eagle
eyes spotted a Dornier Do 217 bomber that had unwittingly
strayed into the combat area and paid the price for its folly.
Dickie submitted a combat report to 72 Squadron for
the interception.

A Bristol Boxkite of the type on which Leonard Dawes learned to fly at the Bristol Flying School, Larkhill, Wiltshire, 1912. (Courtesy BAE SYSTEMS)

Pupils and instructors in front of a Bristol Boxkite, when Leonard Dawes began his flying course at the Bristol School of Flying at Larkhill, Wilts, in May 1912. Standing from left: Lt Ercole (Italy); Lt Antonini (Italy); Senor Campano (Spain); Lt Moore RN; Lt John Graham Bower RN (Instr); Lt Athole Wyness-Stuart; Pierre Prier (Instr); Henri Jullerot (Instr). Seated on the wing is another pupil: Mr Montague Righton Nevill Jennings. Eric Gordon-England (Instr) is seated at the controls of the Boxkite.

Right: Bristol Monoplane of the type operated by the Bristol School of Flying at Larkhill and on which Lt Leonard Dawes took his first steps into the air in May 1912.

Below: A Maurice Farman S7 Longhorn '266' of No. 2 Squadron RFC, with its engine running, at Dysart Farm airfield, Montrose in 1913. (Courtesy Mike Charlton; ukaviationpostcard.co.uk)

Above: *No. 2 Squadron's Royal Aircraft Factory BE 2a '218', modified with a long-range petrol tank in the front cockpit. The pilot, Capt Charles Longcroft, is about to set out on his record flight from Montrose to Farnborough on 22 November 1913.*

Left: *Some of the pilots of No. 2 Squadron at Montrose in 1913, standing in front of a BE2a. From left: Capt Charles Longcroft; Capt George Dawes; Capt John Becke; Lt Francis Waldron; Major Charles Burke (Officer Commanding); Capt George Todd; Lt Leonard Dawes.*

BE 2a '272' was first allocated to No. 3 Squadron at Larkhill in March 1913 then passed to No. 2 Squadron at Montrose in May 1913, where it took part in the squadron deployment to Ireland. It was damaged in a crash-landing en route to the Netheravon camp on 4 June 1914.

Preparations for a day's flying get under way in early morning sunshine at Montrose (Broomfield) aerodrome; home to No. 2 Squadron in 1914. Maurice Farman S7 Longhorn '215' on the left and BE 2a '272' on the right. (Courtesy Mike Charlton; ukaviationpostcard.co.uk)

Above: Four Airco DH 2 single-seat fighters at the Fourth Army Aircraft Park on Beauval aerodrome, France 1916. (Courtesy BAE SYSTEMS)

Below left: 2 (AC) Squadron still going strong in 2019, a BAe Typhoon FGR4, ZK300. (Courtesy Alan Wilson; CCA-SA 2.0 licence)

Below right: 41 Squadron still going strong in the 21st century. BAe Typhoon FGA4, ZJ946, at RAF Coningsby in 2013.

Gloster Grebe, J7583, a single-seat fighter as flown by Plt Off Philip Barwell with 19 Squadron in 1926. (Courtesy Peterborough Museum)

Armstrong Whitworth Siskin IIIA, J8391 and J8382. Fg Off Barwell flew J8382 on several occasions during 1928, while with serving with 19 Squadron.

Fairey Fawn II, J7205. The type flown by Fg Off Barwell when he was posted to 602 (B) City of Glasgow Squadron at RAF Renfrew in 1929. (Courtesy Crown)

Avro Tutor K6115, the aeroplane type most frequently flown by Flt Lt Dickie Barwell during his posting as a staff instructor at Central Flying School, RAF Wittering in 1935. (Courtesy MOD/Crown)

Sqn Ldr Philip 'Dickie' Barwell in his Gloster Gauntlet, K7796, leading 46 Squadron at RAF Digby in 1938. (Courtesy Crown)

RAF Digby operations room laid out exactly as it was during the Battle of Spurn Point on 21 October 1939.

A Heinkel He 115B float-plane of the type operated by I/Kfg 406, encountered by 46 Squadron during the Battle of Spurn Point. (Courtesy Don Hanna)

Images of Hawker Hurricanes operated by 46 Squadron during 1939 are rare. This is a Hurricane Mk I, PO-C of the squadron, being winched onto a lighter prior to being loaded aboard aircraft carrier HMS Glorious for the squadron's deployment to Norway in May 1940. (Courtesy Martyn Chorlton)

Hurricane PO-H of 46 Squadron being re-armed at RAF Digby Oct 1939. (Courtesy RAF Digby records via P H T Green Collection)

Above left: *Flt Lt Jack Leather, left and Fg Off Douglas Watkins, right, of 611 Squadron, whiling away time at readiness at RAF Digby in October 1939. (Courtesy Aldon Ferguson, 611 Sqn Historian)*

Above middle: *Fg Off Desmond Sheen, 72 Squadron, one of the pilots in action during the Battle of Spurn Point on 21 October 1939. (Courtesy Diana Foster-Williams via Kristen Alexander)*

Above right: *Wg Cdr Adolph Gysbert Malan DSO* DFC*, Biggin Hill Wing Leader in 1941. (Courtesy acesofworldwar2.com)*

Sqn Ldr Dickie Barwell DFC, third left, with King George VI, third right, at RAF Digby on 1 November 1939, inspecting aircrew who were involved in the Battle of Spurn Point. Dickie's replacement as OC 46 Squadron, Sqn Ldr Kenneth Brian Boyd ('Bing') Cross is standing between the King and Dickie. (Courtesy Aldon Ferguson, 611 Sqn Historian)

Ex-Battle of Britain Hawker Hurricane I, R4118 in the markings of 605 Squadron. Wg Cdr Dickie Barwell flew Hurricane R4115 with 242 Squadron, as wingman to Sqn Ldr Douglas Bader during the Battle of Britain.

Miles Magister, R1853. In November 1939, three Magisters were taken to Sutton Bridge to enable the pilots of 264 and 266 Squadrons to keep their hand in until their Blenheims and Spitfires turned up. Dickie Barwell and Brian Fern also had flying time on this trainer. (Courtesy A. J. Jackson Collection)

Gp Capt Dickie Barwell's Spitfire Vb, W3365, after its crash-landing due to engine failure on 9 August 1941. (Courtesy John Barwell).

Gp Capt Dickie Barwell, right, accompanies Air Marshal Sholto Douglas, left, and Prime Minister Winston Churchill, centre, on a tour of aircraft dispersal areas at RAF Biggin Hill on 7 July 1941. (Courtesy Norman Franks)

Another VIP inspection. Gp Capt Philip Barwell welcomes Air Cdre HRH The Duke of Kent to Biggin Hill on 3 June 1942. (Courtesy Norman Franks)

Supermarine Spitfire Vb; the type flown by Dickie Barwell on operations with the Biggin Hill Wing over France during 1941/42.

A Wulf in sheep's clothing! Captured on 23 June 1942, Focke Wulf Fw 190A-3, w/n 5313 of III/JG2, is seen in RAF markings as serial PN999, ready for evaluation trials. (Courtesy defenceoftherealm.com)

Above: *A pair of Stearman PT-17 trainers, B218 and B219, from 6 BFTS, Ponca City, Oklahoma, USA in 1941. Brian Fern flew B218 on 15 and 22 August 1942. (Courtesy Paula Denson)*

Left: *Stearman PT-17, B219, 6 BFTS, Ponca City, 1942. (Courtesy Paula Denson).*

Below: *Stearman PT-17, B219, 6 BFTS, Ponca City, 1942. (Courtesy Paula Denson)*

Right: *Stearman PT-17, B217, in which Brian Fern flew at 6 BFTS, with instructor Mr W. B. Kelson climbing down from the wing. (Courtesy Paula Denson)*

Below: *North American AT-6A Texan, Brian Fern flew '278' on 18 November 1942 at 6 BFTS, Ponca City. (Courtesy Paula Denson)*

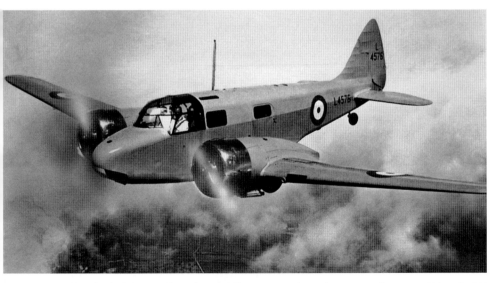

Airspeed Oxford of the type flown by Fg Off Brian Fern during his postings between 1943 and 1945 to 3 (P)AFU, South Cerney; 7 Flying Instructor School, Hullavington; 14 (P)AFU, Banff and 7 (P)AFU, Sutton Bridge. (Courtesy BAE SYSTEMS)

Percival Prentice T1 as flown by Brian Fern at CFS, RAF Little Rissington, in 1951 and 2 FTS Cluntoe in 1954.

Gloster Meteor T7, WA591. Brian Fern joined the jet-age on this two-seat trainer type at CFS Little Rissington in 1951 and 211 FTS at RAF Worksop in 1954.

Percival P56 Provost T1, WW397; the type flown by Brian Fern as an instructor at 2 FTS RAF Hullavington in 1954. (Courtesy BAE SYSTEMS)

English Electric Canberra B2, WH977, showing off its manoeuvrability in a steep diving turn above a snowy landscape. Brian Fern flew the B2 model with 207 Squadron at RAF Marham during 1955/56. (Courtesy MOD/Crown)

Sqn Ldr Brian Fern (left) and his Vickers Valiant crew. (Courtesy Brian Fern collection)

Vickers Valiant XD812 flown by Brian Fern with 214 Squadron in 1958/59. (Courtesy David Whitworth collection)

Above: *Vickers Valiant WZ376 refuels Brian Fern's WZ390. 214 Squadron. (Courtesy Brian Fern collection)*

Right: *Brian Fern, third right, with his crew after their unofficial record flight to Nairobi in April 1959. (Courtesy Brian Fern collection)*

Below: *Sqn Ldr Fern in Vickers Valiant XD870 refuels Valiant WZ390. 214 Squadron 1959. (Courtesy Brian Fern collection)*

Above left: *Sqn Ldr Fern meets Marshal of the Royal Air Force Sir Thomas Pike. (Courtesy Brian Fern collection)*

Above right: *In the mess at RAF Gatow, Berlin, 1964. Sqn Ldr Brian Fern, left, with the wartime fighter ace and OC Gatow Gp Capt Robert 'Bobby' Oxspring, second left, and other BRIXMIS officers. Bobby Oxspring was flying alongside Dickie Barwell when the latter was shot down on 1 July 1942. (Courtesy Brian Fern collection)*

Brian Fern in Vickers Valiant WZ376 refuels Avro Vulcan ZX478, 1959. (Courtesy Brian Fern collection)

Vickers Valiant, XD871, refuelling a Gloster Javelin FAW 9R, XH887. Brian Fern flew XD871 and carried out Javelin refuelling sorties on a number of occasions. (Courtesy Crown)

I was flying as Red 2 to Wg Cdr Rankin who was leading the [Biggin Hill] Wing, which was acting as top cover to six Bostons for an attack on the power station at Le Havre.

As we approached Le Havre at about 10.30 hours I sighted a single aircraft below, to the east and I informed the Wing Leader, who tried to detach Blue and Yellow sections of 72 Squadron [to attack it]. As the leaders of these two sections could not see the enemy aircraft, the Wing Leader called me up and told me to take Red 3 and Red 4 to attack. I broke away, followed by Red 4 only [Plt Off Waters (NZ)], because Red 3 had not received the R/T message and stayed with the Leader.

The E/A was at 12,000 feet just off the coast by Fécamps, flying in a north-easterly direction. I approached from above and got into an up-sun position about 2,000 feet above. I then dived to attack from the starboard quarter, coming in about dead astern and slightly above. I opened fire at about 200 yards range with a rather fast closing speed and I estimate I broke away at 50 yards range. I gave the enemy aircraft one burst of three-seconds with cannon and machine guns [54 cannon and 320 m/g rounds] and saw strikes in the fuselage and port engines and saw several large flashes from the cannon strikes. After breaking away I saw the E/A turn and dive inland with smoke coming from the port engine. I saw several four-star Very lights go off as it went down. Red 4 then went in to attack and I tried to cover him from attack as I thought there were some enemy fighters above. Red 4 saw the port engine on fire and the enemy aircraft going down in a spiral. He fired at it and saw strikes on the fuselage. He last saw it at about 6,500 feet going down nearly inverted.

Blue section witnessed my attack from above and Blue
1 confirms that he saw cannon strikes and the port engine on
fire.' [National Archives AIR 50/30/45].

Dickie submitted a claim for one Dornier Do 217 destroyed.
Because even though it was seen by others to dive earthwards
emitting smoke, no one had actually seen it crash, the Air
Ministry amended his claim to a 'probably destroyed' and there
is no note of his success written against this operation entry in
his logbook. Dickie could be regarded as a reliable witness, both
for aircraft recognition and for not 'over-claiming', but this
'probable' is generally overlooked in modern accounts of his
combat claims – although, curiously, no corroborating evidence
has been found for a 'damaged or destroyed' Do 217 (nor other
twin-fin aircraft) in Luftwaffe records on or near this date.

Meanwhile, the procession of VIP visits to Biggin Hill
continued and Dickie had to switch his mind from the frenzy of
combat sorties to present a calm and efficient air to his illustrious
visitors. On 29 April, high winds caused the morning operation
to be cancelled but Dickie was able to renew acquaintance with
King George VI when he arrived to inspect the Biggin squadrons
and chat to pilots, prior to the Wing setting off on Circus
145 later that afternoon. Dickie did not fly that day, since the
King took precedence over everything.

Wg Cdr Jamie Rankin was back in command of the Biggin
Hill Wing and Dickie Barwell flew some operations as his
wingman. It was on 24 May at 19.20 during an offensive Wing
patrol in the Cap Gris Nez area that Dickie got into a scrap
while flying as 'Red 2' to Rankin. They were at 25,000 feet
when, with Barwell sticking to his wing, Jamie Rankin latched

onto a Bf 109F and chased it in a north-easterly direction. Rankin fired at it without visible result, then Dickie gave it a two-second burst with cannon and machine guns from dead astern at 350 yards range. He saw strikes on the wing and fuselage before he had to break away to re-join Rankin and turn for home. It didn't pay to chase inland for too long on your own. His two-second burst loosed off 48 cannon shells and 480 Browning m/g rounds but could only claim a 'damaged'.

Dickie was back in action during the morning of 27 May, again flying as No. 2 to Wg Cdr Rankin on a Rodeo operation to the Fécamp area. Rankin's combat report provides a view of the action.

After 72 and 133 Squadrons had jumped upon fourteen enemy aircraft, I turned right, with 124 and 401 Squadrons and climbed over the engagement area to give our aircraft cover.

When in position, I saw several E/A at approximately the same height [22,000 feet] in the area, one of which was about ¾ mile off. I chased him with Red section of 124 Squadron. I closed to 400 yards, at which point the E/A saw me and did a slow half-roll. As he rolled, I opened fire with three bursts with all guns and saw many strikes on fuselage as the aircraft rolled. These [strikes] may have been mine or Gp Capt Barwell's, who was firing simultaneously. The E/A went onto its back and commenced to dive. I lost sight of it and pulled away but did not pick it up again. The E/A had been heavily hit and as 'Red 3' and 'Red 4' state that they saw it go down in a vertical dive, turning slowly until out of sight below cloud which was at 1,000 to 2,000 feet base with 4,000 feet top, this E/A is claimed as probably destroyed. [National Archives AIR 50/415/3].

Gp Capt Barwell also submitted a combat report for this incident.

> I was 'Red 2'. Together with Wg Cdr Rankin, I saw several single E/A in the area of Fécamp, one of which I chased. I closed from 300–200 yards and gave two bursts of two seconds each, with cannon and m/g, firing simultaneously with Wg Cdr Rankin. I saw strikes hit this E/A which turned over and went down in a spin.

On 3 June it was the turn of Air Cdre HRH Prince George, Duke of Kent, whose VIP arrival came just prior to a sweep by the Biggin Wing as part of an escort of Boston bombers to Le Havre being planned for later that day. The Duke sat in on the briefing and Dickie stayed on the ground with his guest. He did manage to join Circus 189 on 6 June, which took the Wing to 25,000 feet over the Dieppe area but no battle contact was made. On 7 June there was a return visit by AOC-in-C Fighter Command, Sholto Douglas, this time accompanying Colonel John Jestin Llewellin, the Minister of Aircraft Production. The good news from this visit was that the Wing was promised some of the new Spitfire IXs 'as soon as possible'.

There was a further opportunity to check out a captured enemy aircraft, this time an example of the much-vaunted Focke-Wulf FW 190. It came quite by chance when Oberleutnant Armin Faber, the pilot of FW 190A-3, *werk nummer* 5313 of III/JG2 conveniently misplaced his bearings during an engagement on 23 June 1942 over the western Channel and, around 8.30 p.m., landed by mistake at RAF Pembrey, in west Wales. RAF Fighter Command rubbed its hands with great anticipation because this was the enemy aircraft that had been giving our fighter boys in their Spitfire Vs such a hard time since August 1941. Its performance was superior to the Spitfire Vb so, when he heard one had dropped into our hands completely intact, Dickie lost no time in flying to Pembrey to have a good look at it before it was carted off to Farnborough. There, it would be far less accessible while it underwent a technical assessment prior to it being handed over to the Air Fighting Development Unit (AFDU) based at RAF Duxford.

Once it reached AFDU it was put through its paces in a series of practical flying performance comparisons against current RAF front-line fighters such as the Spitfire V, Hawker Typhoon and the Spitfire IX that was just coming into service. Thus, on 25 June Dickie recorded making the 1-hour trip to Pembrey in his Spitfire AB806. Of course, neither he – nor the small procession of other inquisitive fighter squadron commanders who had heard the news – were permitted to fly the captured machine, but it was helpful just to sit in the cockpit; get a pilot's view and feel for the machine and work out possible 'blind spots'. Dickie then flew over to RAF Fairwood Common, where the hapless Oberleutnant Faber had been taken and where Dickie was allowed by his friend and contemporary Gp Capt David Atcherley – twin brother of Richard, of whom we heard earlier – to meet Faber before he was taken the next day by train to London for interrogation and subsequent shipment to Canada as a POW. Dickie then flew back to Biggin Hill and set about disseminating his first impressions of the FW 190 to his own squadron commanders.

Dickie Barwell participated in his final offensive operation – Circus 195 – on 29 June 1942. Biggin Hill Wing provided high cover to twelve Bostons raiding Hazebrouck marshalling yards. It drew a response from JG 26 which had some success among the other Wings involved but Biggin Hill Wing returned without sustaining any casualties. Interestingly, one of the Bostons was manned by an American crew, which made it the first time Americans had flown from England on combat operations since the end of the First World War. It was also the first time a squadron of Hawker Typhoons was employed as part of the escorting force.

On 1 July 1942 (the day before his thirty-fifth birthday) the only flight recorded in Dickie's log book is a 'local test flight' of 1-hour duration in AB806. All the columns are totalled – of course by another hand – at that point showing that he had amassed a total of 2,905 hours in a flying career spanning fifteen years. In combat Dickie was credited with destroying two enemy aircraft and sharing in the destruction of another, plus one shared probable and one damaged. Behind that terse description, though, is a tragic ending to this story of a brave and distinguished airman.

As the RAF's policy of attacking the enemy on his own territory entered its second year, the Luftwaffe stepped up its own retaliation by carrying out hit-and-run operations by fighters and fighter-bombers over the south coast of England. In Biggin Hill sector the brunt of handling these incursions fell upon 91 Squadron based at Hawkinge but by the middle of the year it had achieved little by way of success against these swift and elusive raiders. Perplexed by the situation, the CO of 91, Sqn Ldr Robert Wardlow 'Bobby' Oxspring DFC (later Gp Capt DFC** AFC), flew over to Biggin Hill to discuss this issue with Dickie Barwell and his Sector Controller, Bill Igoe.

The outcome was that Dickie suggested that he and Oxspring should fly a patrol between Dungeness and Beachy Head that very evening, under the control of Bill Igoe and see if they could work out what was causing the difficulty in intercepting these enemy raids.

About an hour before sunset on 1 July, with Dickie flying in company with Sqn Ldr Oxspring, the two aircraft were nearing Beachy Head at 16,000 feet, just above the evening haze, when the controller warned them of unidentified plots approaching their position. Scanning the sky, Oxspring spotted a pair of fighters coming out of the sun and shouted a warning to Dickie, who was positioned between him and the fighters. Oxspring identified them as Spitfires and watched in dismay as one disappeared behind him while the second curved in behind Dickie's aircraft and opened fire at him. Barwell's aircraft was hit and burst into flames. Oxspring himself was then attacked by the first Spitfire so he had to take evasive action, going hard down into the haze to shake it off. When he emerged again from the haze he found the two attackers had disappeared but there was also no sign of Group Captain Barwell's aircraft, AB806, nor any response from him to radio calls. Despite an intensive air and sea search no sign of Dickie or his aircraft was found and it was presumed he had gone to the bottom of the Channel with his aircraft. Group Captain Barwell's body was, however, some days later washed ashore on the French side of the Channel and he was buried in Calais Canadian War Cemetery at Leubringhen. At the inevitable court of inquiry which followed this tragedy, it was alleged that of the two 'attacking' pilots – both Canadians from 129 Squadron based at Westhampnett – Sgt Richard Leonard Reeves was on his second war patrol and Sgt Maurice William Frith was on his first. Both pilots claimed their aircraft were attacked first but Sqn Ldr Oxspring claimed it was the other way around. It was a tragic end to a brilliant career.

Group Captain Philip Reginald Barwell DFC is remembered on both Swavesey (St Andrew) and Peterborough war memorials. It has been suggested that Dickie was 'from' Peterborough and this view is perhaps encouraged by his name appearing on the Peterborough City Memorial. It appears, however, that because Dickie's wife Mary was a Peterborough girl, she asked that her husband be remembered in that city. He was also commemorated in more recent times, too, when in 2006 a road in a new housing estate in Biggin Hill, off the A233 road close by the airfield, was named Barwell Crescent in his honour.

Part 3

THE COLD WAR WARRIOR, 1941–1967

Squadron Leader Brian Fern, RAF

3.1

IN OKLAHOMA SKIES

Brian Edward Fern was born on 26 September 1923 in Mafeking, that historically famous town in South Africa located close to its border with Botswana. Brian's flying career brings our story into the modern era with an indication of how RAF training was conducted during the latter part of the Second World War and the part he played in the development of the post-war RAF to reach its goal as a strategic global-reach air force.

His parents, Edward and Dorothy, were both of British nationality and they migrated from England when his father obtained a post in South Africa as a government veterinary officer. Brian spent his early years in Mafeking before being sent back to England at the age of seven to continue his education at Junior King's School, an independent preparatory school at Milner Court, Sturry, in Kent, where he remained from 1931 to 1936. At the age of thirteen he moved on to the senior King's School in Canterbury where, by 1941, he had achieved an Oxford & Cambridge Joint Matriculation Certificate.

It was here, too, that in 1938 he joined the school's Junior Training Corps unit and, when it was formed in 1941, the Air Training Corps, in which he reached the rank of cadet sergeant. Brian was keen on sport, playing cricket and rugby at school and had a keen interest in the world of nature.

With the onset of the German *Blitz* in 1940, the city of Canterbury was in a vulnerable location so the headmaster of King's, in consultation with government education authorities, decided it was in the interests of pupil safety to evacuate the whole school to Cornwall to escape this bombing threat. Brian was one of those pupils evacuated and this is confirmed by the 'home address' he gave to the RAF when he applied to join up, *viz*: c/o Mrs Tidy, Cornish Riviera Hotel, Carlyon Bay, near St Austell, Cornwell. He also gave an address for his next of kin, his father, as: Central Veterinary Research Institute, Mazabuka, Northern Rhodesia (now Zambia).

Like many of his contemporaries, with the onset of war Brian volunteered for aircrew in the Royal Air Force. At the age of seventeen years and ten months, he was physically and mentally tested before being inducted into the service at the Combined Recruitment Centre (CRC) in Euston, London, as 1394486 Aircraftman Second Class (AC 2) Fern on 5 August 1941 having been accepted as an ACH (aircraft-hand) candidate for pilot/observer training and placed on the reserve to await mobilisation. However, having reached his eighteenth birthday, his service record shows him as being attached to Glasgow University Air Squadron (UAS) from 10 October 1941 until his full mobilisation on 11 April 1942. Being attached to a UAS is explained by the fact that, like the vast numbers of men going through the same process around this time, the then-current

RAF training system simply could not cope with the quantity and Brian was obliged to wait for a place at a flying training school. Having gained his Matriculation Certificate at school, at his Air Crew Selection Board (ACSB, also at Euston) he was recommended for pilot training and offered a place on what was known as an RAF University Short Course (USC). In addition, the minimum age for general call-up was eighteen but candidates for aircrew were not called up until they were at least eighteen-and-a-quarter years of age. Therefore, for those young men such as Brian, whose education was up to university entrance standard, it was an effective utilisation both of a recruit's waiting time and the universities' 'spare' wartime capacity.

The UAS course reflected the air crew ground school syllabus that would have been found at the RAF Initial Training Wings (ITW) – the alternative route into the aircrew training process – but several of the academic subjects were taught to a higher level than at ITW. During this period with Glasgow UAS, Brian would have received instruction in basic RAF training such as drill, weapons, signals and aircraft identification. In addition, he would have received lectures at the university on such subjects as meteorology, aircraft engineering and principles of flight, physics and mathematics. There would have been some tuition in a Link Trainer (an early flight-simulator) although there is no evidence of any airborne air-experience flights in Brian's case. The USC scheme was also aimed towards those who might be of commissionable material and/or if a sufficiently high standard of subject results were achieved, a candidate might be given some sort of preference to re-enter the university after the war – if they had the opportunity to do so. Accommodation was in the university halls of residence.

Upon completion of his course in Glasgow, along with thousands of other airmen, Brian's first taste of real service life came when he was called forward to attend No. 3 Air Crew Reception Centre (ACRC) in Regent's Park, London, on 12 April 1942. Arriving in 'civvies' clutching his meagre personal possessions, over the next two weeks he was issued with uniform and kit, marched from pillar to post, medically examined, inoculated and he filled in numerous forms of paperwork that turned him from a civilian into an airman. Uniform was issued at Lord's Cricket Ground – requisitioned for the duration – where information lectures were taken in the stands and PT was carried out on the former hallowed turf itself. Accommodation was in RAF standard (i.e. Spartan!), dormitory style rooms in requisitioned, converted housing and flats in the surrounding London streets, while airmen were marched to take meals in the restaurant of London Zoo.

Now the ball was rolling and elevated to the dizzy rank of Leading Aircraftman (LAC), his next posting was to the Air Crew Disposal Wing (ACDW) in Brighton for allocation to a flying training unit. ACDW was formed in October 1941 to deal with personnel including, among others, those like Brian who had attended a UAS and who were being sorted out into the various aircrew categories. Brian arrived in Brighton on 27 April 1942 but it was almost a month before a slot became available for him at 7 Elementary Flying Training School (EFTS), a 'Class A+2' flying grading school run by the aircraft components manufacturer Reid & Sigrist Ltd from their airfield at Desford, Leicestershire. This was a large school with a pupil population of around 180 organised into six Flights with overlapping courses going through on a 'conveyor belt' system.

Here aspiring aircrew were given basic flying training in the DH Tiger Moth to find out who was considered capable of further training as a service pilot, or who would not make the grade as a pilot – but who might make it as an observer or navigator. Brian was at Desford for three weeks but there is no formal record of what flying time he put in or when he went solo, although it was customary for those who were graded as potential pilots to demonstrate they could fly solo after no more than about 10–12 hours' instruction. A clue to Brian's participation in this phase comes from his own comprehensive analysis of his flying hours, made when he retired from the service in 1967 and noted at the end of his current log book. In that summary, among all the different aircraft types, he noted that he had flown 13 hours and 20 minutes in a Tiger Moth, of which 20 minutes was solo. Since his very first log book entry is dated 11 August 1942 and relates to his time in the USA, and there are no entries for Tiger Moths in any of his surviving log books after that date, it must be assumed that those solitary '13h 20m' relate to his 'grading time' at 7 EFTS, part of No. 51 Group Pool, which his service record shows he attended from 21 May to 13 June 1942. We can reasonably assume, therefore, that he went solo for the first time a few days prior to 13 June 1942.

Having passed this first hurdle to becoming a pilot, Brian was informed he was part of Draft 4596 due to be sent to Canada to continue his flying training and on 24 June 1942 he was ordered to present himself at the Air Crew Dispatch Centre (ACDC) in Heaton Park, Manchester. There he had to kick his heels for about a week while the process of being consolidated into a transit batch with other aspiring aircrew took place.

He left ACDC on 2 July for Scotland to embark on the SS *Letitia*, a troopship of 13,600 tons and capable of a speed of 15 knots, for the Atlantic crossing. The ship sailed 'independently' (i.e. not in a convoy) from the Clyde on 3 July 1942 bound for Halifax, Nova Scotia, which was reached without incident on 11 July. From Halifax he travelled 150 miles north by troop-train to reach 31 Personnel Despatch (PD) Centre, based at Moncton on the shore of the Bay of Fundy in the province of New Brunswick. 31 PD was a huge reception centre dealing with RAF personnel moving between Canada, the USA and England and so, again, Brian had to wait patiently for the wheels of officialdom to grind out his next posting – which took until the first week of August to sort out.

On the move again, Brian Fern found himself as one of a group of forty-three cadets put aboard a train – this time a far more comfortable regular express rather than a rackety old troop train – that would, with some changes *en route*, take them on a journey of over 2,000 miles through Canada and into the USA, to the warmer climes of the mid-western state of Oklahoma. Their final destination was Ponca City airfield, home to 6 British Flying Training School (6 BFTS), which was run by the Darr School of Aeronautics. The following outline of the background to this Anglo-US arrangement is derived from information kindly provided by Paula K. Denson, an historian from Oklahoma; Mike Igglesden, himself a former RAF pupil at 6 BFTS during the Second World War, and from records of the US Dept of the Interior National Park Service.

Prior to the US entry into the war and before the passage of its 'Act to Promote the Defense of the United States' which incorporated what became known as the 'Lend-Lease Bill',

Deputy Chief of Staff and Chief of the US Army Air Corps (USAAC) – which, after 1941, became US Army Air Force (USAAF) – General Henry Harley 'Hap' Arnold, put an interesting idea to Air Cdre George Pirie, the British Air Attaché in Washington. Arnold's overall idea – later dubbed the 'Arnold Scheme' – had two components. One involved RAF pilots being trained under the USAAC three-phase flight-training system – primary, basic and advanced – at existing USAAC schools. The other part of Arnold's idea involved setting up six civilian-run flying schools in the USA to undertake training of RAF pilots to the RAF's own Flying Training School syllabus. The latter would be known as British Flying Training Schools (BFTS) and although they, too, began by operating a three-phase syllabus, part way through it was changed to two phases only – primary and advanced. In addition to this two-phase system, the BFTS also differed from their USAAC counterparts by having students complete each British course entirely at the BFTS location to which they were initially attached. In May 1941 approval was finally given by President Franklin D. Roosevelt, under the umbrella of that ingenious creation of his, the Lend-Lease Act, to a scheme that provided facilities for thousands of RAF airmen to be trained as pilots in the USA.

The USAAC was prepared to supply 260 primary and 285 advanced, standard US trainer aircraft to these civilian schools whose owners and those organisations that owned the property or land, would invest substantial sums of money in the construction of appropriate new facilities at each airfield selected. Technically, the aeroplanes would be purchased by the Federal Government and 'loaned' to the British under the terms of the Lend-Lease Act. The investors would recoup their expenditure through the rates they charged the RAF for expertise provided, e.g. for flying hours, which were reported to be around $25 per hour for Primary and $35 per hour for Advanced. In 2019 terms, these sums are equivalent to $437 or £340 and $612 or £476 per flying hour respectively.

At Ponca City municipal airport there already existed in 1941 aviation service businesses such as Braniff Airways (it was a staging point in its airline network); Continental Oil Company and the Ponca City School of Aeronautics – a flying school run by Tom Smyer. This latter company was unsuccessful in negotiating for one of the new contracts, although it and the other service companies still continued to operate from the premises even when 6 BFTS eventually arrived.

It was Harold S. Darr of Chicago, the owner of the Darr School of Aeronautics, who successfully bid, on 4 August 1941, for the contract that resulted – within the space of just one week – in construction work to create 6 BFTS commencing at Ponca City Airport. The City Chamber of Commerce also agreed to enlarge the airport acreage to accommodate new buildings, which included three huge new hangars. Harold Darr was an ex-First World War flight instructor who, between the wars, worked variously for the Curtiss-Wright Company; as manager of St Louis municipal airport; as a flight engineer for American Airlines before, in 1938, opening his first aviation school: the Chicago School of Aeronautics. At the time of the 'Arnold Scheme' he owned and operated three other military flight training schools in the southern states of the USA.

Seven new schools, known as British Flying Training Schools, were set up in double-quick time across the southern states of the USA and with its prospect of plentiful good, clear, flying weather it was expected that the schools together would turn out at least 1,300 pilots per year. This figure was well exceeded by the end of the scheme.

1 BFTS	Terrell, Texas	Opened 9 June 1941.
2 BFTS	Lancaster, California	9 June 1941.
3 BFTS	Miami, Ottawa County, Oklahoma	16 June 1941.
4 BFTS	Mesa, Arizona	16 June 1941.
5 BFTS	Clewiston, Florida	17 July 1941.
6 BFTS	Ponca City, Oklahoma	23 August 1941.
7 BFTS	Sweetwater, Texas	May 1942 (closed Aug 1942).

Each course was similar between the schools and – unlike the USAAC's own flight schools – these British courses were designed to be fully completed at the same location. A course was scheduled to last twenty-eight weeks and originally comprised three parts: primary tuition was given on the Stearman PT-17 aeroplane; basic tuition on the Vultee BT-13 Valiant and advanced tuition on the North American AT-6 Texan, a type known as the Harvard in RAF service. However, at Ponca City, from course 9 onwards the basic (BT-13) component was deleted from the syllabus and cadets went from twelve weeks primary on the PT-17, directly onto sixteen weeks advanced on the AT-6.

The Stearman PT-17 was a rugged single-engine bi-plane of 32-feet wingspan with a fixed/tail-wheel undercarriage and two open cockpits in tandem. Powered by a Continental R670 air-cooled radial engine of 220 hp it had a maximum speed of 135 mph and a service ceiling of 13,000 feet. The North American AT-6A & C models (mostly the 'A') used at 6 BFTS were single-engine, low-wing monoplanes of 42-feet span; a retracting undercarriage with tail-wheel and two seats in tandem under sliding canopies. A Pratt & Whitney R-1340-49 air-cooled radial engine of 550 hp gave the AT-6 a maximum speed of 200 mph and a service ceiling of 24,000 feet. Aircraft at each BFTS were identified by a large code letter on the fuselage. For example, the code for 6 BFTS at Ponca City was 'B', followed by an aircraft number, e.g. B123.

After an initial, staggered, build-up to bring about 180 to 200 students in to Ponca City, courses consisting of around fifty cadets then arrived at roughly seven-week intervals but from course 11 onwards, the BFTS in general increased their intake to about 100 cadets at nine-week intervals and also began to include around 20 per cent USAAC cadets among their number. Brian Fern joined course 9 at 6 BFTS in Ponca City, which ran from 8 August 1942 to 19 February 1943 and his training followed the revised primary/advanced syllabus.

All Darr's instructors, ground crew and support staff were American civilians. Key air and ground personnel were brought in from Darr's other schools but many had to be recruited locally. This latter situation applied to flight instructors too, because there was a shortfall in numbers available, although some of those locally recruited – even though they were experienced fliers – did not have an instructor rating. In his typical 'can-do' attitude Harold Darr took immediate steps to address this difficulty by arranging for potential instructors to be retained on a salary while they undertook instructor-rating tuition courses set up at the school itself. After passing Federal

Civil Aviation Authority (CAA) exams the successful candidates were then taken on as flight instructors by the school.

Each school also had a small RAF administrative staff, comprising a commanding officer, three or four other officers, and non-commissioned officers (NCOs) for armaments, signals and other specialist RAF training. Matters of discipline and pay were also dealt with by the RAF staff. The RAF OC Ponca City for most of the time that Brian Fern was in residence was Wg Cdr Charles A. Ball – although the latter did not arrive on site until May 1942. Prior to the USA entering the war on 8 December 1941, RAF cadets were required to wear civilian clothing but after that date, cadets wore appropriate RAF uniform. With Saturday afternoons and Sunday free, a great many cadets were 'adopted' by Oklahoma families and all airmen were greeted with warmth, hospitality and generosity wherever they went. It was not long before RAF airmen, at first somewhat taken aback, were soon enjoying the abundance of good food, including steaks, hamburgers, malts, sodas and bacon and eggs. In the town, T. J. Cuzalina's Drug Store was a favourite off-duty hangout and dancing was a frequent pastime that could be enjoyed with the local ladies at the Club Lido.

Cadets for the first RAF course arrived on the evening train into Ponca City on 26 August 1941. The instructional programme at Ponca City was fast-paced and rigorous, in what amounted to cramming a year's instruction into five months. Classes for ground subjects were attended for 4 hours a day, and cadets were expected to do another 4 hours a day homework in their barracks and these tyros spent either a morning or an afternoon in the air every day, weather permitting. The Link trainer was a valuable piece of equipment, used at all stages to supplement real flying and to correct problems encountered. Two auxiliary landing fields were also constructed a few miles away to relieve the pressure on the main airport. In April 1942 the US War Department took over Darr's contract with the British and the property was sold to a government-related organisation known as the Defense Plant Corporation. The now federally owned property was then leased back to Harold Darr to carry on the training programme as before. Later in 1942 the school was further enlarged to accommodate an increase in student population from around 200 to 400.

Brian Fern began his own flying training on 11 August 1942 with a 40-minute flight in PT-17, B206, with instructor Mr Artis, who was to remain his tutor throughout the primary phase. This first flight covered RAF numbered exercises:

1. Air experience.
2. Effect of controls.
3. Straight and level.
4. Climb and descend.
5. Taxying.
6. Medium level turns.
8. Stalling.

Between this first flight on 11 August and the end of the month, Brian flew on fifteen days putting in 22 hours, of which 14 were dual and 8 solo, a flying rate that he would have been quite unlikely to achieve in English skies. His big day arrived on 17 August when Mr Artis sent him off solo for 25 minutes of circuits (exercise 11) in PT-17, B205, after just 4 hours 40 minutes of dual. This proved to be 'a bit hairy' because the throttle kept sticking during the circuit but he made it round without mishap. Over the next eleven weeks Brian carried out a variety of air exercises under the watchful eye of Mr Artis, who interspersed the exercises with 'co-ordination' practice and assessment to ensure his pupil continually pulled together all the individual components of his tuition into his flying technique.

Twelve weeks after arriving at Ponca City, Brian was deemed competent with the PT-17 by day, by night, on instruments, spinning and recovering, engine-off forced landings and could top it off with basic aerobatics (Brian claimed to have done one loop 'without straps!') – all in just over 90 flying hours. He was 'signed off' by Mr C. E. Barr, OC 'F' Flight, on 2 November 1942 by which date his 'end of primary' totals were:

Daylight dual	37.
Daylight solo	46.
Night dual	3.
Night solo	5.

Brian also noted that 10 of his dual hours were on instruments and he had put in 14 hours in the Link Trainer. His 91 hours was not far removed from RAF expectations, in that the Royal Air Force considered 70 hours primary and 80 hours advanced was an absolute minimum needed to train a pilot to its standard but in the relatively unpressured environment of this 'all-through' system in the US, the RAF gratefully accepted that total hours could and should, be in the order of a more ideal figure of 180, split in roughly the same proportions.

After a week's leave Brian moved onto the advanced stage and had his introduction to the far more powerful AT-6A on 14 November when he had an hour in the air with Mr Kannewurf, his new instructor. A couple of weeks and 8 flying hours later, Mr Kannewurf sent Brian off on his own to complete a 45-minute first solo on the AT-6A in B278. Then it was into the same sort of flying routine for a month until instructor Mr Clyde W. Fellers took Brian up for a check ride in B265 on 14 December. Mr Fellers first put him through his paces on stalls, steep turns, spins, precautionary landings and aerobatics for three-quarters-of-an-hour then sent him off solo in B299 to practise steep turns and aerobatics. Back with Mr Kannewurf, the next month became more intensive, including air gunnery and covering instrument flying (I/F), I/F take-offs and landings, flying beam approaches and night flying that included night navigation exercises and navigation with another pupil in the back seat.

After a further month, on 12 January, his progress was assessed by another check ride – this time for an hour in B290 with Mr Gordon H. Horlick. Then it was back to polishing up the more demanding elements of the course such as navigation by day and on instruments, instrument flying, armaments, night flying, low-level flying and aerobatics – the last of which was not Brian's favourite element. On 9th in B240 and on 10 February in B236 (both AT-6Cs rather than the usual 'A' model), Brian's instrument flying was put under scrutiny by instructor Clarence J. Wootton, but must have been found satisfactory as Mr Wootton also checked out his aerobatics for an hour in B265 on the morning of 11 February. This was followed by a 2-hour cross-country navigation exercise in B273 with LAC Allen acting as navigator and – since having returned intact and having clearly not become lost – this was Brian's final flight at 6 BFTS; his advanced course came to a formal end on 15 February 1943 with the presentation of his Wings and his promotion to sergeant. He had logged 100 hours on the advanced course and thus accumulated a total of 191 hours in total during his time at Ponca City. This airtime was augmented by 28 hours in the Link Trainer.

It was during an analysis of Brian's primary flying hours from his log book that it first became evident that the 'grand total' flying hours he first noted, actually differed from the 'breakdown' hours (log book columns 1–10) by 13h 20m – for which there are no individual entries and which as mentioned earlier, are assumed to be those hours flown at his UK grading school.

By the time 6 BFTS Ponca City closed in April 1944, seventeen courses had passed through its portals. A total of 1,245 pilots – 1,107 RAF and 138 USAAC – had undergone training during its thirty-three months of operation. As a matter of interest, at the hourly rates mentioned above, the cost of this would have been in the order of $7 million and even though the Darr School was obliged to invest in the region of half a million dollars in the property, allowing for salaries, lease and running costs etc., there was clearly a good return on investment for the School and for the local Chamber of Commerce. But, of course, the value to the RAF of this unfettered flow of trained pilots cannot be measured in such simplistic terms. It has been estimated that over their lifetime the BFTS and US Arnold Scheme schools trained some 12,000 pilots in total for the RAF.

Sadly, 7 RAF students were killed at Ponca City during training as well as 3 US airmen and 5 civilian instructors. Of these, LAC Joseph Nield and his instructor Mr M. Hill, died on 30 September while on the same course (No. 9) as Brian Fern.

Another way to not finish the course was to be 'washed out', or eliminated from the programme due to inadequate progress or unsuitability for further pilot training. Over the period 6 BFTS was open, 267 students were eliminated and of the 43 students starting on Brian's course No. 9, 17 were 'washed out' (40 per cent) which was almost double the average course failure rate of 21 per cent for the school.

In his end-of-course assessment, by CFI Henry 'Hank' Jerger, Brian's flying ability was rated as 'average' with the comment 'rough on aerobatics' but this was a satisfactory outcome and now Brian could look forward to his next posting. Sadly, Henry Jerger died on 21 June 1943 in a flying accident that cost him his life and that of a mechanic, Mr E. Murray, who went along with him as a passenger at the time.

Now Brian had to make the long rail journey back to 31 PD Moncton in Canada, where he could reclaim his stored personal clothing items and equipment and wait to be allocated a place on a ship back to dear old Blighty. Two weeks elapsed between his arrival at Moncton and his departure by ship from New York, which of course required yet another rail journey back into the USA to go aboard no less a vessel than the RMS *Queen Elizabeth* (83,000 tons). On 10 March 1943, *Queen Elizabeth* set sail from New York harbour – alone – as convoy AT-38; she was unescorted because with her service speed of 28 knots she was considered to be safe from interception by enemy U-boats. Indeed, she arrived in the Clyde on 16 March without incident and next day Brian was back in a cold, wet English winter, *en route* by train to 7 Personnel Reception Centre in Harrogate.

After a month's well-earned leave, Sgt Brian Fern was posted to attend a training course for senior NCOs in the seaside town of Whitley Bay, Northumberland (re-designated: the Aircrew NCO's School later that same year) which occupied him for another four weeks until 12 May. The course was intended to 'toughen-up' aircrew SNCOs by giving them instruction on what was expected of such beings, accompanied by bags of drill and 'good healthy outdoor exercise' – which included swimming in the North Sea – courtesy of slightly sadistic Army instructors. However, after this little 'holiday', 25 May saw Sgt Brian Fern beginning his next phase of flying training having been posted to 3 (Pilot) Advanced Flying Unit (3 (P)AFU) at RAF South Cerney in Gloucestershire. Upon his return from the USA, he was designated for what was known as 'multi-engine' aircraft and he knew he would be flying the twin-engine Airspeed Oxford trainer from South Cerney.

The role of a (Pilot) Advanced Flying Unit (AFU) was to receive pilots who were already qualified to 'wings' standard – most often from the overseas flying schools in the Empire Air Training Scheme (EATS) or, as in Brian's case, the BFTS and Arnold Schemes (and other similar schemes) in the USA – and advance their general flying skill to the standard required for operational flying. In the case of the multi-engine AFUs these pupils, who were likely to be posted to bomber squadrons or possibly twin-engine fighters, would learn the flying characteristics of a heavier aircraft than they had experienced so far. They would be encouraged to develop a 'feel' for aircraft in which they flew before being turned loose on, for example, Vickers Wellington or Bristol Beaufighter or the new four-engine 'heavies' such as Short Stirling, Handley Page Halifax and Avro Lancaster. Another important aspect of the AFU courses was to allow pilots to experience and learn to adapt their flying to cope with European weather conditions, which were likely to be very different indeed to those in which they had trained overseas.

In addition to more ground school, the flying side of AFU courses fell into three phases. First, a pilot was taken through a series of standard exercises so that he could become familiar with the Oxford. After soloing on the Oxford, several cross-country flights were made to brush up navigational skills. These flights of 200–300 miles were done initially under the eye of an instructor then with a fellow pupil acting as 'safety' pilot and 'critic'. Next phase of training involved beam approach flying, which was intended to prepare the pilot for phase three which was the night flying part of the course. The pace was a busy one, both on the ground and in the air. Instrument flying and in particular the beam approach element, was also very demanding both mentally and physically on the pilot.

At 7,500 lbs weight fully loaded, the Airspeed Oxford was by no means as heavy as the operational types mentioned earlier but it was a reasonably demanding and reliable twin-engine advanced trainer. Brian flew in two versions of the Oxford: Mark I and Mark II, the former powered by two 355 hp Armstrong Siddeley Cheetah IX seven-cylinder radial engines and the latter 375 hp Cheetah X. It had a wingspan of 53 feet, a top speed of around 180 mph and would cruise at about 140 mph.

Brian Fern's introduction to the Airspeed Oxford came on 1 June 1943 and followed an established pattern of basic exercises with 5 hours of instruction from Sgt Owen in Oxford I, V3230 over the next three days. With a short check flight with 'B' Flight commander, Fg Off Candler, Brian was then sent off solo for an hour in an Oxford II, X6980. From then on, he made rapid progress, doing much of his flying from Cerney's Relief Landing Ground (RLG) at RAF Bibury, 10 miles to the north. Bibury was a grass airfield that had two Sommerfeld Track runways laid out on it. These were made from metal/wire netting that, when laid and secured over the grass, helped to stabilise the airstrip surface and reduce erosion by weather and aircraft usage.

With just 3 more hours dual and solo flying Brian was 'put through the hoop' on 13 June, first with a navigation test in Oxford II, BM844, then a 2-hour cross-country navigation exercise in R6160, followed by a progress test and an instrument flying test by the Chief Flying Instructor, Flt Lt Graham-Smith, in V3740. The instrument test was a precursor to Brian then spending a couple of weeks on No. 7 course at 1539 Beam Approach Training (1539 BAT) Flight also based at RAF Bibury. The Flight was affiliated to 3 SFTS and kept six Oxfords equipped to receive ground-to-air beam- (or 'blind-') approach landing signals.

Beam approach (or blind approach) was introduced to pilots so that they were taught to listen for and interpret several audible radio signals emitted by ground radio transmitters set up on an airfield. It was designed to facilitate aircraft landings in darkness or poor visibility. Tuning in to the appropriate frequency for Bibury, the Morse Code letters 'A' (dot-dash) and 'N' (dash-dot) were radiated from transmitters on the airfield out to a distance of 30 or more miles. The airfield was divided into four 'quadrants' and alternate quadrants broadcast directionally the signal 'A' or an 'N'. By listening to the signals, their regularity and strength, in his headset, a pilot could first establish which side of the airfield he was approaching or on and establish his direction of flight in relation the known details of that particular airfield. By applying all his concentration and considerable mental agility, he would be able to judge how close he was coming to the runway centre line and when to make a correctly rated turn onto the approach path.

At Bibury the landing system also used two beacons, one located at each end of runway 04/22, that each emitted along the line of approach two audible 'A' and 'N' signals that could be picked up by a pilot during descent to the runway. When both letters merged into a continuous single tone, he knew he was 'on the beam' and would need to keep his aeroplane at the required angle of approach by maintaining the single tone during a specified angle and rate of descent, from about 600 feet down to about 100 feet; at which point he would hope to see the runway threshold. Judging distance to the threshold was also aided by two more transmitters, whose beams were oriented vertically upwards at two known points on the approach path; emitting their own distinctive signal for an 'outer marker' and 'inner marker' point. Passing over these markers also caused a different coloured lamp to light on the instrument panel in the cockpit. All in all, this course was very demanding of a pilot's flying ability but whose mastery would be of immense value to, for example, bomber pilots returning to base in bad weather after operations.

Almost immediately after take-off, the instructor would pull a screen across the pupil's side of the cockpit which prevented him from seeing anything but his instruments and controls. From then on, he was on instruments and headset signals only, until he was – hopefully – almost onto the runway, when the instructor would whip the screen away and a visual landing could be made.

Sgt Brian Fern began his BAT course with Bibury's 'Y' Flight on 16 June and over the next five days underwent a series of daytime dual familiarisation flights with his instructor Fg Off Staples in Oxford Is: V4267, DF534, LB422, MP373 and MP400. By 23 June Brian had mastered the beam system sufficiently to begin getting to grips with dual circuits and landings and precision landings at night. As his confidence and ability improved, on 28 April his skill level at precision approach and landing was checked out in LW751 by Flt Sgt Waller, after which Brian spent the remainder of the course honing his skill with solo flights. Having flown 25 hours day and 20 hours night on his BAT course, on 7 July he was finally assessed by the OC 3 (P)AFU, Sqn Ldr Harold Swanston, as 'above the average on Oxfords'.

This assessment was probably the catalyst for a significant change of direction in Brian Fern's flying career, since it marked the point at which he took the road to becoming a qualified flying instructor.

In this mid-war year of 1943, the demand for multi-engine pilots was increasing as Bomber Command rapidly stepped up its air campaign against the German homeland. This demand for pilots naturally had a similar effect on the numbers of instructors required to teach potential operational pilots at various stages of their training. During his own training Brian Fern had displayed the personal disposition and ability to become one of these instructors and this is a measure of the value the RAF placed upon him; but first, of course, he had to learn the techniques of his trade. To this end he was posted to 7 Flying Instructors School (7 FIS) based at RAF Upavon in Wiltshire.

Since 1912, the name of Upavon had been long associated with the RAF, with the Central Flying School (CFS) – of which we have heard much already – being the principal long-term resident unit at the station. However, in March 1942 a new unit called the Empire Central Flying School (EFCS) was created at RAF Hullavington, near Chippenham. As it was essentially an expanded version of CFS, many of the staff from Upavon found themselves transferred to the new unit but there were sufficient staff left behind at Upavon to form the nucleus of 7 Flying Instructors School which came into being on 1 April 1942. A few weeks later it was re-designated as 7 FIS (Advanced) and was equipped with Airspeed Oxford (45), Miles Master (40) and Miles Magister (20) aircraft and had 1537 BAT Flight, which operated ten of the Oxfords, affiliated to it. During August 1942, all the Masters and many of the Oxfords were transferred to another FIS and were replaced by a similar quantity of Miles Magisters which, during 1943, gradually became the predominant aircraft at 7 FIS.

Brian Fern, now with a grand total of 247 flying hours in his log book, joined No. 45 (War) Flying Instructor course at 7 FIS on 6 July and next day presented himself at 1537 BAT Flight dispersal to undergo tuition on the finer points of how to teach other people to fly beam approaches. His tuition began with an hour in Oxford BG149 with Fg Off Weber going through a series of standard numbered exercises, but this time from the viewpoint of an instructor rather than a pupil. On the 12th, back at the main School, Brian took up Miles Magister T9697, again with Fg Off Weber in the back seat, to go through the standard training exercises relevant to this single-engine type.

Over the course of the next five weeks Brian alternated with the Oxford and Magister and the gaze of Fg Off Weber and Sgt Turner, not only improving his own flying skill but also acquiring the 'patter' and the techniques of how to demonstrate each standard exercise effectively to a pupil and then how to monitor, assess and correct a pupil's performance. By 15 August, having put in 15 hours with 1537 BAT Flight, his attention was now directed to a spell of night flying (N/F) tuition in 7 FIS's Oxfords until the end of August. This required him to fly a series of dual N/F circuits and landings, N/F cross-country navigation exercises and N/F precision instrument approaches with his instructor, before his own progress was checked out by the CFI, Sqn Ldr Henry Crommelin on 26 August. Between 3 and 10 September there followed more of the same routine at the end of which Brian had another CFI check flight, this time with Sqn Ldr Booker. On 14 September 1943, after nine weeks and 104 flying hours tuition at 7 FIS, he passed out as a Qualified Flying Instructor (QFI) on multi-engine (ME) aircraft with a rating of category C (ME) to await his next posting.

Refreshed by two weeks leave, Sgt Brian Fern was duly notified of his next posting and on 22 September 1943, reported to 14 (Pilot) Advanced Flying Unit (14 (P)AFU) which was based at RAF Banff on the banks of the Moray Firth in Scotland, where he would begin work as a flying instructor on the ubiquitous Airspeed Oxford.

Created during 1942, when Service Flying Training Units (SFTS) were re-designated as AFUs, 14 (P)AFU was a large organisation with an aircraft establishment of around 112 Oxfords plus another fifty-six on reserve. Banff airfield was not large enough to accommodate all the aircraft and in order for the (P)AFU to maintain its extensive flying programme, it operated Oxfords from Relief Landing Grounds (RLG) along the Moray coast at Dallachy and Fraserburgh. Brian was allocated to 'Y' Flight of '2 Squadron' at Fraserburgh, where he arrived on 26 September. His first sortie with his new unit in this bleak corner of Scotland came on the 28th when he was checked out in V3237 by Fg Off Wheeler for an hour of dual, followed by an hour solo, getting used to the aircraft, the airfield and the local area.

Next day though was a busy one; it was down to the real business when he took up his first pupil, Plt Off Welsh – another new arrival – putting him through his paces on the initial flying exercise programme, in Oxford DF400. He then took up another pupil, Sgt Hart, who was at a later stage in the training programme, following that with a pupil Plt Off Steinman, who was at yet another different stage and had to carry out a dual navigational test, this time in BG222. This first 'real' day was rounded off by Brian flying an hour's dual check in V3568 under the eagle eye of OC '2 Squadron', Sqn Ldr J. R. Watt, followed by a couple of circuits solo in the gathering darkness before Sqn Ldr Watt took him up again for his sixth and final flight of the day checking out his technique during 80 minutes of night-flying circuits. Nothing was left to chance.

From then on it was an almost daily routine, weather permitting, of anything up to eight flights by day or night, dual with pupil pilots. Some pupils – usually those who were allocated to him from the beginning of their courses – he flew with several times, while others – generally those at later stages of training – he just took up on single occasions. After a month or so with the newer pupils he seems to have been given a change at the end of December 1943 when he had a spell of a couple of months doing night-flying tuition. The list of pupil names in Brian's log book is long and varied and one might well wonder: what happened to these young men he helped to train? Considering also the number of these budding tyros he had to nurse in the air and the quantity of different Oxford aeroplanes in which he flew, Brian appears to have enjoyed good fortune by not having any mishaps to his name. His closest call seems to have occurred on the night of 18 January 1944 when he noted simply: 'attempted circuit – kite u/s'. That night he was flying as instructor to Sgt Donald Franko, a nineteen-year- old Canadian who was working through the final, night-flying, stage in his training. Sgt Franko had in fact gone solo at night about a month earlier – during the middle of December 1943 – but as the following anecdote shows, he was a very lucky chap to be in a position to continue his training.

Sgt Franko's escapade on 16 December 1943 is an indication of how fine a line it was between routine flying and potential disaster for these inexperienced pilots. His adventure began in winter darkness at RAF Fraserburgh when he took off on a night navigation training sortie in Oxford HN600. Unexpected tail winds and thick cloud forced him off his intended course and he was being pushed in a generally northerly direction, flying roughly parallel with the Scottish coast but well out over the featureless North Sea. Time passed by, but still there was no sign of the coastal landmarks he expected – he was lost and only the inhospitable sea glinted below. His next worry was the fuel; it was running pretty low. After about an hour, searching the inky blackness and the sea below, he spotted breakers on rocks of the first piece of land he'd seen since take-off. He had no idea where he was but, now almost out of fuel, he decided there was no option but to make a forced landing, wheels up on this, the only piece of land within sight. Sgt Franko pulled off a good belly landing on grass and heather and slithered to a stop, right way up and intact.

Spending the night in the relative warmth of his aeroplane, he emerged into the cold light of dawn to find himself and his aeroplane perched upon a tiny island. It appeared uninhabited except for a lighthouse. He had dropped on to the only piece of friendly ground on Auskerry, a pocket-handkerchief sized island – just one-third of a square mile in area – on the eastern fringe of the Orkney Islands, 100 miles due north of Fraserburgh! The two lighthouse keepers found him standing by his practically undamaged aeroplane and welcomed him into the sanctuary of the lighthouse where, because foul weather prevented any boats from landing, he was forced to remain on the island until beyond that Christmas. Eventually, Sgt Franko was picked up by motor launch, twelve days later, on 28 December when the weather finally abated and he returned to 14 (P)AFU to finish his training. The RAF considered it was impracticable to salvage the Oxford and after removing some useful equipment, it was burned in situ. In partial answer to the original question: what happened to these pilots; well, in Donald Franko's case he went on to complete thirty-four operations in Halifax bombers and survived the war to return to his native Canada, where he died peacefully in 2011.

Around May 1944, Brian Fern was given another change of routine when he taught instrument flying until the end of June, by which time he noted that, out of his overall total of 760 flying hours, he had done 391 hours as an instructor in the nine months since arriving at 14 (P)AFU. Brian had by that time also logged instructional time with eighty (P)AFU students. In February 1944 he was promoted to temporary flight sergeant which was made substantive in July, during which month he was re-graded as an 'average' Category B (ME) instructor. That month also marked another step up the promotion ladder when he was put forward for a commission, which was confirmed on 29 July when he became 182356 Pilot Officer Fern.

Brian played no more part in proceedings at RAF Fraserburgh, since he was posted on 1 September 1944, as a supernumerary, briefly to 16 (P)AFU which was based at RAF Newton, near Nottingham and then, on 13 September, to 7 Service Flying Training School (SFTS) at RAF Sutton Bridge, in Lincolnshire.

For two years prior to this point, the Central Gunnery School (CGS) was the resident unit at RAF Sutton Bridge. However, with the skies around The Wash becoming ever busier, it was decided to re-locate CGS from Sutton Bridge to RAF Catfoss in Yorkshire, a move that was completed by the end of February 1944. This left RAF Sutton Bridge on a Care & Maintenance basis under the control of 7 (P)AFU at RAF Peterborough for a short period until a new role could be found for it. This matter was not long in being resolved in a change that would result in the sound of foreign tongues again being heard in the small town adjacent to the station. Another change that came into effect during that summer was for RAF Sutton Bridge to be re-classified as a satellite station, first parented by RAF Newton while the latter's water-logged grass surface was repaired, before reverting once more to the control of RAF Peterborough. Since 7 (P)AFU directed its efforts towards mainly single-engine fighter pilots, its establishment was upwards of 130 Miles Masters plus 15 Hawker Hurricanes while it had over 200 pilots to cope with. Resources at Peterborough were therefore stretched to the limit at this time and this is why RAF Sutton Bridge became involved in relieving the pressure on RAF Peterborough.

Yet another change of system on 21 June 1944 saw night-flying training for 7 (P)AFU – previously conducted from Peterborough airfield, with occasional use of Sibson RLG and RAF Wittering – also being transferred to RAF Sutton Bridge. This was, however, only a temporary relief arrangement for Peterborough as shortly afterwards Sutton Bridge actually went back onto a Care & Maintenance basis, pending yet another re-assessment of its future. It was, though, the demise of Peterborough's current satellite, RAF Sibson, that finally brought this C & M period to a close in August 1944 and with it brought a modicum of stability for a couple of years. Two main factors were responsible for this latest change.

First, on 4 July, in order to speed up throughput of aircrew, the basis of flying training at 7 (P)AFU Peterborough was altered to a 'course-based' system. This meant that each 'Flight' at Peterborough was made responsible for both day and night training of a complete 'course' of (at that time) about thirty-seven pilots for a four-week period. Various administrative changes were also proposed, all with the aim of using main and satellite airfields more effectively, particularly in respect of accommodation issues.

Second, at the end of July, Sibson airfield's grass surface, having taken a lot of wear and tear, was declared unfit for use and in need of re-seeding. This was a lengthy, time-consuming process so Flying Training Command took the easier option of giving up Sibson and declaring that Sutton Bridge, being immediately available, would take on the role of satellite for Peterborough.

That decision was implemented on 8 August 1944, although Sibson strangely enough still remained designated as a Relief Landing Ground (RLG).

With the rapid decline in the flow of aircrew from the overseas EATS system at this stage of the war – there was an air of optimism following D-Day – the need for AFUs was also diminishing and in September 1944, the content of flying training at 7 (P)AFU at RAF Peterborough and Sutton Bridge took on a more general nature than before. This now manifested itself with the introduction of courses that handled the training of only French pilots at 7 (P)AFU – thus accounting for it gaining the additional title of 'the French SFTS'; its No. 1 course which began – spread between both stations – in September 1944. Flying activity in this new role, however, was far less intensive around The Wash than during the old CGS days, because Sutton Bridge dealt mainly with the night-flying training syllabus. It transpired that between September 1944 and November 1945, 198 French airmen passed through Peterborough and Sutton Bridge to reach RAF Wings standard on single- and twin-engine aeroplanes.

To cope with the new, twin-engine workload at RAF Sutton Bridge, fifteen new flying instructors – one of whom was Pilot Officer Brian Fern – were posted from RAF Newton to the French SFTS on 13 September, for the specific purpose of training French pilots who would go on to form the nucleus of the post-war Armée de l'Air (French Air Force) and Aéronavale (French Fleet Air Arm). Airspeed Oxford twin-engine trainer aeroplanes would be transferred from Peterborough to Sutton Bridge although – at least initially – servicing work on them would be carried out at the parent station. By mid-November there were located at Sutton Bridge sufficient aeroplanes to equip three Oxford Flights, plus a few specialist Oxfords for bombing and beam-approach duties and some Masters for gunnery training – which was still being conducted over The Wash range. Over at Peterborough another three Flights had also been established, equipped with Masters, to handle those pilots destined for single-engine aircraft.

The final major organisational change came on 21 December 1944, when 7 (P)AFU was re-titled 7 SFTS and the term 'French SFTS' disappeared from usage. At this time Gp Capt James Ramage Addams AFC was commandant of 7 SFTS at RAF Peterborough, chief flying instructor was Wg Cdr J. H. M. Smith AFC and Wg Cdr David Kinnear AFC AFM was in overall command of RAF Sutton Bridge.

By the time No. 1 course of thirty-two pilots passed out in February 1945, the pattern of training French pilots had evolved into single-engine students (one-third of each course complement) being based at Peterborough and twin-engine students (two-thirds) based at Sutton Bridge. Miles Masters were gradually phased out up to June 1945, being replaced by the North American Harvard. Brian was involved with most of the pilots who graduated on No. 1 course, although he had himself had to take time out to attend the Aircrew Officers School at RAF Hereford (a non-flying station) between 18 October and 15 November, where he was 'taught how to behave like an officer'. It is interesting to note that upon his return to Sutton Bridge, the CFI did not let him into the air alone until he, Sqn Ldr McCarthy, and Brian's 'D' Flight Commander, Flt Lt White, had both checked out that he had not become 'rusty' during his absence.

While epitomising this period of Sutton Bridge history, one fatal air accident in particular also played its part in forging a permanent bond between the community of Sutton Bridge and the French nation. By this time, the war was over but No. 6 (French) course of 7 SFTS was well into its stride. From Sutton Bridge on 13 August 1945 Oxford PH414 took off, with Caporal Vincent Maestracci and Matelot (Seaman) Charles Georges Moitessier aboard. Briefed for a routine dual sortie of 45 minutes duration in the local area, they were to land at the end of that time and change places, prior to making another sortie. It was quite usual for competent pupils to be briefed to fly as a 'safety pilot' during exercises with one of their compatriots. This exercise, though, was destined never to be completed. Cpl Maestracci was, albeit briefly, one of Brian pupils and his log book shows he flew with Maestracci in PH426 on 7 June for 40 minutes.

Nearing the village of Clenchwarton, PH414 was last seen emerging from low cloud in a spin from which it did not recover. Hitting the ground at speed it was completely destroyed and both Frenchmen died instantly. Despite speculation, as on so many occasions, no real cause for the accident could be established. Maestracci's body was returned to France for burial while Moitessier, whose family home was in Morocco, was buried with full military honours in Sutton Bridge churchyard. In the immediate post-war years, in common with towns and villages across the nation, monuments to the fallen were being erected. Particularly with its connections to the RAF airfield, Sutton Bridge was no exception and the churchyard, last resting place of so many brave young men from all parts of the world, was honoured with a Commonwealth War Graves Commission memorial cross.

During his time at Sutton Bridge, Brian had helped to train fifty French pilots, almost one quarter of the total number of French pupils passing through the SFTS. In contrast to the way his workload at previous schools was organised, at 7 SFTS he had a greater opportunity to spend more flying time with individual pilots and was thus able to guide these Frenchmen through substantial parts of their tuition. Brian also had the good fortune to avoid being involved with the crop of mishaps that inevitably accompany all training activities and out of the fifty Frenchmen he dealt with, only two of them had relatively minor accidents.

Sous Lieutenant G. L. H. Rivière – whom Brian had taken up on 15 December for beam approach training and again on 15 January '45 for a cross-country – blotted his copybook during a solo night-flying practice sortie on 7 January. Bringing in Oxford P8911 to land, Rivière made an error of judgement and undershot, crashing into a field short of the runway and turning the Oxford over onto its back. He scrambled out unhurt. On 15 January S/Lt Rivière was receiving instruction from Flt Lt White on over-shoots during landing. Rivière's descent rate on approach was too rapid and the undercarriage of Oxford V4126 struck the barbed wire perimeter fence. The instructor was unable to intervene in time to check the rate of descent and the aeroplane hit the ground hard, causing its port wheel to buckle and the port wing tip to dig into the ground. Both men fortunately emerged unhurt.

Sgt J. Jouet was one of Brian's first French pupils on 3 October 1944. By 22 January 1945, Jouet was nearing the end of his course and that afternoon was practising forced landings in Oxford LX746 near the village of Sutterton. Picking out a suitable field, he started his glide at 3,000 feet but in the very cold weather, he forgot to keep warming the engine during the prolonged glide. When he opened up the throttle to pull away, the starboard engine failed to respond and he could not gain any height with just one engine – so he had to force land for real! The aircraft was damaged but Jouet was unhurt.

Brian Fern was promoted to flying officer on 29 January 1945 and remained at Sutton Bridge with 7 SFTS Sutton Bridge until 29 June 1945 when he – along with thousands of his contemporaries – became 'surplus to requirements' and he was declared redundant.

His 'hostilities-only' services no longer required, Brian reported to 1 Aircrew Holding Unit at RAF Kidlington on 2 July to await what was euphemistically referred to as 'disposal'. He had 1,056 flying hours in his log book and was graded 'average' as an STFS instructor but 'above average' as a pilot. Probably realising what employment prospects might be like in post-war England and in view of his roots in South Africa, Brian took decisive action and applied successfully to the British Colonial Service for potential employment abroad. Thousands of RAF personnel – air and ground-crew – were going through the process of de-mobilisation which usually meant weeks of hanging about and Brian appears to have used this time effectively. On 29 August he reported to No. 100 Personnel Dispersal Centre at RAF Uxbridge where, after yet more hanging around, at the ripe old age of twenty-two, he was offered a Class B Release from the Royal Air Force on 29 September 1945. Class B Release was usually granted to skilled tradesmen or professionals who were deemed most likely to meet the needs of civilian industry or services and his intention to join the Colonial Service would have satisfied the criteria of this category.

3.2

COLD WAR COCKPIT

Following his discharge from the RAF, Brian travelled to the Isle De France (Mauritius) and thence to Mombasa on the coast of Kenya. From September 1945 to May 1951 he served as a Colonial Police Officer in the Tanganyika Police Force, based variously at Dar-es-Salaam on the coast then at Bukoba, a large port on the west shore of Lake Victoria; Musoma on the east shore of the Lake and finally, Kasulu near Kigoma close to the border with Burundi. During his colonial service he rose to the rank of assistant superintendent but police work in the tropics was not destined to become an occupation for the rest of his working life. By 1951, for reasons that are not entirely clear, it seems he wished to return to flying and applied for a Short Service Commission in the RAF once more. His action is most likely to have been prompted by the global political and Cold War situation; the creation of the North Atlantic Treaty Organisation (NATO: 1949) and the outbreak of the Korean War in June 1950 in particular.

This was a time when the RAF, having declined considerably in size since the end of the Second World War, was now advertising its expansion to such an extent that it would reach a post-war peak by the end of the Korean conflict. On 29 January 1951 the British Prime Minister announced proposals to accelerate the re-armament of all three armed services. The RAF budget reached its highest level since the end of the Second World War and twenty Royal Auxiliary Air Force (RAuxAF) Squadrons were mobilised for active duty within Fighter Command. There also began a decade when the RAF became caught up in a variety of relatively minor – although some, like Operation *Firedog* in Malaya, were long-lasting – conflicts around the world. As such, it rapidly needed aircrew and, of course, the men to train them. The RAF requirement for student pilots, for example, rose in 1951 to 750 per year and Brian, with his wartime background in flying instruction, was just the sort of man the RAF was looking for.

Brian Fern returned to England and on 5 March 1951 reported to the Air Ministry in London to be interviewed for a short service commission (SSC). He had a medical the same day and on the 10th received a letter confirming his appointment for an eight-year SSC (plus four years on reserve) in his old rank. Thus it was on 4 June 1951 that Brian reported to RAF Training Command at Hendon as a 'supernumerary on recall' and was offered a post as a flying instructor – in effect carrying on where he had left off nearly six years earlier, albeit with some catching-up to do. A week later, on 12 June 1951, as a general duties (GD) pilot with the rank of flying officer (service number: 182356) he found himself posted to the Central Flying School (CFS) detachment at RAF Moreton-in-Marsh.

Re-organised in May 1951 the CFS operated a ground-training squadron, two Harvard Squadrons and a Gloster Meteor Flight & Examining Wing from RAF Little Rissington. In addition, a Qualified Flying Instructor (QFI) Refresher Flight and two Percival Prentice Squadrons were located at RAF South Cerney while its re-entrant 'pre-CFS' course and a Harvard Squadron operated from Moreton-in-Marsh. It was to the latter that Brian was posted to, attend No. 9 flying refresher course.

His reborn flying career began on 18 June 1951 with 45 minutes dual familiarisation in a North American Harvard IIB under the watchful eye of Fg Off Jindřich Skirka, a Czech pilot who had seen active service with 310 Squadron during the Second World War. Brian had lost none of his familiarity with the Harvard – after all he had learned to fly on the AT-6 as it was known in the USA – and after another 50 minutes with Skirka on 20 June he was sent off solo for an hour. Over the next three weeks, under the guidance of instructors Fg Off Albert Twigger and Flt Lt Shafe, Brian flew 17 hours dual and 22 hours solo to complete the Harvard course at Moreton. During this course he put in 6 hours of instrument flying and on 13 July was tested by Fg Off Robinson who awarded him an initial 'Green' instrument rating.

Following a spot of leave Brian returned in mid-August to South Cerney to continue his refresher training as an instructor, now with CFS's 2 FTS which was equipped with the Percival Prentice T1. Flying got under way on 16 August and after an hour's dual in the Prentice with Flt Lt Pressland he went off solo for another 30 minutes and from then on practised the correct procedures and 'running patter' for all the basic flying training numbered exercises with Flt Lts Pressland, Haslop, Crouch and

Sunderland-Cooper. As this was during the school holidays, South Cerney became a summer camp venue for a number of Air Training Corps squadrons and as a pleasant diversion, Brian took several pairs of cadets up for air experience flights in the Prentice.

With 19 hours dual and 25 hours solo on the Prentice, by the end of October Brian was due to move on to the next, more advanced, stage of his CFS programme. At the beginning of October he joined No. 131 course in 'E' Flight of CFS's 3 Squadron at RAF Little Rissington, flying the Harvard again. Throughout October, flying sorties of between 30 and 70 minutes, up to three times by day or night, Brian built up his expertise. There came, on 10 October, a great milestone when he was allowed to fly a 40-minute dual sortie (he noted it as 'Exercise I') with Flt Lt Severne in a CFS Gloster Meteor T7 ('MQ') – his first time in a jet aeroplane. Further Meteor opportunities came during the month: on the 19th, Exercise II in 'JY' with Flt Lt Severne, then Exercises III and IV on the 3rd during two sorties in 'JD' with Flt Lt Price. After landing from the second sortie on the 23rd, after 2h 40m dual, Brian was sent off solo for a 15-minute circuit in Meteor 'JD'. He had joined the jet age!

Brian's spell at CFS came to an end on 13 November 1951 after spending five months learning to be a flying instructor in the 'modern age'. His course had included 39 hours dual and 44 hours solo flying; he had 1,183 hours in his log book at this time and was assessed as a QFI with an 'Average' (B1) category. There was little time for celebration though as there was a war on, albeit on the other side of the world, and the RAF needed pilots – quickly.

In its wisdom the RAF now posted Brian to convert to
the twin-engine Vickers Wellington, and to this end he was
posted north to join No. 93 course at 101 Flying Refresher
School based at RAF Finningley, Yorkshire, where he was to
convert to type on the Wellington T10 version. It seems odd
that the RAF still employed the rather ancient Wellington but
the purpose of this unit was to provide 'regular' pilots with a
course designed to update their flying experience in the light
of new developments in aircraft and operating procedures.
In addition to the Wellington T10, the unit also operated
an eclectic mix of the Harvard, Spitfire, Meteor F4 and
T7, Oxford and Tiger Moth. In particular 101 FRS was to
contribute to achieving the training expansion aims of the RAF
in the wake of the Korean War and in effect back-pedal on its
post-Second World War decline.

Brian's first trip at 101 FRS came on 21 November in
Wellington NC836, 'RD'. It was 45-minutes dual with Fg
Off Kennedy going over the instructor patter for twin-engine
numbered exercises and this was followed by further trips over
the next couple of days. Then, after 3 hours dual, Brian went solo
in NC836 and there followed more dual instruction flights over
the next two weeks, progressively going over the procedure for
teaching students the basics of handling multi-engine aircraft.
Practice force-landings featured towards the close and there
was one rather intriguing entry on 26 November which read:
'PF989; Flt Lt Oldham / Self; Ex 19/22 (Crashed).' No flying
hours were recorded and no explanation noted. The accident
occurred during a single-engine approach to Finningley, with
Flt Lt Oldham flying the aeroplane. Oldham lost control of the
aircraft and, while trying to regain control, he stalled and the

aircraft crash-landed in a field about 1 mile east of the airfield. There were four people on board but no one was injured. The Wellington was, however, damaged beyond repair and written off. Brian was back in the air the next day – although Flt Lt Oldham never appeared again as a pupil in his log book after that incident!

After about 20 hours flying, Brian satisfactorily completed his conversion to the Wellington on 7 December 1951 and was posted to 'F' Flight of 104 FRS at RAF Lichfield. This unit trained Reserve pilots for postings to bomber units – which were still operating propeller-driven aeroplanes – and it provided Brian with a means of honing his instructional skill. Longer duration flights, of 1–2 hours, gave him more time in command of this dual-control aircraft so that he could put his 'patter' and instructional technique to the test on Reserve pilots going through the FRS course. December 1951 turned into January 1952 and by the end of February, Brian had flown 59 hours by day and night in command and after eight months his re-introduction to the post-war RAF was complete. During his time at Lichfield, Brian lived in a caravan which must have been a bit 'parky' that winter. Now his total flying hours stood at 1,266 and he was about to embark on his first QFI posting.

This new phase of Fg Off Brian Fern's flying career began on 10 March 1952 when he was posted to 14 Advanced Flying Training School (AFTS) at RAF Holme-on-Spalding-Moor. The station was one of several former surplus wartime airfields re-activated at this time and 14 AFTS had also just been reformed a week earlier – all arising from this pressure to expand the RAF quickly – and Brian was one of the new batch of flying instructors who were drafted in. The Air Ministry decided that as part of the RAF response to the global political situation and events in Korea, the need for pilots was so pressing that it would re-open and refurbish nine old, closed RAF stations, a process which it deemed would be far quicker and cheaper than building new airfields.

The station and the unit took a few weeks to settle down and blow the cobwebs away and it was almost the end of March before the flying training programme commenced. Again Brian lived in a caravan, which may have been a reasonable option compared to re-furbished ex-wartime buildings! The aircraft used were the Airspeed Oxford and Percival Prentice, both of which of course were familiar to Brian. His first flight back behind the controls of an Oxford was an hour in T1044 on the 26th and with another 90-minute flight the next day that was all the air time he managed in March. However, between April 1952 and January 1953, Brian Fern accumulated 217 instructional hours in almost twenty different Oxfords imparting his skill to a long list of tyro pilot officers. In January 1953, with his own total now just short of 1,500 hours it was time to move on again.

Brian's professional skill and personal attributes – competent and reliable – seemed to have the confidence of his superiors in that he was again posted to a re-formed unit: 2 FTS, based at RAF Cluntoe in Tyrone, Northern Ireland. This station, too, was closed after the war but when the Korean War caused a drastic rethink, it was one of the nine refurbished stations mentioned above and re-opened in January 1953, equipped with the Harvard IIB and Prentice T1. Brian commenced work at 2 FTS on 2 February 1953 and lived in a caravan at first before moving in to rented accommodation in nearby Cookstown.

A week after joining he was made course commander of the Ground Training School with the acting rank of flight lieutenant. It was 23 April before he managed a check flight in Harvard KF449 but that was his only flight that month; and with just three trips, he fared little better in May. However, there was some compensation when Brian was offered a permanent commission as a General Duties Pilot. In accepting this, with effect from 1 April 1953, it gave him a more settled future in the RAF, in which he saw his long-term future career.

As a result, during the next twelve months he appears to have moved slightly away from purely instructional duties and was being directed towards acquiring a wider view of the RAF, possibly with his further promotion in mind. Between 3 November and 15 December 1953, he attended No. 58 Intelligence Course at RAF Uxbridge. This was followed by attendance on No. 73 course at the Officers Advanced Training School at RAF Bircham Newton, a staff school whose role was to provide training for officers being groomed to take the first steps up the command ladder in posts such as flight or squadron commander.

By early March 1954 Brian was back in instructor mode at 2 FTS Cluntoe where he put in a few week's instructional duties with young acting pilot officers attempting to learn to fly the Prentice T1. However, times were changing and the Prentice was no longer suitable for the pilots of the future and a new aeroplane in the shape of another Percival product appeared: the piston-engine P56 Provost T1, which was now being issued to the Flying Training Schools. 2 FTS was also destined for a change of scenery, too, when, in June 1954, it left Northern Ireland and moved to RAF Hullavington where it was re-equipped with the Provost T1. This side-by-side two-seat basic trainer was powered by a 550hp Alvis Leonides piston engine, giving it twice the power of the Prentice together with higher performance, manoeuvrability and good aerobatic qualities.

Having gone solo on the Provost, Brian was soon into the routine of the training programme, with anything up to four sorties a day during the months up to October. Then, yet again, it was time to move on. In his time with 2 FTS, by 21 October 1954 Brian had logged 9 hours on the Harvard, 25 on the Prentice and 89 on the Provost. On 27 October his commanding officer assessed him as 'average' both as a pilot and a QFI (B1) and confirmed his 'Green' instrument rating.

Although while at CFS Brian had managed to log a small number of jet aircraft hours in a Meteor, his next posting, to 211 FTS was to place him finally and firmly in the jet age. Now promoted to flight lieutenant, on 2 November 1954 he joined the All-Weather Jet Familiarisation course at RAF Worksop near Sheffield. RAF Worksop was one of those nine stations, mentioned above, that re-opened at the start of the Korean conflict and designated first as an Advanced Flying School (AFS), it catered for fast-jet training related to the Gloster Meteor, which at that time was in front-line service with the RAF and the Commonwealth air forces. His course was designed to take pilots who had trained on piston-engine aircraft through the principles of flying jet aircraft before they went onto an Operational Conversion Unit (OCU) and subsequently to an operational squadron. The course consisted of ground and air instruction components and the latter, involving about 50 hours, would use the Gloster Meteor. At Worksop, pilots would begin in the tandem two-seat Meteor T7, of which there were about twenty-five on charge, before moving on to gain experience in the Meteor F8, which numbered about thirty.

It was on 9 November that Brian, attached to 'C' Flight of the FTS's 2 Squadron, took to the air in Meteor T7, WL456 for an hour's familiarisation under the watchful eye of Fg Off Lowe. With the exception of a second dual trip in 456, to get the feel of the aircraft with Flt Sgt Harper on the 29th, that month was devoted to ground school. The flying programme got under way on 2 December with Fg Off E. E. Kortens demonstrating asymmetric flying to Brian in VW414. A wise precaution no doubt but, that this particular exercise featured at the beginning of training, is a reminder of the inherent fragility of early jet engines. This was followed the next day by Kortens demonstrating circuit procedure and asymmetric circuits then for his final flight of the day Brian was sent off for 30-minute solo in WA736. Undoubtedly Brian's wealth of flying experience stood him in great stead and this is quickly reflected in his log book entries. Just three more sorties, dealing with instrument flying, height climbing and a 'speed run', then on 10 December Brian was let loose in a single-seat Meteor F8, WK733.

Over the next two-month period, Brian was instructed in, practised, and was tested in, the T7 and F8 on exercises such as aerobatics, at medium and high level; circuit procedures by day, night and in bad weather; height climbs; speed runs; engine 'failures'; instrument practice and rating test; ground-controlled approaches (GCA); formations and cross-country flights. His final handling test came on 14 February 1955 when he flew with Sqn Ldr Ormiston (OC Flying Wing) for an hour in T7, VW456. After 33 hours (T7:20; F8:13) – substantially less than the course average – Brian was passed out on 22 February as 'proficient' on the Meteor and 'above average' for his instrument rating. He had 1,642 total flying hours to date and was off to his next posting. This would normally be an OCU but before Brian took that step, he first had to attend another short course.

Bomber Command Bombing School (BCBS) formed in October 1952 at RAF Scampton and re-located to RAF Lindholme a month later. It was to Lindholme that Brian was posted to attend No. 34 pilots bombing course from 9 to 30 March 1955 to receive instruction in the theory and practice of radar and visual bombing – from a pilot's viewpoint. In addition to ground instruction, during the middle of the course he made four 2½-hour duration flights in Vickers Varsity aircraft (WJ897, WL623 and WL689) to put the theory into practice over the Theddlethorpe weapons range on the Lincolnshire coast. Upon completion of the course Brian was posted next to 231 OCU at RAF Bassingbourn for No. 62 Canberra course, where he would train to become a Canberra bomber captain. His arrival at Bassingbourn on 30 March 1955 marked the beginning of a major new phase in Flt Lt Brian Fern's flying career as he now embarked upon a path that would see him serving initially as an operational jet bomber squadron pilot, then as a flight commander. During this posting he lived in rented accommodation in Saffron Walden.

The English Electric Canberra T4, which Brian first encountered at 231 OCU, was a dual-control version of the Canberra B2 bomber – mainstay of the RAF bomber force – and was brought into service in 1952 to help train aircrew destined for the bomber version. The crew for the B2 was three in number – pilot, navigator and bomb-aimer – but in the T4 a second pilot seat and control yoke were installed in a cosy side-by-side arrangement under the cockpit canopy, while the rear compartment housed a single navigator in a seat located directly behind the left-hand pilot.

Brian's first familiarisation flights in a Canberra were 2-hour sorties on 22 and 25 April 1955 with Sgt Dobbins in command of T4s WJ871 and WH847. On 28 April Flt Lt Moore took him up in '871 and on 4 May 'C' Sqn Commander Sqn Ldr Walker gave him his first taste at the controls of a B2 with an hour in WH716. Over the following week Brian and his crew of Flt Lt McGowan and Plt Off Chapman put in more practice until 19 May when Flt Lt Harrington checked his progress in T4 WH845, then it was back to the training programme numbered exercises through May and June including: medium level bombing, (simulated) high level bombing, cross-country flights, GH tracking, instrument rating practice and test and night-flying. With all twenty-seven exercises – each of an average of about two flying hours in duration – in the programme complete, it was time for the final handling tests on 23, 24 and 27 June in T4s: WH847 (under Flt Lt Gordon), WH846 and WH840 (under Plt Off Spokes). Brian passed these with an assessment of 'above average' as a jet bomber pilot having logged 60 flying hours on the course comprising: T4: day 11h 40m; night 6h 50m; B2 day 27h 30m; night 14h 15m. The course ended on 28 June and after a week's leave, on 11 July 1955 Brian reported to his first operational squadron: 207 based at RAF Marham, Norfolk, where he would become a Canberra bomber squadron pilot with his own crew of Flt Lt R. B. McGowan (Navigator/Plotter; responsible for position and timing) and Plt Off P. G. Chapman (Navigator/Observer; responsible for operating radar and bomb-aiming).

Although 207 Squadron had been in existence almost continuously since the First World War, it was disbanded in March 1950. Re-forming at RAF Marham in July 1951 with the Boeing B-29 Washington it operated this stop-gap American bomber until delivery of its first English Electric Canberra bombers in March 1954. Brian Fern and his crew joined the squadron in July 1955 and remained with it until March 1956 when – technically – it was disbanded in order to reform and to re-equip with the Vickers Valiant.

Two months of visual and GH bombing practice sorties enabled Brian's crew to participate in the major air defence exercise of 1955 – Exercise *Beware*, the largest-but-one since the Second World War. The exercise took place over the UK and continental NATO countries and was designed to test the performance of air defence fighters and new radar and controlling techniques against an all-out bomber offensive on the UK. The 'threat' was perceived to be atomic, so interceptions would be made ideally at least 30 miles from the UK coast. Canberra bombers, including Brian's and those of 207 Squadron, would make up the major part of the RAF contribution to the attacking force, which would also include bombers (e.g. B-47; B-45) and fighter-bombers (e.g. F-84; F-86) from the 7th and 49th Air Divisions of the USAF; 2nd and 4th Allied Tactical Air Forces (ATAF); France; Belgium; Holland and Italy; NATO Mediterranean Commands; RAF Flying Training Command and the Fleet Air Arm. Thus there would be aircraft of many nationalities (90 per cent of them jets, compared to 75 per cent the previous year) operating over an area of the UK stretching from Inverness, down the East Coast and west to Devon.

The defenders, including Hunters, Meteors, Vampires and US F-86D Sabres by day, with Meteor, Venoms and Sea Venoms and a couple of Javelins operating at night – one of the latter claiming no less than eight 'kills' – mounted over 7,500 sorties between them. More than 1,000 bomber sorties were launched against the UK at all altitudes, with the Hunters taking on anything over 40,000 feet – such as the Canberras. On 24 September Brian's crew made one 3-hour night '*Beware*' sortie in Canberra B2, WJ978 followed on the 27th by another 4-hour sortie in WH904 on which he took along Mr Lee, a civilian from the BBC. The first BBC live TV-broadcast involving Hunters, a Venom, a Meteor NF12 and a Canberra, flying alongside a Varsity from RAF Watton, went out on 22 August 1955 and it is believed Mr Lee was in some way involved in a further, similar broadcast or recording project during this major air exercise.

While Exercise *Beware* tested the responses of the UK air defence fighters, it was followed immediately by Exercise *Fox Paw* which assessed the fighter interception risk to the Canberra bomber during day- and night-time operations. *Fox Paw* also included units of the USAF flying the RB-57A, the US version of the British Canberra bomber, which were tested during night reconnaissance sorties. For this exercise Brian and his crew was detached to RAF Geilenkirchen, Germany, in WK142 on 30 September, returning to Marham on 1 October with Brian occupying the jump seat while the CO, Sqn Ldr Peter H. Gibbs, flew the aircraft home.

It was around this time that Brian, now a fully operational 'Combat Star'-rated pilot, began to spread his wings and carry out the first of many overseas flights on 28 October, when he flew WJ618 from Marham on a Lone Ranger sortie, number

147, to RAF Luqa, Malta, via Gibraltar; 3h 30m for the leg there then 2h 35 to Malta. On the 30th he took off from Luqa to make a 3h 35m flight to Wunstorf in West Germany – from where, after refuelling, he made the 1-hour flight back to Marham later the same day.

'Lone Ranger' was the RAF's generic name for overseas flights carried out by single crews. These independent deployments often used non-RAF or civilian airfields overseas and were regarded in a somewhat light-hearted manner as a welcome relief to the tedium of routine duties – indeed they have sometimes been referred to as 'RAF DIY holidays' – away from base but with all expenses paid! However, far from being light-hearted, their purpose was to accustom a crew to operating independently away from its own base, something it might very well be called upon to do at short notice in a war emergency situation.

Upon its return from the Lone Ranger trip, Brian's crew were back on more routine continuation training with the occasional 'co-operation' exercise with various fighter squadrons during such as 'King Pin' and 'Bombex' (or 'Bomex') exercises. On 17 November, for example, Brian flew B2, WK142 on a 3h 20m Bombex sortie during which he was required to simulate a bombing attack at 450 mph above 40,000 feet altitude so that some fighters could practise interceptions upon his Canberra target. A 'King Pin' exercise, such as the 3h 50m sortie he flew on the 24th in B2, WH886, was another version of acting as a target during which the Canberra would fly simulated bombing runs at a variety of altitudes and use electronic jamming techniques against fighters attempting to intercept it.

The year 1956 saw a major change in the composition of the RAF; the era of the four-engine jet V-bombers was about to begin and this in turn saw a gradual run-down of the Canberra squadrons which, at its peak of twenty-eight squadrons, had up to then formed the backbone of the bomber force. By February 1956 Brian, now with 1,900 flying hours in his log book, was assessed as 'above average' as a jet bomber pilot and he and his crew of Flt Lt McGowan and Fg Off Chapman were posted to 90 Squadron, a move that coincided with the disbandment of 207 Squadron. 207 was almost immediately re-activated in April 1956 to become the third squadron to be equipped with the new Vickers Valiant bomber. Brian and his crew were classed as supernumerary for a couple of weeks until on 14 March 1956 they joined 90 Squadron, another Canberra unit still located at RAF Marham. The only highlight of this 'transient' period came on 20 March when Brian and his crew took off in B2, WK115, for a Lone Ranger trip to Gibraltar-Luqa-Wunstorf-base.

The remainder of March and April was pretty bereft of flying except for a few hours in a T4 doing continuation training and providing some excitement for the crowd at a Homes & Garden Exhibition in Birmingham. After this light relief, 90 Squadron, too, came up for disbandment and Brian and his crew found themselves moved on to 35 Squadron, which was also based at RAF Marham. 90's demise was again connected with the Valiant programme and the squadron would be re-activated on 1 January 1957 at RAF Honington when it became part of the Valiant force.

This new posting itself lasted just one month and when 35 Squadron re-located its Canberras from Marham to Upwood, Brian found himself posted yet again, this time to 115 Squadron on 4 June 1956. Still located at Marham, for the first month he and his crew were occupied with more continuation training of which the majority was instrument rating practice and testing. This was quite normal on Canberra bomber squadrons, where life for a crew would be split between honing basic crew duty skills and acquiring a Bomber Command Classification to enable it to become operational with 'Combat' status, then flying and practising to maintain or improve its classification towards the coveted 'Select' status. On 26 June Brian had the now rare opportunity to put in some piston-engine time when he took up Anson VM342 while his navigator Fg Off Chapman underwent some instrument training of his own.

In October 1956 the political situation over the Suez Canal issue came to a head with military action that involved British forces, including the RAF. Thirteen Canberra bomber squadrons were despatched to Malta and Cyprus for operations over Egypt but 115 was not one of those deployed. However, during the preceding months it was becoming clear to the RAF that action was not far off and in as part of the general preparations, Brian flew out to Luqa and back on 10 August as part of Exercise *Accumulate*. He flew Canberra B2, WH718, on the 3h 10m each-way deployment trial with newly promoted Sqn Ldr McGowan as his plotter and Fg Off Wilding as observer. 115 was put on standby at Marham but in the event was not called upon and after the brief Suez Campaign ended, it was back to a routine of practice flying again. For Brian and his crew most of August and September were taken up with practice bombing sorties, usually carried out at altitudes of 35–45,000 feet and speeds of about 450 mph. Canberras flown included WH718, WH705, WH905, WK110 and WJ631. A typical bomb load was eight 25-lb practice bombs, which would be dropped over one or other of the UK coastal ranges, such as Wainfleet or Holbeach Marsh in The Wash. Bombing runs involved the use of a radar bombing aid called 'GH' but sometimes the bombs were dropped visually using the Mk XIV bombsight.

September 1956 saw the year's biggest air exercises with Exercise *Stronghold* which, over several days, tested the UK air defences and was co-ordinated with Exercise *Whip Saw*, a large NATO exercise directed by SACEUR (Supreme Allied Commander, Europe). It was similar in concept to the previous year's '*Beware*' in which the main task for the RAF fighters was to intercept as many as possible of the attacking bomber force. Brian's involvement, with his crew of Flt Lt Stevens and Fg Off Chapman, was to fly one *Stronghold* sortie at night in B2, WH905, on the 21st followed by another night sortie for *Whip Saw* on the 26th. The latter was flown in WJ631 with a civilian, Mr Fulton, in the jump seat, but no reason for this was noted. The weather was poor for most of the exercise period and they finished on 28 September then, after a two-day deployment to Luqa, Malta, on 2/3 October it was back to the grind of routine training again.

On a couple of occasions during November and December 1956, Brian became involved in the testing of target acquisition radar relating to a new ground-to-air missile called Sea Slug. This was an anti-aircraft weapon destined for the Royal Navy and trials of the first fully working system were taking place aboard HMS *Girdle Ness* off the south coast at this time. Air targets for the Sea Slug were picked up by a beam from a Type 901 fire-control radar that 'illuminated' the target, whose signals were then relayed to the missile and guided it onto the target after being fired from special carriers on the deck of the ship. The Navy needed some 'tame (sitting?) ducks' for the radar acquisition trials, which were carried out under the title of Exercise *Girdle Ness* and Brian flew one of these on 12 November, in WJ980, and another on 6 December, in WK140.

During 1956 the squadrons at RAF Marham were subjected to changes directly connected to the major reshape taking place in the RAF as a whole; it was beginning to transform itself into a global strike force – a process spurred on by the chill wind blowing through the world political arena. These changes, among others, were designed to ensure that RAF Marham was 'cleared out' so that the station could support squadrons operating the new Vickers Valiant bomber. In January, 214 Squadron re-formed at Marham with the Vickers Valiant and this squadron would emerge with a key role to play in how the RAF achieved its global aim. It was with this squadron that we shall see how Flt Lt Brian Fern also plays a significant part in helping to achieve those global ambitions.

As we have read above, 207 Squadron remained at Marham and was already in the process of re-equipping with the Valiant bomber at the station. 90 Squadron was deactivated but would in later years reform with the Valiant at RAF Honington. 35 Squadron moved out to RAF Upwood, where it would soldier on with its Canberras until 1961 when it too would de-activate and reform the following year at RAF Cottesmore with the Avro Vulcan. 115 Squadron, with whom Brian was currently serving, hung on to its Canberras until June 1957 then it was de-activated. It re-formed at RAF Watton in August 1958 by re-numbering 116 Squadron to become the new 115 Squadron and operated as a Radar Calibration Unit, subsequently moving down to RAF Tangmere.

3·3

VALIANT COMMANDER

There were signs during January 1957 that things were about to change for Brian when he and his squadron, went through a period of two weeks of intensive flying while detached to Luqa, Malta; Nicosia, Cyprus, and El Adem in the Libyan Desert. There was another week on detachment to Luqa during February after which Brian was put through his general flying assessment and instrument rating paces over quite a lengthy period. This all earned him an 'above average' rating as a jet bomber pilot, a 'green' instrument pass and confirmation of his Combat Star classification and after a flight to RAF Gaydon – home of the Valiant OCU (Operational Conversion Unit) – and back, it became pretty obvious that he was going to be posted the V-bomber force. A posting eventually came through with effect from 10 April 1957 and he was indeed off to RAF Gaydon to join 19 Medium Bomber course with 'B' Squadron at 232 (Valiant) OCU.

Brian was as meticulous in his record keeping as he was in his approach to flying and his flying log book is a model of neatness in which – co-incident with all the above assessments – he analysed his flying to date – all 2,126 hours of it – and tabulated it in his log book. In the words of a senior RAF officer at that time: 'If you have a man with a £1 million aeroplane strapped to his bottom, you have to get the best.' 'The best' meant that potential Valiant captains were required to have at least 1,750 hours as a first pilot, an 'above average' rating, come 'highly recommended' and have completed at least one tour on Canberras. They would be required to remain with a V-bomber squadron for a tour of five years, so it was a long-term investment that was being made in these men.

Brian Fern: Analysis of flying hours as at 1 February 1957

Single engine

Type	Hours
Miles Master	3
DH Tiger Moth	13
Stearman PT-17	91
N. A. AT-6 Texan	200
Miles Magister	25
Percival Prentice	66
Percival Provost	91
Total Single engine	**489**

Multi-Engine.

Airspeed Oxford	1,047
Vickers Varsity	9
Avro Anson	1
Vickers Wellington	85

Gloster Meteor Mk.7	22
Gloster Meteor Mk.8	13
E E Canberra T4	71
E E Canberra B2	389
Total Multi engine	**1,637**

The Vickers Valiant B1, the pure bomber variant, was a big beast; the first four-engine jet to equip the RAF, in whose service it and the later Avro Vulcan and Handley Page Victor, would become known as 'V-Bombers'. This production model first went into squadron service in January 1955 with 138 Squadron at RAF Gaydon. Powered by four Rolls-Royce Avon engines of 10,000 lbs static thrust each, the Valiant had a wingspan of 114 feet, a length of 108 feet and stood 32 feet to the tip of the fin. It weighed in at 76,000 lbs empty, with an all-up weight of 140,000 lb that allowed it to carry a load of 1 x 10,000 lb nuclear weapon or 21 x 1,000 lb conventional bombs. Maximum speed was 567 mph at 30,000 feet; its service ceiling was 54,000 feet and with under-wing fuel tanks, it had a range of almost 4,500 miles. Manned by a crew of two pilots, two navigators and one air electronics engineer, the Valiant was indeed a formidable addition to the RAF inventory, bringing with it a strategic capability that, when air-to-air refuelling (AAR) was introduced – two additional crew members were carried for this function – the distances over which it operated became truly world-wide.

After a spot of leave between the postings, Brian arrived at 232 OCU in early April 1957 but he had to first apply his mind to the intensive Valiant ground school curriculum before he would be let loose in one of these monsters in the air.

Pilots were expected to spend several months studying the Valiant and its systems; over 20 hours were allocated to the simulator, and they had to fly lots of Instrument Landing System (ILS) practice in Canberras. A month elapsed before the flying training stage began on 9 May and Brian's next sorties were flown in the familiar Canberra T4, at first being checked out by 'B' Squadron commander then brushing up his ILS technique along with two trainee Valiant navigators. On 25 June, Brian got his hands on a Valiant for the first time, going up as co-pilot to Sqn Ldr Gale in WZ364 for a 2h 45m familiarisation sortie.

With more dual on the 27th, interspersed with more ground school, it was 1 July 1957 when Brian finally went solo in Valiant WZ364. In between yet more ground school sessions, there then followed longer solo flights lasting 3–4 hours, until exercise No. 10 came round which, in WZ361, was his introduction to flying the big bomber at night. From then on, he practised night flying and ILS landings, including a 6-hour sortie in WZ374 on 22nd which set him up for a check flight the next night as aircraft captain of WZ368, with Sqn Ldr Laird as co-pilot and assessor. Brian's instrument rating test came on 26 July and he graduated from his conversion course with a grading of 'Proficient' as a medium bomber First Pilot and an 'MG' instrument rating. (The 'MG' or 'Master Green' is one of various, ascending, colour grades that authorise pilots to do flying of varying difficulty in poor visibility; an MG instrument rating is a high one.) During this course he had flown 44 hours in the Valiant of which 26 were by day and 18 by night and he was now a fully fledged V-bomber pilot.

On 26 July 1957 Flt Lt Brian Fern received his posting to 214 (Federated Malay States) Squadron at RAF Marham, a station with which he was entirely familiar and which was to become a major V-bomber station. Over the next three years, Brian too would play a significant role in the life of the squadron and the subsequent development of the Valiant, guided as it was by events during the Cold War. When Brian joined the squadron, it was commanded by the illustrious Wg Cdr Leonard Trent VC, DFC, who was awarded the VC for his courage and leadership while flying a Lockheed Ventura with 487 (NZ) Squadron on an epic bombing raid on 3 May 1943, during which he was shot down and spent the rest of the war as a POW.

Brian's operational V-bomber flying began on 14 August 1957 with a check flight in Valiant XD870 under the watchful eye of his flight commander Sqn Ldr John Wynne. His five-man crew had been formed at the OCU and comprised himself as pilot and aircraft captain; Flt Lt Burleigh, as co-pilot; Flt Lt Hartland, navigator/plotter (nav/plotter); Fg Off Hewson, nav/ bomber and Sgt Gastrell, air electronics operator. Training, as a crew on their own, began on 21 August with a practice diversion down to RAF St Mawgan in WZ395. Two days later this was followed by a trip in the opposite direction, to RAF Kinloss and back. But there was as much work to be done on the ground as in the air since sortie planning, de-briefing and analysis of their work and performance was vital to crew proficiency as both a single team and part of an operational squadron. The crew's flying hours, at 13 hours for the month, was therefore relatively low at this stage of their training. However, although the number of sorties was low the sortie durations expected of Valiant crews were quite long at around 4 hours each.

September 1957 provided a little variety though, as mixed in with practice radar-controlled bombing sorties in WP212 and

WZ395 on 3, 4 and 5 September, Brian participated in a mass Bomber Command flypast over the Farnborough Air Show. On Saturday 7 September he flew XD870 as part of a large formation of high-flying Valiants and Canberras of RAF Bomber Command, through an almost cloudless sky over Farnborough and a week later, on the 14th, he flew XD870, its flight crew and a ground crew chief, Chief Technician (C/T) Terry, down to London Airport to put the aircraft on display as part of the annual Battle of Britain Day celebrations, remaining there until the 16th.

Then it was back to Marham to take part in the biggest NATO exercise of the year: Exercise *Strikeback*. This was actually a major naval exercise, one of a series, which simulated an all-out attack by Soviet forces upon NATO. It took place over a vast area of the North Atlantic, the Iceland Gap and Norwegian Sea and involved over 200 warships, 650 aircraft – mainly carrier-based types – and 75,000 personnel from all the NATO countries. NATO was known as 'Blue Force' and various surface and air units were designated as 'Orange Force', which represented the Soviet threat. Valiant bombers from the RAF were part of Orange Force and tasked with simulating high-level bombing attacks on several Blue Force carrier groups, including that of HMS *Ark Royal*. Brian carried out one 6-hour sortie in WP212 on just one day, 19 September, of the ten-day exercise.

October 1957 brought a significant change for both the squadron and Brian and his crew, when long overseas detachment flights began, initially to the Middle and Far East. During the afternoon of 3 October, five Valiant crews left Marham bound for Akrotiri in Cyprus, including Brian and his regular crew together with Chief Tech Prior in the jump seat, who made the trip from Marham in WP212 in just under 5 hours. Three other Valiants, captained by Wg Cdr Trent, with Sqn Ldr Wynne and Flt Lt Price, flew out to RAF Changi, Singapore, the same day, their objective being to gain experience of operating the Valiant under Far East flying conditions.

While at Akrotiri, Brian and his crew took over WZ379 and on the 7th, 8th and 10th they flew three 4-hour, round-trip, visual bombing sorties to RAF El Adem Bombing Range in the Libyan Desert. Back at Akrotiri they then spent a few days preparing to move on, this time as a VIP transport! On the 14th, now with AVM (later Sir) Leslie Bower, Senior Air Staff Officer (SASO) at HQ Middle East Air Force occupying the jump seat and Fg Off Parr taking the place of Fg Off Hartland – who is believed to have been unwell – Brian flew WZ379 to Bahrain (3h 20m) then on to Khormaksar (4h 15m), Aden – now part of Yemen. After an overnight stop there, Brian took WZ379 and the AVM on to RAF Eastleigh (2h 25m) on the outskirts of Nairobi, Kenya, arriving on 15 October. Another overnight stop and then he was off back to Khormaksar and Bahrain before finally delivering the AVM back to Akrotiri on the evening of 16 October.

After a few day's rest, on 21 October, this time with Flt Sgt Kerans standing in for Fg Off Hartland, Brian made a 5½-hour cross-country flight over the eastern Mediterranean in WP212 with Sqn Ldr Garstin, in the jump seat. October was brought to a close with two more 5-hour visual bombing sorties – one by day and the other by night, out to El Adem range and back, both in XD869; the second of which on the 28th saw Fg Off Hartland back in his usual place as nav/plotter.

On 1 and 2 November Brian and his crew flew two 5-hour sorties in NATO Exercise *Red Epoch* in WP212 and with their detachment at an end, they brought WP212 and their crew chief back to Marham. With more bombing practice flights completed during mid-November, Brian yet again set off on a three-day Lone Ranger (with Chief Tech Partridge aboard) from Marham for sunnier climes, this time to RAF Idris, a station on the Libyan coast formerly known as Castel Benito and in 2019, Tripoli International Airport. These were 6-hour trips each way, made in XD859.

By the end of January 1958 Brian was classified as a 'Combat' category first-pilot in a 'Combat' category crew. Now, with 2,370 hours in his log book Brian was a fully fledged operational member of the elite V-bomber force. 214 Squadron itself was now under the command of Wg Cdr Michael Beetham DFC (later MRAF Sir Michael GCB CBE AFC), a Second World War veteran who would rise to command the RAF in years to come. The squadron was also about to undergo a major role-change and Brian Fern would get his chance to play an important part in its next task. In the first half of 1958, though, it was practice, practice, practice, by day and night, including another 'Lone Ranger' detachment to El Adem, Eastleigh (Kenya), Aden, Bahrain, Akrotiri and back to Marham, the whole round trip being completed in the space of a week. But this, of course, was what the V-bomber force was all about – the ability to reach out across the globe.

There was, however, still a missing piece in the V-Force jig-saw; in order to achieve this global commitment of its bombers, in a world of ever-changing geo-politics, the RAF could no longer afford to rely on being able to use its existing network of airfields around the world. If unrefuelled in the air, the Valiant could remain airborne for a maximum of just under 7 hours. It was clear, therefore, that to fulfil its strategic aims the RAF must have a means of refuelling its aircraft in flight and 214 Squadron was selected as the first service unit to undertake this role. Strategic thinking also considered that extending the V-bomber range in this way would expose more potential enemy targets and also gave crews a wider choice of routes to a target. It was intended that Vulcan and Victor bombers then currently in service would be converted to in-flight 'receivers' and future deliveries of these bombers would come off the production line with that facility built-in. Furthermore, by using an aircraft with the performance of the jet-powered Valiant as a tanker, flight-refuelling could be carried out far more efficiently at high altitudes compared with similar operations using propeller-driven tankers.

In-flight re-fuelling – the transfer of fuel from one aircraft to another in flight in order to extend flying range – was not a new concept even in 1957. Indeed, the idea had been around since just after the First World War. One of the leading British developers and exponents of this technique was Sir Alan Cobham whose successful experiments, pre- and post-World War Two, led to the creation of his company, Flight Refuelling Ltd (FRL). During the early 1950s the RAF decided to equip its V-bomber force with air refuelling capability and used FRL to carry out development work to this end and to come up with an equipment solution. FRL's preferred option was for equipment based on its 'Probe and Drogue' system that used a fixed, nose mounted rigid 'probe' on a 'receiver' aircraft, which engaged a flexible hosepipe trailed from a 'tanker'.

A prototype of FRL's Mark 16 Hose Drum Unit (HDU) intended for the Valiant was manufactured and trialled successfully in a Canberra. During 1956 one Valiant bomber (WZ376) was modified to carry the Mk 16 HDU while another (WZ390) was fitted with a receiver probe and trials were undertaken by the Aircraft and Armament Experimental Establishment (A&AEE) at Boscombe Down. By early 1957, since all the Valiant bombers ordered were now actually in service, it was accepted that an operational squadron had to be tasked with bringing this new system into operational service. This was the background to how 214 Squadron was selected as the service trials and development unit for the RAF while Marham, its base, became the location of the RAF's Air-to-Air Refuelling (AAR) School. FRL provided initial training at its Tarrant Rushton site for the first RAF tanker crews.

At first, 214 was required to retain its primary bombing commitment as well as conduct flight-refuelling trials and to this end, its 'B' Flight carried out the former and 'A' Flight the latter. The flight-refuelling trials, which were conducted over a period of about two years, were given two designations. The first phase was Trial Number 306, which was a programme designed to test the capability of the tanker and receiver equipment under service conditions and under which 214 was to convert solely to that role. The second phase was Trial Number 306A, which was to develop an effective navigational aid 'rendezvous' system that would assist tanker and receiver aircraft to come together so that fuel could be transferred between them. This change of role was not popular with the 214 Squadron crews, who saw it as something of a second-rate activity compared to their V-Force bombing duties. However, after a while it became clear to them that in 'tanking' they had quite a lot of freedom of action while flying Trial 306 operations, whereas their pure bomber compatriots were frequently tied up on the ground on QRA (Quick Reaction Alert) duties 'waiting for the nuclear balloon to go up'.

In December 1957 the squadron shuffled aircraft between its two Flights so that those that had been modified to carry under-wing fuel tanks were all moved to 'A' Flight, which then began the process of converting first itself, and eventually the rest of the squadron, to refuelling mode. The under-wing tanks simply maximised the standard fuel capacity, which – in the case of a 'tanker' as opposed to a 'receiver' – was further increased by the installation of a 4,500 lb capacity extra tank suspended in the bomb-bay forward of the HDU. In a 'tanker' Valiant, certain fuel tanks were allocated for transfers and a 'tanker' could transfer the contents from this particular set of its fuel tanks to a 'receiver'. These 'transfer' tanks were fitted with an extra pump that delivered fuel directly to the HDU at the pressure required for the refuelling process. When not working as a 'tanker' aircraft, the fuel in those transfer tanks could be used by the Valiant for its own purposes.

TANKERS AWAY!

As part of this Flight re-organisation, at the end of May 1958, Brian (and his crew) was transferred from 'B' Flight to 'A' Flight and thus he was to become one of the first of the jet-age pilots involved with flight-refuelling in the RAF. In view of the subsequent training of pilots in this new technique, that had to actually take place on the squadron and on the aeroplane flight deck in the air, it seems very likely that Brian's considerable past experience as an instructor would have been a factor in his selection at this critical time for the squadron.

All Valiant aircraft in service at the end of 1957 were capable of being modified to both dispense (tanker) and receive (receiver) fuel in flight. Indeed, many Valiants had rolled off the production line with the basic internal components already installed. A receiver probe could be fitted in less than an hour and full conversion of an aircraft to tanker mode could be completed on-squadron in a matter of a few hours. 214 Squadron's Valiants underwent conversion to 'receivers' by installing a tubular external probe to the front of the

Navigation & Bombing System (NBS) scanner bay and then connecting that probe to a series of internal pipes linking it to the bomber's own fuel system. A control panel for the HDU was installed in the instrument panel at the navigator/radar (nav/rad)'s position and he acted as the fuel panel operator during any in-flight refuelling activity. External floodlights were also installed to assist refuelling operations at night. The whole system was designed to allow the transfer, between Valiant tanker and receiver, of up to 45,000 lbs of fuel at a rate of 4,000 lbs per minute under a maximum hose pressure of 50 psi (pounds per square inch).

Things began to change for the squadron from January 1958 when the first converted Valiant BK1s began to arrive at Marham. The Valiant B1 was the basic bomber variant (Vickers Type 706). The BK1 was a B1 model modified to receive fuel in-flight and with built-in equipment that enabled it to be converted to a fuel tanker when required (Vickers Type 758). The B(PR)1 was a B1 but with built-in equipment that allowed it to be adapted to a photo-recce role when required (Vickers Type 710). A BK(PR)1 was again based on the standard bomber that was modified for in-flight refuelling as a receiver but also capable of being converted to a photo-recce or fuel tanker role when required (Vickers Type 733).

A variety of problems emerged during the pre-service trials, such as severe air turbulence around the receiver when the tanker bomb bay doors were opened. This was fixed by the installation of a fairing behind the bay. Turbulence behind the hose drogue-cone caused vibration on hook-up but this was eliminated by installing a cone with many slots cut into it. Some technical faults with the fuel transfer pumps materialised from the outset of the service trials and although this did not inhibit flying training, it meant that only what were known as 'dry hook-ups' could be practiced until it was resolved. It would be nearly a year before the technical hitches were sorted out and 'wet' transfers could begin.

On 3 June 1958, now with 300 flying hours on the Valiant in his logbook, Brian began his part in the Trial 306 operations with a 3-hour air test in Valiant B(K)1 XD869. The following day he was co-pilot to Sqn Ldr John Garstin, 'B' Flight commander, in XD816 for 4 hours on their first practice at receiving fuel. Most of the sortie was taken up with trying out the manoeuvres necessary to line up the probe during which he made what he noted later as 'two below', signifying that he had made two 'dry' connections. On this occasion, Mr Ken Wickenden, a very experienced technician from FRL, was supernumerary on the flight deck to offer words of wisdom about how to go about the task.

A few days later Brian was off again, this time for another 4-hour sortie as co-pilot to his 'A' Flight commander, Sqn Ldr Peter Coventry, in XD869, in which they completed three contacts 'below' as receiver. It was the same again next day with Sqn Ldr Coventry for 4 hours in XD812 during which they completed two contacts 'above', as tanker and eight 'below' as receiver. On 12 June Brian was let loose to practise on his own, in XD816, taking along a couple of nav/rads from other crews to get some experience on the control panel. They completed seven contacts 'below' (receiver) during the 4-hour sortie. On 13 June Brian took his own crew up in XD812 for some more mundane continuation training, before returning to refuelling practice in the same aircraft on the 16th with a 4-hour trip as a tanker for ten contacts. On 27 June, Ken Wickenden accompanied Brian's crew on a daylight 4-hour 'tanker' sortie in XD816, which included 30 minutes of simulated flying on instruments, which must have made it an interesting test of Brian's ability. June came to a close with Brian having flown a total 30 hours during which he made 32 'hook-ups,' of which 12 were in the tanker position.

A fuel transfer operation entailed both aircraft flying in a 'trail' formation for about 10–15 minutes at a steady speed of 250 mph. For the receiver aircraft, the process of hooking-up involved approaching the trailing hose drogue (basket) and flying the probe into the drogue at an overtaking speed no greater than about 5 mph. If the docking speed was higher than that, there was a risk that the hose re-wind mechanism would not respond quickly enough and it would 'kink' and perhaps cause it to fly off the end of the probe. If the docking speed was lower than 5 mph, the connection between probe and drogue might be loose and a leak might occur when the fuel began to flow.

Brian and his colleagues in 'A' Flight were clearly getting the hang of these 'dry' hook-ups but practice was still very much the order of the day. On 3 July Brian and his crew, in XD816, acted as 'tanker' for others in the Flight to make ten hook-ups. On the 8th, Ken Wickenden from FRL joined Brian on the flight deck of XD816 again, this time with a camera set up for filming a flight-refuelling sortie, although it is not clear what aspect of the operation was being filmed. However, on the internet, there is a short piece of film, credited to British Pathé and dated 1958, that is filmed from the port side of what appears to be a Valiant formatting on two other Valiants that are hooked-up as for refuelling. Could it be that Brian's aircraft was photo-ship for this event? Unfortunately, no aircraft serial numbers can be deciphered.

There was more light relief when Brian and his crew was ordered to fly XD859 to Coventry (Baginton) Airport on Saturday 12 July, to entertain the crowd during the final day of the annual three-day Air Pageant. After sparkling clear sunshine on the earlier days, Saturday's weather was overcast and drizzly, forcing Brian to get down pretty low to get beneath the 400-foot overcast. The Air Pageant was venue for the British National Air Races and an international aerobatic competition but the weather put paid to the latter event, although the annual King's Cup race was still, just, able to be flown. A couple of days later Sqn Ldr Garstin took Brian up in XD816 for an instrument rating test and the month was rounded off with a flight in WZ390, a BK(PR)1, from Wisley airfield to Marham, with Ken Wickenden in the jump seat.

It was almost a month before Brian was airborne again and most of his flying during August was taken up with practising for the Farnborough Air Show, at which 214 Squadron was going to show off its flight-refuelling expertise to the crowds. There was, of course, a great deal of pride involved in this event and the eyes of the RAF and the public would be upon the squadron so there was pressure to perform well for the honour of the squadron. In this respect, Brian was airborne first as co-pilot to the CO, Wg Cdr Michael Beetham, in B(K)1 XD816 to practise receiving. No doubt the CO wanted to lead the whole 'show' and was anxious to get things just right, so Mr Frank Russell, another technician from FRL, was taken to offer advice. On 23 August, Brian also took along Sqn Ldr Garstin as his co-pilot in WZ395, a BK(PR)1, for seven receiver hook-ups as practice for Farnborough and again on 25th in XD812, with Frank Russell on board too. The next day he was back in WZ395 for more Air Show practice and the following day the intense practising was rounded off when he flew in XD816 as co-pilot to Wg Cdr Beetham once again.

On every one of the seven days of the show, a pair of Valiants from 214 Squadron carried out 'hooked-up' flypasts over the Farnborough Air Show, which that year took place in front of immense crowds between Monday 1 and Sunday 7 September in generally warm and sunny weather. Brian's log book does not mention which position his aircraft occupied in the daily formation but on the 1st he flew as co-pilot to Sqn Ldr Wynne in XD816 (with Frank Russell on board as well to see everything went smoothly); on the 2nd he flew XD816 as aircraft captain, while on the 4th (in XD821), 5th and 6th (XD816) and 7th (WZ390) he flew as co-pilot to Sqn Ldr Wynne. It looks as if he had a day off on the 3rd. It seems perfectly reasonable that the Squadron CO and his Flight Commanders would task themselves to fly these highly prestigious, public sorties and since Sqn Ldr Wynne was 'B' Flight commander, this tends to suggest he may have taken the lower, receiver slot. Brian, from 'A' Flight, was almost certainly selected for the co-pilot's job because of his overall experience of refuelling – and without doubt, his utter reliability on such occasions. He also flew with his regular 'back-seaters' of Flt Lts Hewson and Adamson and Flt Sgt Gastrell.

The 1958 show was one of those vintage Farnborough years, including lots of helicopters and fast jets, among which was the sight of no less than twenty-two Hawker Hunters from

111 Squadron ('Treble-One') being looped – not once, but twice – in formation, a feat never seen since those heady, far-off days. The bombers then made their stately flypasts. First to run in at 1,000 feet was a 'vic' of three V-bombers: a Vulcan of 83 Squadron, a Victor of 10 squadron and a Valiant of 90 Squadron. Then came the turn of a pair of Valiants from 214 Squadron, – including XD816 with Brian Fern on board – 'hooked' together at 1,400 feet to demonstrate flight-refuelling and followed a few minutes later by nine Canberra jets from Nos. 9 and 12 Squadrons. On Brian's sortie on the 2nd he took the squadron's newly appointed OC Admin Wing, Wg Cdr H. K. Rees, along for the ride and on the final Sunday of the show Ken Wickenden occupied the jump seat.

After the effort put into the Farnborough show it was necessary to get back to normal training for V-force bombing operations and Brian made several 5-hour 'profile' sorties by day and night in WZ390 and XD821 over the next couple of weeks. However, his refuelling expertise was called upon again later that month when, in XD821, he provided the 'top half' (tanker) of a hooked-up flypast at one of the annual Battle of Britain air shows. Then it was back to more bombing training with sorties of 4–6 hours becoming the norm, all in preparation for a Lone Ranger detachment to Luqa in Malta in November.

Brian flew out to Luqa, with his ground crew line chief C/T (Chief Technician) Smithers occupying the spare seat, on 5 November in XD858 and returned on the 21st in XD812. During this detachment Brian flew a number of day and night visual bombing practice sorties over the El Adem range in Libya. One significant 5-hour trip from Luqa on 18 November involved carrying out a rendezvous exercise as part of a refuelling Trial 306 sortie. As 214 Squadron's expertise at the 'standard' refuelling task increased, so its attention would turn more towards the second phase of flight-refuelling – 'Trial 306A' – which addressed the issues of rendezvous techniques and how to enable tanker and receiver to meet up in their three-dimensional workplace.

Brian's co-pilot for the spell at Luqa was a new pilot on the squadron, Plt Off Peter Wormall, with whom he flew only during that detachment. Plt Off Wormall flew with other crews in subsequent months but sadly died in an accident during take-off from Marham on 11 September 1959, in which he and all his crew perished. The Valiant in which Fg Off Wormall was flying as co-pilot, XD869, was taking off, in poor weather conditions, at the start of a Lone Ranger detachment to Nairobi (Eastleigh), during which it was scheduled to be refuelled in flight over Malta by a 214 Squadron tanker Valiant operating from Luqa. It is interesting to note in Brian Fern's log book that, a few days prior to the Lone Ranger, on 8 September 1959, he made transit to Luqa where he remained for three weeks on refuelling duties and to participate in Exercise *Crescent Mace*. Two tankers were normally made ready at Luqa to deal with a Lone Ranger flight-refuelling operation and it was recalled by a crew chief that word came through from Marham that they would not be needed that night. It is believed Brian's aircraft would have been the tanker that Fg Off Wormall's ill-fated Valiant was due to meet up with *en route* to Nairobi.

As 1958 drew to a close it was clear that the flight-refuelling trials had gone well and the problems arising from them – which kept them as 'dry' simulations – had been resolved. Plans were now in place to begin what became known as 'wet' transfers, when fuel would actually be passed from one Valiant to another. As we have seen above, senior officers were anxious to keep up with the technique and none more so than the OC Marham, Group Captain (later ACM Sir) Lewis Hodges. Popularly known as 'Bob', Gp Capt Hodges was a highly decorated and colourful Second World War veteran and he was placed in Brian's capable hands to see for himself how refuelling operations were carried out. For the benefit of the group captain, who took the left-hand seat of WZ395, on 22 December, Brian carried out nine Trial 306 hook-ups; two as tanker and seven as receiver.

Then the big day finally arrived. Wet transfers were finally approved and the first transfer of fuel was scheduled to take place in daylight conditions on 23 January 1959. Gremlins, however, caused some problems with the aircraft which were not fully serviceable until well after dark. Although Group HQ had stipulated that the first 'go' was to be made in daylight, Wg Cdr Beetham, ever keen to press on, conveniently overlooked that aspect of his orders and decreed the test sortie was to go ahead in darkness that evening.

The honour of making that first RAF all-jet 'wet' transfer fell to 'A' Flight's Flt Lt Brian Fern as tanker pilot of WZ390 and 'B' Flight's Sqn Ldr John Garstin (in April, Garstin would be appointed 'A' Flight commander) as receiver pilot. Brian's crew for the momentous occasion was: Flt Lt Fisher, co-pilot; Flt Lts Hewson and Turner, Flt Sgt Gastrell and, keeping a watchful eye on the proceedings, was Frank Russell from FRL. John Garstin also had Ken Wickenden of FRL on board his aircraft and the test was a resounding success. This was a significant milestone not only for 214 Squadron but also for the RAF and the forthcoming months of 1959 would see many long-distance flights being flown across the world by the RAF jet V-Force, courtesy of 214 Squadron tankers.

Brian flew two more Trial 306 'wet' sorties that month, one on 26 January in WZ390 with Ken Wickenden on board and the other on the 28th in XD816, during which he made ten contacts and eight contacts respectively. Of course, the fuel transferred during these trial wet hook-ups would only be nominal quantity to test the aircraft systems during each of the hook-ups that were made. Now, with a grand total of 2,628 flying hours and 86 refuelling hook-ups to his name, Brian's flying skill was assessed by Wg Cdr Beetham as 'Above Average', and he had acquired something of a reputation as a flight-refuelling expert and a pilot who could always be relied upon.

Since the introduction of long-distance deployments known as 'Lone Rangers' there arose a more pressing need for the Valiant crews to be able to understand the workings of its systems that were more usually the preserve of ground maintenance personnel, so that they could help keep their aircraft serviceable while operating independently away from base for quite long periods. On these deployments it was therefore usual to take along a ground crew chief technician as an extra, important, member of the crew. This aspect also accounts for Brian's attendance at Rolls-Royce's Aero Engine School in Derby for a week from 9 to 12 February 1959 to learn something of the construction, operation and flight handling characteristics of the Rolls-Royce Avon 200 Series jet engine as installed in the Vickers Valiant.

February and March saw Brian making trial tanking rendezvous sorties and practice 'wet' transfers, by day and night, so that other pilots and crews could become proficient and bring the squadron fully up to speed. When he was not 'tanking' he was flying practice bombing and navigation exercises to maintain his own crew's V-Force proficiency. During April, Trial 306 occupied most of the squadron with one notable exception when Flt Lt P. Butler took Valiant XD859 on a 'Polar Bear' detachment to Gardermoen airfield, near Oslo in Norway, for a couple of days.

April 1959 was also the time for 214 Squadron to 'stretch its legs' and show the world what the RAF was capable of doing. Wg Cdr Beetham, to some extent left by higher authority to his own devices in this new role, set in train plans for the squadron to undertake a number of long-distance air-refuelled flights to distant parts of the British Empire and Brian Fern was to play a significant part in that programme. Sqn Ldr Price was first to fly out to Embakasi, Nairobi, on 6 April. Next to fly out was Brian and his crew of Flt Lts Fox, co-pilot; Hewson, nav/plot and Turner, nav/radar with Flt Sgt Gastrell, signaller and C/T Partridge, crew chief. During their non-stop, flight-refuelled 'Tankex' mission, they achieved an unofficial record for the flight from Marham to Embakasi, Nairobi, on 7 April 1959. Taking off in XD859, Brian's Valiant was refuelled over Malta by one of two 214 Squadron tankers (XD861: Sqn Ldr J. Wynne and XD870: Sqn Ldr J. Slessor) that had been temporarily detached to RAF Luqa. He landed 7 hours 40 minutes and 4,350 miles later at Nairobi airport and with an average speed of 567 mph, and was credited with setting a new (unofficial) record for that particular journey.

Three days later he flew XD859 back to Marham non-stop in 10 hours with another in-flight top-up over Malta, as did Sqn Ldr Price during his own return journey. These two receivers were followed home by the two tankers. Brian had demonstrated what could be done – almost in a quite routine way – and now the squadron rose to even greater heights – or perhaps that should be 'distances'!

On 16 April it was the turn of Wg Cdr Michael Beetham. At 02.30 GMT (Greenwich Mean Time) that morning Beetham in XD861 and a few minutes later, Brian Fern in XD859 took off from RAF Marham bound for Salisbury (Harare) in Southern Rhodesia (Zimbabwe) – or at least that was the destination for Michael Beetham. Brian's role was to act as an in-flight reserve aircraft to back-up his Squadron Commander. If all went well, XD861 would be flight-refuelled over the Libyan Desert by a tanker, XD870, flown by Sqn Ldr Garstin who, together with his own reserve tanker, a day or so earlier had repositioned from Marham to RAF Idris in order to be on station when Wg Cdr Beetham required more fuel. All did indeed go well and at 05.30 XD861 made a rendezvous at 40,000 feet altitude with the tanker over Libya, made a first-go hook-up for a 15-minute transfer of fuel, then pressed on southwards towards Salisbury. Sqn Ldr Garstin, his task completed, returned to Idris, where he was joined by Brian Fern in XD859, whose back-up receiver duty was also finished.

Wg Cdr Beetham in XD861 flew over the official timing point at Salisbury at 12.42 GMT, having flown a distance of 5,320 miles in a time of 10 hours and 12 minutes at an average speed of 521 mph, to complete the first non-stop flight between the two points and the longest non-stop flight by an RAF jet to date. Although obviously delighted with his record, Wg Cdr Beetham was quick to point out that the principal purpose of this and other flights like it, was to perfect team-work, planning, navigation, rendezvous and communications techniques that would improve flight re-fuelling operations as a whole. Brian returned to Marham in XD859 the next day and for the remainder of April life returned to normal with continuation and bombing training sorties. Wg Cdr Beetham refuelled twice, over Lake Victoria and Idris, and returned to Marham on 20 April.

There was much publicity for the RAF to be gained from these long-distance, refuelled flights. On 15 April, the day before Wg Cdr Beetham's flight, a press conference was held at Marham to brief the local and national press. Also present were the TV cameras of BBC and ITV, as well as film cameras from Pathé News that were there for the benefit of cinema audiences. The black-and-white Pathé film is still (in 2019) able to be viewed on that company's internet site and it contains a glimpse of Brian Fern and his crew seated at the briefing. An account of the exercise also appears in (archived) editions of *Flight* magazine.

May saw Wg Cdr Beetham make a Lone Ranger trip to Kano in Nigeria to check out the possibility of using that airfield as a tanker base while, on 28 May 1959, Sqn Ldr Garstin flew a Lone Ranger to Salisbury, Rhodesia. Refuelled over Idris, his flight time of 9 hours and 40 minutes at an average speed of 548 mph was another distance and speed record for the squadron. In support of Garstin's run, Brian took XD870 on a 'Tankex' op from Marham to Idris on the 26th, then he flew down to Embakasi from Idris on the 27th – a flying time of 6½ hours. He made the 10-minute hop from Embakasi to Eastleigh on the 29th, remaining at Eastleigh until 4 June. Repositioning again to Embakasi, Brian set off for home on 6 June and a 7-hour flight brought him to Luqa for a refuelling stop before continuing to Marham later that same day.

With this Squadron thirst for long-distance flying, still under the auspices of Trial 306, Brian was off to Africa again on 19 June in XD858, this time as a 'receiver' on a 'Tankex' mission direct to Salisbury, Rhodesia. Twice refuelled in flight, he completed the trip in 11 hours 30 minutes and remained there until 23 June when he completed the return to Marham again in one, air-refuelled sortie, lasting 11 hours 35 minutes. Flying sorties such as this was becoming quite routine for the sixteen tanker Valiants of 214 and it would become evident in the months to come that just one squadron of tankers would not be enough to meet the strategic demands of the RAF. But it was back to more mundane flying matters when Brian had to fit in his instrument rating check, do more Trial 306 practice and keep himself and his crew current in the use and application of the RBS on standard bombing practice sorties.

Wg Cdr Beetham was ever anxious to stretch the reach of the V-bomber force further and further and to this end he had his eye on one of the 'Blue Riband' records, the prestigious London to Cape Town route. Having checked out the airfield at Kano in Nigeria in May, Wg Cdr Beetham scheduled an air-refuelled run to the Cape for July 1959.

Sqn Ldr Brian Fern – promoted to squadron leader on 1 July 1959 – and his crew were selected as part of the refuelling support team for the squadron commander's record attempt and he flew down to Kano in XD869 on 7 July to make ready. Beetham made the non-stop flight in XD858 on 9 July crossing the official start-time point over London Airport, covering 6,060 miles in 11 hours 28 minutes at a speed of 530 mph by the time he had reached overhead D. F. Malan Airport, Cape Town; an official record. That day Brian was airborne over Kano acting as the secondary (standby) tanker for Wg Cdr Beetham's re-fuelling point but, in the event, he was not required to dispense any fuel and returned to Kano to await the CO's return trip. Beetham returned from Cape Town on 14 June and was, this time, flight-refuelled by Brian in XD869 over Kano. Wg Cdr Michael Beetham completed the return journey in 12 hours 20 minutes at an average speed of 492 mph, thereby beating the previous record, set by a Canberra, on both legs, and for which he received an Air Force Cross (AFC).

Feeding the flight crews on these long-duration sorties was a primitive affair. The Valiant was equipped with a small electric oven that was just about big enough to heat up food in tin cans. The personal ration for each member of the crew was one tin of chopped pork and one tin of soup for each 4-hour sortie, or multiples thereof, topped up with some sandwiches. Thus on a 12-hour trip, with six on board, the few storage spaces available would be crammed with upwards of thirty-six cans to be heated up and consumed in cramped conditions. On 15 June, Brian returned to Marham from Kano after what had been the highlight of the squadron's tanking exploits to date.

During September 1959 Brian made two more trips out to Luqa to practise tanking rendezvous and refuelling techniques with other Valiants on 'Sunspot' detachments. (Sunspot is a frequently used exercise enabling crews to experience oprating from Mediterranean or Middle East bases, e.g. Malta, Cyprus, Lybia; and to carry out high-level – 30,00+ feet – visual bombing practice.) While based in Malta he also participated in Exercise *Crescent Mace,* which was a major US Navy fleet exercise in the Mediterranean area. The US Sixth Fleet mounted simulated atomic strikes against its list of war targets, while Valiants of the RAF acted as 'enemy' bombers operating against the US surface vessels – in the event quite successfully, too.

For Sqn Ldr Brian Fern, things now began to turn interesting on the flight-refuelling front and having been designated in 214 Squadron as a flight-refuelling instructor, his undoubted expertise in this role was recognised when he became involved with the expansion of flight-refuelling to the Vulcan element of the RAF V-Force. This development represented a major step forward for the global aspirations of the RAF.

It was on 16 October 1959 that Brian went on a two-week temporary detachment to '17A' course run by 230 OCU at RAF Waddington to receive training as a co-pilot in an Avro Vulcan. His first dual sortie was a 3-hour session of circuits and bumps under the watchful eye of Flt Lt Thomas in Vulcan B1, XA898, during which he managed nine 'rollers', six instrument approaches and a full-stop landing. A week later he was sent up to RAF Finningley, to 101 Squadron, where he spent another few days on the flight deck of Vulcan B1, XA910, instructing Flt Lts Green and Wilson in the art of receiving fuel in-flight from a 214 Squadron Valiant tanker.

This interesting diversion was over by mid-November and Brian was back at Marham on routine bombing practice, flight-refuelling and sharing duties as 'A' Flight commander with Sqn Ldr Robert Furze. At the end of November 1959, a report was issued declaring the flight-refuelling Trial 306, which had kept 214 Squadron occupied since January 1958, was now complete. Although there was still work to be done on Trial 306A – the 'refuelling rendezvous' element – this was the point at which the RAF's V-Force flight-refuelling capability was officially declared operational. Only once does

Brian specifically mention the rendezvous aspect; when he flew a Trial 306A sortie on 26 November to test *Rebecca* and *Eureka* apparatus. This refers to development of the wartime radio navigational aid where the modern Mark X *Rebecca* was installed in a fuel-receiver aircraft and a *Eureka* beacon, with a 30–40-mile signal range, in the fuel-tanker. *Rebecca* had distance-measuring and directional capability and, in theory, enabled a receiver aircraft to home onto a *Eureka* signal emitted by a tanker while, for example, maintaining radio silence. The final outcome of Trial 306A is unclear.

According to those aircrew involved with flight-refuelling, in the pre-satellite navigation 1960s-era, the rendezvous (RV) point(s) for flight-refuelling were usually very well pre-planned jointly between the crews and squadrons involved, so that the RV point, time, altitude and heading was agreed between all parties. It would then be up to the navigator to enable his pilot to reach that point at the agreed time. The two aircraft involved would be in radio contact and able to keep each other informed of progress and timing. In clear air it would also be possible to spot a contrail from a substantial distance. One unpredictable factor could be the presence of cloud at the planned height and would sometimes require a last-minute adjustment to the refuelling altitude. Another factor was air turbulence, which had to be avoided if possible since it would make the hose and drogue unstable, and contact more difficult. Achieving precise position and timing accuracy was a challenging task for the navigators.

February 1960 saw Brian on his travels again when, on the 13th, he flew XD861 on a Tankex sortie out to Nairobi, receiving fuel *en route* during the 9-hour flight. On the 16th he flew on to El Adem, Libya, a 6-hour trip during which the tanker that was supposed to top him up could not get its hose to trail. Having reached El Adem, he refuelled on the ground and was back in Marham that evening, a round trip with 20 hours in the air. By the end of May 1960 Brian had a total of 3,000 flying hours in his log book and he seemed quite at ease hopping into a Valiant and flying to the other side of the world – but then, of course, he was not alone in this as it was only what had come to be expected of pilots in the elite V-bomber force. This strategic versatility was amply demonstrated again by 214 Squadron when it despatched Sqn Ldr John Garstin on a non-stop flight from Marham to Singapore on 26 May 1960.

With co-pilot Flt Lt Robert Pattullo and his crew: Flt Lt Hewson, Flt Sgt Terry, Sgt James and Fg Off Jeremiah, Brian set off on what turned out to be a one-month Tankex deployment to the Middle East as part of the tanker support for Sqn Ldr Garstin's long-distance Singapore Tankex flight. Brian left Marham on 22 May in XD860, in company with Sqn Ldr Furze's Valiant plus two spare aircraft, bound for Akrotiri, Cyprus. Furze and one spare plane would remain at Akrotiri as the first tanker for Garstin, while Brian and his spare aircraft refuelled and pressed on the next day with another 5-hour leg to RAF Mauripur (now Masroor air base) just outside Karachi in Pakistan. There Brian would take up the role of second tanker.

Fully fuelled, Brian took off from Mauripur on 26 May to rendezvous with Sqn Ldr Garstin and top him up. All went well; the two met up successfully and 80 minutes later Brian was back on the ground while Sqn Ldr Garstin winged his way eastwards. Sqn Ldr Garstin reached his destination at RAF Changi, Singapore, in 15 hours 35 minutes, having covered a non-stop distance of 8,110 miles at an average speed of 523 mph. He made the return trip on 1 June, being refuelled again by Brian Fern over Mauripur and Robert Furze over Cyprus. Sqn Ldr Garstin was awarded an AFC for this prodigious achievement. Brian, too, had to return home and he made an 11-hour non-stop flight from Karachi back to Marham on 2 June, meeting up with his tanker at RV9 over Nicosia's NDB (non-directional beacon). As a result of this – the longest flight-refuelled deployment by the RAF to date – the Air Ministry was satisfied with the way 214 Squadron had proved the effectiveness of the system and declared Trial 306 had been completed successfully.

After some leave Brian was back at Marham by 21 June and found himself selected to initiate the AOC 3 Group Bomber Command, AVM Michael Dwyer CBE, in the gentle art of receiving fuel in flight. This was achieved over a couple of days using WZ390 and XD870, by which time the AOC had successfully carried out eleven hook-ups. Brushing up his practice under Brian's careful eye, with another seven hook-ups on 1 July, AVM Dwyer was now considered competent enough to captain a Valiant on a goodwill flight to Vancouver, Canada, taking along Brian Fern as his co-pilot. It was to be the first time that an RAF jet would make a non-stop flight across the Atlantic and all the way to the west coast of Canada.

In common with the other long-distance flight recently undertaken, two Valiants that would act as primary and secondary tankers for AVM Dwyer's aircraft, were despatched a few days prior to the main event. These were XD859 with Flt Lt A. McDonald in command and XD860 captained by Flt Lt Alan Fisher. They departed RAF Marham at 11.00 on 2 July to deploy to the Canadian Air Force Base (AFB) at Goose Bay in Labrador where they would be fully refuelled and await the approach of AVM Dwyer. Unfortunately, there was a false start to events on 4 July; WZ390 went unserviceable (u/s) less than an hour into this Tankex sortie to Vancouver and AVM Dwyer was obliged to return to Marham. However, he, Brian and the crew set off again at 09.20 the next day (the 5th) in XD870 and rendezvoused with and took on fuel from both tankers during the course of the 5,060-mile westward journey to Sea Island Airport near Vancouver (now Vancouver International Airport). Dwyer hooked-up successfully to McDonald's XD859 around 12.00 over the Atlantic and later to Fisher's XD860 at 15.00 as progress was made across Canada. Valiant XD870 finally touched down at Sea Island at 19.58 on 5 July after a non-stop flight lasting 10 hours 38 minutes flown at an average speed of 483 mph. Both tankers returned to Goose Bay to await the return leg.

In the meantime, suitably refreshed from being strapped into an ejector seat for over 10 hours, the next afternoon AVM Dwyer and his crew took XD870 over to Comox AFB, less than an hour's flying time across the Strait of Georgia from Vancouver. There the Valiant was parked in the static display line for the annual air show while AVM Dwyer, Brian and the crew sampled the renowned British Columbian salmon fishing in the locality. Next day, 7 July, they flew XD870 back to Vancouver to prepare for the long flight home and an early start.

XD870 lifted off Vancouver runway at 03.55 and 4 hours later met up with Flt Lt McDonald's XD859 that had taken off from Goose Bay at 08.15 to make the refuelling rendezvous over the Canadian east coast. His tanker duty done, Flt Lt McDonald was back on the ground at Goose Bay at 09.41, his own aircraft was refuelled and 2 hours later he too was on his way back to Marham. Due to favourable winds and weather, Flt Lt Fisher was not needed to provide another top-up on AVM Dwyer's east-bound flight so, after accompanying McDonald to the rendezvous to act as backup in case of a problem, Fisher in XD860 independently made his way back to Marham. AVM Dwyer's XD870 landed at Marham at 13.45, just ahead of Fisher, down at 14.05, and McDonald coming in at 16.48, thus accounting for everyone safely back from this highly successful long-distance deployment. Dwyer and Brian had made the return non-stop flight from Vancouver to Marham in 9 hours 35 minutes at an average speed of 523 mph, thereby completing, with the first leg too, a double unofficial record for the distance.

For Sqn Ldr Brian Fern it was then back to more routine matters. He delivered XD812 to Hurn for modifications on 12 July then on the 14th he had his standardisation and tanker QFI check ride in WZ390 with Sqn Ldr Welford who put him through his paces for an aircraft captain check, six dry hook-ups and a manual landing. The remainder of the month it was back to more mundane bombing practice sorties until another small milestone in Brian's career was reached.

After a short leave, Sqn Ldr Brian Fern was posted to 49 Squadron as a Flight Commander and moved to take up his new job at RAF Wittering with effect from 29 August 1960. At this point in his RAF service, Brian had accumulated 3,062 flying hours, of which 884 were in the Vickers Valiant. During his time in a 'tanking' capacity with 214 Squadron he had carried out 219 'dry' contacts and 61 'wet' contacts, which led him to reach a high degree of experience in the practice of flight-refuelling, including gaining QFI status in the art. He had also played a significant role in 214's conversion to become the first V-Force air refuelling unit. The RAF, though, had not forgotten that Brian was a cog in its V-Force machine and that his reliability and wide experience could be put to great use in another squadron while allowing him to regain full currency in his primary V-Force role of strategic bomber captain.

As 'A' Flight commander, Brian began flying with his new squadron – commanded by Wg Cdr Ronald Payne AFC – in September 1960 and over the next few months, settled into a crew with Fg Off Fuller, co-pilot; Flt Lt Davidson; Flt Lt Holton and Flt Sgt Chilton and, although other names appeared in his crew from time to time, these became his most 'regular' companions. For several months there is little of great note in his log book entries, other than the constant RBS (Radar Bombing System) and navigation practice flights, cross-country exercises and diversions to other UK airfields. However, it is worthy of recording that Brian's first flight, on 6 September, in a 49 Squadron aircraft, was made in what is undoubtedly its most famous Valiant: XD818 – the bomber that dropped the first British atomic weapon in October 1956. It was 1 February 1961 before Brian flew XD818 again, on the occasion of doing various flying checks under the eye of the new commanding officer of the squadron: Wg Cdr Alan Chamberlain.

At the beginning of May 1961, however, came a Lone Ranger, No. 327, to break the monotony. On 1 May 1961 Brian and his regular crew took XD825 out to RAF Idris in Libya, a place Brian had flown to several times before. The following day they made the 6-hour flight from Idris down to Nairobi and the next day it was on to Salisbury (still in Rhodesia in those days) with Brian giving co-pilot Fuller – now a flight lieutenant – some time in the left-hand (captain's) seat. A couple of days rest and then the crew set off for Nairobi, again with Flt Lt Fuller taking the left-hand seat for this first leg of the return journey. From Nairobi, the next day Brian headed for Idris again but had to divert to Khartoum for the overnight stop but was able to fly to Idris early the following day, refuel and continue to Marham where he touched down later that same evening.

Between the 10th and 16 May 1961 there were two major UK air exercises to test both the offensive and defensive capability of the RAF. The offensive exercise was code-named *Mayflight* and tested, according to a government press release reported in Hansard:

> Bomber Command's ability to alert, disperse and subsequently to 'scramble' the V-bomber force and also to alert the Thor missile force. After being dispersed to pre-arranged airfields, the V-bombers will be scrambled on simulated operational missions and on their return to bases they will 'attack' targets in the UK to test the air defence system [comprising] control & reporting organisation, fighters and Bloodhound surface-to-air missiles.

The second phase exercise was code-named *Matador* and involved testing UK Fighter Command air defences against simulated retaliatory strikes by enemy forces, the latter being aircraft from RAF Germany, USAF, RCAF and the French Air Force. Needless to say, 49 Squadron was involved in all this excitement and on the 13th Brian flew one 5-hour day/night sortie in WP210.

The end of Brian's posting to 49 Squadron more or less coincided with the relocation of the squadron from Wittering to Marham on 26 June 1961, although he did not officially transfer to 214 Squadron until 25 August. The arrival of 49 Squadron at Marham brought the number of Valiant squadrons on the station to four. Unfortunately, Brian just missed almost certain involvement with what was regarded by many as the zenith of V-Force refuelling operations. That momentous – nay, monumental – event occurred on 20/21 June 1961 when Vulcan B1A, XH481 of 617 Squadron, captained by Sqn Ldr Mike Beavis, flew non-stop the 11,500 miles from RAF Scampton in Lincolnshire to Royal Australian Air Force (RAAF) base Richmond, Sydney, Australia, in 20 hours and 5 minutes at an average speed of 573 mph. It was supported by nine Valiant tankers of 214 Squadron topping up the Vulcan at four points down the route (which was obliged to avoid Russian and Chinese airspace) and this combined feat showed the world that the RAF indeed had a global reach. This bum-numbing, non-stop distance remains a record within the RAF – earning Sqn Ldr Beavis an AFC – and far exceeds even the mileage flown by the *Black Buck* Vulcan missions of the Falklands War. Beavis later became ACM Sir Michael, KCB CBE AFC.

With the completion of Trial 306, 214 Squadron now turned its attention to helping Fighter Command stretch its much smaller wings, by testing flight-refuelling for such aircraft as the two-seat Gloster Javelin. Training for Javelin FAW Mk 9 crews from 23 Squadron in how to receive fuel in-flight began in June 1960 and within a few months, trials had progressed to the extent that refuelled by 214 Squadron, four Javelin FAW Mk 9Rs ('R' indicated refuelling capability) from 23 Squadron were able to make a non-stop deployment to the RAAF base at Butterworth near Penang, Malaya. In addition to providing fuel in flight, the Valiants also acted as navigators for the Javelins as those aircraft were not equipped with long-range navigation aids. These trials were still ongoing when Brian rejoined 214 and he quickly became involved with Javelin refuelling training sorties. In December 1960 the Javelin pilots of 64 Squadron were also receiving AAR training using 214 Squadron tankers.

During August 1961, 90 Squadron, another Valiant unit based at RAF Honington, began training to undertake the flight-refuelling (FR) role and Brian became involved with that transition, too. On 29 August, he took up XD861 for quite a varied 4-hour sortie during which he gave 'dry' hook-ups to Javelins from 23 and Valiants of 90 Squadrons then rounded of the sortie with some RBS (bombing by radar) practice. On 5 September, in WZ390, he and his crew gave some instruction to Flt Lt Warwick who went along as co-pilot and Flt Lt Fisher (nav/rad), both from 90 Squadron, to see how a 'wet' hook-up was handled from the pilot and fuel-flow controller viewpoints. This was the order of things throughout September, October and November as the Javelin trials continued and 90 Squadron's crews were converted to refuelling operations. On 16 October, for example, Brian flew in 90 Squadron's XD813 with Flt Lt Shelley and his crew to check them out as a receiver crew, during which 4-hour sortie they carried out no less than twenty-four 'dry' contacts. On the 30th it was back to the Javelin boys, with Brian and his own crew flying XD860 to give them twelve contacts by night.

His own crew was now more or less settled as Flt Lt Robert Pattullo, co-pilot – a familiar face from his earlier posting – Flt Lts Mills and Wellen, and Master Signaller (MS) Fraser. Just to make sure he had not become 'rusty' and indeed to maintain his coveted 'Above Average' first pilot assessment,

14 December saw Brian complete a day/night, 10-hour full battle-profile flight that included three navigational stages, a full-transfer in-flight refuelling and a simulated RBS attack. Then the year was rounded off with yet more Javelin refuelling sorties. Brian's work with the Javelins of 23 Squadron had already paid off during mid-1961 when the fighters and tankers were tasked with making a rapid, simulated war deployment to Bahrain and back, via Cyprus and Karachi, as part of the British response to a crisis that had arisen between Kuwait and Iraq.

Avro Vulcan bombers had recently begun to have refuelling probes installed and in January 1962 this development again brought Brian into contact with the Vulcans of 101 Squadron, now based at RAF Waddington, when he had a short spell of instructing some of its pilots in the art of air-to-air refuelling. The instructional flights took the form of 3- to 4-hour AAR sorties with Brian in the co-pilot's seat flying with Flt Lt (later Gp Capt CBE AFC) Edward 'Ned' Frith in Vulcan XA913 on 8 January, followed by Flt Lt (later Gp Capt) John Ward in XH477 on the 9th and Sqn Ldr Malcolm Laidlay in XH477 on the 10th; Ward again on the 17th in XH477 and finally Frith again in XA913. Between them they practised seventy-three 'dry' contacts during the 17 flying hours of instruction. Brian also had a flight in XH481 on 13 March 1962 when he provided some AAR instruction to Sqn Ldr Wilson and Flt Lt Shepherd.

As mentioned above, Brian missed being involved with Beavis's Vulcan flight to Australia but it will be noted from the serial numbers shown here that he did at least have the opportunity to fly Vulcan XH481, the aircraft Beavis used, since it had been transferred to 101 Squadron subsequent to its record flight. In another small twist, Brian can also claim to have flown the 'film-star' Vulcan, XA913, which actually made a fleeting appearance in the James Bond movie *Thunderball*. Part of the film's plot featured the hijacking of a Vulcan bomber over the Caribbean. Images of XA913 were used in the ground filming sequences for the film, which was released in 1965.

It was in late-March 1962 that Brian was again actively involved in supporting another record attempt, this time an official one made by a Vulcan of 101 Squadron between London and Aden. The Vulcan involved was XH483, flown by Flt Lt John Ward who, it will be recalled, had received AAR instruction from Brian a couple of months earlier. Writing on the 'blog.aerco.co.uk' site in 2009, Group Captain John Ward recalled that instruction and his record flight.

101 squadron, which still had the Mk 1A, was to take over the [Vulcan] flight-refuelling role in January 1962. I was one of three captains chosen to train in this role. The first flights were undertaken under the guidance of experienced Valiant tanker captains but we were soon on our own, building up skill and confidence.

In March 1962, HQ Bomber Command agreed to send a Vulcan to participate in the Annual Open Day at RAF Khormaksar, Aden, and by employing in-flight refuelling, attempt to break the existing official point-to-point speed record from London to Aden. Aden would have been within the Vulcan's 3,000-mile range at normal cruising speed, but by flying faster with increased fuel consumption, an in-flight refuel was essential. I was chosen to do this flight, which took place

on 30 April [1962] and we [flight-] refuelled once near Malta
and arrived at Aden after six hours and thirteen minutes at an
average speed of 590 mph.

On return to Waddington I was congratulated by the
squadron commander who told me the Royal Aero Club
[RAeC] had confirmed the establishment of a new world speed
record between London and Aden. In due course I received the
Record Certificate but what was much greater surprise was
the news that I had been awarded the Geoffrey de Havilland
Trophy for 1962. The Trophy had been created in memory
of Geoffrey de Havilland junior who, as the de Havilland
Company's chief test pilot, had been killed in the experimental
Swallow aircraft in 1946. Subsequently the Trophy was
awarded annually to the British pilot setting the fastest time in
any official race or record.

The official FAI statistics for John Ward's record run were:
distance, 3,673.7 statute miles; time, 6h 13m 59.7s; average
speed, 589.4 statute miles per hour. It was also the first
record-bid to have its start timed by radar. The Vulcan took
off from Waddington and flew across London at 38,000 feet
altitude where the start of its record run was timed over the
centre of the city by Sopley radar control centre.

Needless to say, the re-fuelling component of this record
attempt was vital to its success and Brian played his part. As
part of a 214 Squadron refuelling detachment, on 25 March
Brian and his crew flew out from Marham to El Adem. On
27 March he carried out a Javex (Javelin) refuelling sortie in the
vicinity of El Adem then, the next day, flew to Luqa in Malta to
await the passing 101 Squadron Vulcan. Brian was designated

as secondary (back-up) tanker for the refuel over Malta that John Ward mentioned above.

On 31 March Brian flew his Valiant, XD860, from Luqa to Khormaksar, Aden, where on 2 April he carried out another Javex sortie, landing back at Khormaksar the same day. Transferring to XD812 Brian and his crew, this time with crew chief C/T Partridge on board, flew back to Marham next day in a single, flight-refuelled, trip lasting 9 hours and 30 minutes. It had certainly been a busy and varied ten-day deployment.

Brian visited 101 Squadron at RAF Waddington again on 11 April. On this occasion he flew one sortie in Vulcan XH479 with Flt Lt John Ward who had, since Brian's last visit, had been categorised as a Vulcan AAR Qualified Instructor – as indeed had Flt Lt Ned Frith too. On this particular flight another 101 Squadron Vulcan captain, Flt Lt Bernie Revnell, was being converted to the AAR role under instruction from John Ward. Brian Fern's presence on the flight deck was to assess John Ward's performance and formally authorise him to carry out the conversion of the rest of 101 Squadron – including his CO, Wg Cdr Arthur Griffiths! During this authorisation flight, they carried out twenty contacts as a receiver aircraft and in order to monitor what both pilots were doing, Brian would have had to have stood at the top of the crew entry ladder just behind them.

In April 1962, Nos. 214 and 90 Squadrons officially lost their 'bomber' role entirely and were re-designated as flight-refuelling squadrons. It was intended to designate a third Valiant unit for flight-refuelling but government funding was not forthcoming and by the time that situation changed, the Valiant force had been struck down by its well-documented main-spar fatigue problem, so the third unit did not materialise.

Brian became involved in yet another experimental operation during July 1962 that required the services of all the tankers that the RAF could muster at that time. The test, referred to as Trial 448, was the RAF's attempt to emulate the USAF Strategic Air Command (SAC) policy of keeping a number of armed strategic bombers in the sky continuously. The RAF's Trial 448 set out to test the feasibility of and logistics required to keep Vulcan bombers – not just a single aircraft of course – airborne continuously for fourteen days. This was at the time when the United Kingdom had agreed to purchase a thermo-nuclear armed, air-launched ballistic missile (ALBM) called 'Skybolt' from the USA. It was realised that the possession of such a weapon made RAF bomber bases targets for possible pre-emptive strikes by a potential enemy and it was with this in mind the RAF decided to examine what was referred to as Continuous Airborne Alert. The trials called for the current Vulcan force to operate an aircraft in an orbit over the North Sea. It would be refuelled at intervals to extend its time on station and replacement sorties were planned to overlap so that one aircraft would be airborne in the prescribed pattern at all times.

Brian began his stint on Trial 448 in WZ390, as primary tanker to the 'duty' Vulcan, with a 90-minute refuelling sortie on 3 July. He repeated this procedure in XD859 on the 4th; in XD871 on the 6th; twice on the 7th in WZ390 and XD870 and twice more in those aircraft on the 10th. He then made one refuelling sortie in WZ390 on the 12th before his last for the trial on the 13th. The trial was brought to a close and the Continuous Airborne Alert idea was shelved. The main difficulties encountered were a lack of adequate resources in the form of both bombers and AAR tankers; tying-up aircraft and aircrew on a limited mission; crew fatigue; cost of fuel and aircraft maintenance issues. Avro had even proposed an improved version of the Vulcan, which included an enlarged cockpit space for additional crew but when the American government decided unilaterally to scrap 'Skybolt' in late-1962, none of this ever materialised.

For Brian Fern, the end of Trial 448 also drew a line under his own long involvement with flight-refuelling and he bowed out from squadron service. He flew his last tanker flight on 23 July 1962 in XD812 and had the privilege of giving the station commander of RAF Marham, Gp Capt Ian Campbell AFC, some AAR instruction during which they carried out twelve 'dry' receiver contacts in a 3½-hour sortie.

At the end of his time with 214 Squadron, Brian's log book showed a total of 3,584 flying hours. As meticulous as ever, he had analysed his tanker sorties and noted that during his two postings with 214 Squadron – August 1957 to August 1960 and July 1961 to July 1962 – he had carried out 680 'dry' contacts and 138 'wet' contacts; a grand total of 818 hook-ups since he flew his first Trial 306 sortie back in June 1958. This marked the end of his jet-flying career and at the end of July 1962, Sqn Ldr Brian Fern was posted to Headquarters Bomber Command (Air 1 d) at High Wycombe to fly a desk for a couple of years as an Air Staff Officer.

RAF Gatow had played a vital role during the Berlin Airlift of 1948/49 when it was the termination point for thousands of supply flights made by the RAF from RAF Wunstorf in Allied West Germany to the beleaguered British-controlled sector of Berlin. After the blockade was lifted, Gatow became the base for the British Army's Berlin Infantry Brigade and the airfield handled transport aircraft carrying out flights that conveyed troops to and from the Brigade and the Berlin garrison. Under the wartime Potsdam Agreement made between the four main Allied countries: Great Britain, USA, France and Russia, although Berlin was inside Russian-controlled East Germany, Britain (and the others) had the legal right to use the airspace over both West and East Berlin and to have access to its sector of Berlin by means of an air corridor each. In the case of Britain this was a corridor from West Germany in the vicinity of Wunstorf to RAF Gatow in the city of Berlin itself.

Soon after the end of the Second World War, airspace over the city was designated as the Berlin Control Zone (BCZ) and aircraft from all the Allied Powers were permitted to fly within that area. BCZ was a circular area with a 20 nautical mile radius centred on what was known as the Berlin Air Safety Centre (BASC), a building occupied by the Allied Control Authority located on the Kleistpark in Berlin. Here, Air Force officer representatives from all four Allied Powers were accommodated and they were tasked to co-ordinate with each other, the approval, control and safety of air movements within BCZ and the three 20-mile-wide air corridors to the West. BASC was also required to work closely with the Berlin Air Route Traffic Control Centre (BARTCC) located at Templehof Air Base.

After his two-and-a-half-year stint at HQBC was up in January 1965, Brian Fern was posted to RAF Gatow, initially as Senior Administration Officer and deputy to the station commander, Gp Capt Robert 'Bobby' Oxspring DFC** AFC, the renowned Battle of Britain fighter pilot. Later, Brian took on the roles of Admin/Air officer and OC Flying at the station. He had done no flying during his spell at HQBC and at Gatow there was no resident flying unit except the grandly named Station Flight.

This latter was composed of just two DHC Chipmunk T10s, an aircraft which was a single-engine, fixed undercarriage, two-seat trainer in service with the RAF. During the time Brian was at Gatow, the two Chipmunks operated were WG303 and WK587and he flew both these aircraft during his time at the station. Ostensibly these two innocuous small aircraft were on charge so that any pilots posted to the station could maintain their flying currency and thus be eligible to draw flying pay. However, there was another clandestine task for which these two Chipmunks – and their replacements in later years – were employed and in which Brian appears to have been involved.

From time to time these aircraft were used for low-level reconnaissance sorties inside the authorised BCZ. Such sorties were made at the request of and in co-ordination with an organisation called the British Commander-in-Chief's Mission to the Soviet Forces of Occupation in Germany, otherwise known as BRIXMIS. BCZ naturally covered an area occupied on the ground by both Russian and East German military forces and installations and as such was of considerable interest to the West. The British took advantage of the Agreement and not only regularly exercised its right to fly over Russian territory within the BCZ but also, from 1956 at irregular intervals, used these flights – classified as Top Secret – to gather intelligence under various code names such as Operation *Schooner*; *Nylon* and later, *Oberon*. As far as the Chipmunk flights were concerned intelligence gathering usually took the form of photography and/or visual observation of potential interesting-looking installations and troop activity and the flights were often co-ordinated with BRIXMIS intelligence-gathering activity (sometimes described as 'Tours') on the ground. This is where Brian's flying experience came in.

The crew of the Chipmunks consisted of a staff pilot – such as Brian – who usually flew the aeroplane from the rear cockpit and an 'observer' in the front seat. The observer was a member of BRIXMIS – usually someone of non-commissioned rank with experience in an RAF photography trade – and who was equipped with a hand-held camera sporting a high-quality telephoto lens. The sorties were flown at about 500 feet altitude and WG303 and WK587 were used between 1958 and 1967 for this task and were found to be a stable platform and ideal for the purpose. According to entries in his log book, these were the two aircraft flown by Brian at various times during his posting at Gatow from January 1965 to August 1967. Chipmunks WP850 and WP971 were operated from Gatow between 1967 and 1974, then WZ862 and WD289 from 1974 to the mid-1980s, followed finally by WG466 and WG486 until 1989 when the Berlin Wall came down and the Soviet Warsaw Pact Alliance changed fundamentally. WG486 is now (2019) still flying in the UK as part of the RAF Battle of Britain Memorial Flight at RAF Coningsby.

There is little doubt that the Russians knew exactly what was going on and no doubt were also doing their own version of this covert operation. Every Chipmunk flight, whatever its purpose, had to be cleared at BASC and it is reported that the Russian controller always endorsed the Chipmunk flight notification cards: 'Safety of flight Not Guaranteed', because the Russians – rather conveniently for them – interpreted the terms of the 1946 Agreement to mean the exclusion of any flight in airspace outside that immediately over West Berlin Sector. In effect this gave the Russians leave to take a potshot, if they so wished, at an aircraft wandering about in their airspace over East Berlin – even though it might still be within BCZ airspace!

Brian had his first flight in a Chipmunk on 9 March 1965 when Flt Lt Youngs took him up for 45 minutes in WK587 to get his air-legs back again. The pair made another similar flight the next day and then Brian took it up solo for an hour, after which he was declared as checked out on the 'Chippie'. Unsurprisingly, Brian's log book entries give no indication of anything of a covert nature and all are simply noted as 'Local' with occasional reference to a 'GCA approach'; air test or the occasional 'joy-riding' passenger (e.g. the local padres). During his posting to RAF Gatow, Brian flew Chipmunk WK587 on seventeen occasions and WG303 on eighteen occasions, so the quantity of flights is actually quite small and averages about one a month – but they are quite random and of course there would have been other pilots on the station who could have taken the two Chipmunks up on these spy flights on other occasions.

To keep the clandestine nature of a flight from prying eyes, the crew climbed aboard the aircraft while it was in a closed hangar. The pilot would start-up with the crew already in place; the doors would be opened for the Chipmunk to emerge innocuously and trundle out for take-off. Landing after about a 90-minute sortie, the reverse procedure would be carried out and all the photographer needed to do was to put his camera kit into a bag and both crewmen would leave the hangar by a back door. It probably fooled no one – but these spy sorties were flown about two or three times a week for thirty-five years without any serious mishaps.

For most of the time Brian's duties were administrative in nature, he himself noting that this included: 'Daily contact with British Foreign Office officials and other members of the British Military Government. Close liaison with United States and French military personnel; civilian officials and members of the West Berlin German authorities.'

On 8 May 1967 Brian wrote to the Ministry of Defence to apply for an early retirement, which was approved and a date for his retirement set at 8 September 1967. At that date he was a month short of his 44th birthday; had completed twenty years and four months in his two periods of service with the RAF and his log book total stood at 3,601 flying hours.

Brian joined Barclays Bank under an ex-officer recruitment scheme and initially worked as a cashier in charge of a number of sub-branches of the bank. It was not long before he was promoted to Premises Assistant in Barclays Exeter Head Office and he was employed by the bank for twelve years. During the latter part of these years, though, the health of Brian's wife deteriorated and during 1979 her illness became so serious that she was totally incapacitated. In June 1979, therefore, in order to care for his wife, Brian took early retirement from the bank but sadly his wife died in October of that same year. Picking up his life again, Brian joined Abbey Life Assurance Co in 1979 and as an associate, helped to set up a branch office in Lincoln where he remained until 1984 when he resigned from Abbey Life. Between 1984 and 1995 he held the post of Financial Planning Manager with an investment consultancy in Brighton. Brian re-married and finally retired to Lincolnshire, where he died in 2005 at the age of eighty-one.

As far as the V-Bomber force was concerned, by the end of 1964 it had been established that all Vickers Valiant aircraft were suffering from metal fatigue in the wing spars and attachments and the aircraft was retired from RAF service by the end of 1965. The final Valiant tanker sortie was flown on 9 December 1964 by XD812 of 214 Squadron and the last Valiant bomber sortie was made on the same date by XD818, both of which aeroplanes had been flown at some point by Brian Fern. Air-to-air refuelling duties were passed on to the Handley Page Victor squadrons but in 1966, even though this facility still gave the RAF a global reach, control and responsibility for the global delivery of the British nuclear weapon was passed to the Royal Navy in the form of its Polaris missile-equipped nuclear submarine force. The first operational patrol of a Polaris submarine began in June 1968. Brian's flying career therefore drew to a close in effect at the time as the V-force went into decline and the RAF could be said to revert to the more tactical, battlefield support concept that Leonard Dawes helped to create all those years ago, although air-to-air refuelling (AAR) still remains the key to enabling the RAF's aircraft to 'fight these fires' around the world.

Vickers Valiant and Avro Vulcan aircraft flown by Brian Fern.
232 OCU Valiant: WZ361; WZ362; WZ364; WZ368; WZ371.

214 Sqn Valiant: WP212; WP217; WP219; WZ367**; WZ379; WZ390; WZ395; WZ404; XD812; XD816; XD821; XD858; XD859; XD860; XD861;

XD869; XD870; XD871; XD874.

The aircraft marked ** was one of two Valiant detached to Maralinga, Australia, in 1956 for the first air-dropped A-bomb tests. The cockpit of XD816 is preserved in Brooklands Museum (as at 2019).

49 Sqn Valiant: WP210; WP218; XD818*; XD822*; XD823*; XD824*; XD825*; XD829; XD857.

Those marked * are aircraft that dropped H-bombs during Operation *Grapple* atomic weapons tests at Christmas Island in 1957. XD818 is now (2019) on display in the RAF Museum Cosford as the only remaining fully-intact Vickers Valiant in the world. The cockpit of XD857 is owned by and awaiting restoration at the Norfolk & Suffolk Air Museum, Flixton, Norfolk (as at 2019).

90 Sqn Valiant: XD813.

101 Sqn Vulcan: XA898; XA910; XA913; XH477; XH479; XH481.

BIBLIOGRAPHY

Brett, R. Dallas, *History of British Aviation, 1908–1914*, Vols 1 & 2 (London: The Aviation Book Club, 1934).

Brookes, Andrew, *Valiant Units of The Cold War* (London: Osprey Publishing, 2012).

Caldwell, Donald, *JG26; Luftwaffe Fighter Wing War Diary 1939–42* (London: Grub Street, 1996).

Caygill, Peter, *The Biggin Hill Wing 1941, From Defence To Attack* (Barnsley: Pen & Sword, 2008).

Cross, Kenneth & Orange, Vincent, *Straight and Level* (London: Grub Street, 1993).

Denson, Paula K., *The RAF in Oklahoma* (USA: Oklahoma Heritage Association, 2005).

Docherty, Tom, *Swift to Battle, 72 Squadron RAF in Action, Vol 1: 1937–1942* (Barnsley: Pen & Sword, 2009).

Franks, Norman, *Fighter Command's Air War 1941; RAF Circus Operations & Fighter Sweeps against the Luftwaffe* (Barnsley: Pen & Sword, 2016).

Goodrum, Alastair, *Dying To Fly* (Stroud: The History Press, 2011).

Goodrum, Alastair, *No Place for Chivalry* (London: Grub Street, 2005).

Guttman, Jon, *Zeppelin vs British Home Defence 1915–1918* (London: Osprey Publishing, 2018).

Hiller, Mark, *A Fighter Command Station at War; Westhampnett* (Barnsley: Frontline Books, 2015).

Igglesden, Mike, *A Brief History of No. 6 BFTS* (self-published).

Jacobs, Peter, *Stay the Distance; Life & Times of MRAF M. Beetham* (Barnsley: Frontline Books, 2011).

Jane, Fred, *Jane's All the World's Aircraft, 1913* (Project Gutenberg archive)

Jefford, Wg Cdr C. G., *Observers and Navigators in RFC, RNAS and RAF* (London: Grub Street, 2014).

Killegrew, Tom, *The Royal Air Force in American Skies* (Denton Tx, USA: University of North Texas Press, 2015).

Lake, Deborah, *Tartan Air Force; Scotland and a century of military aviation 1907–2007* (Edinburgh: Birlinn Ltd, 2009).

McInnes, I, & Webb, J. V., *A Contemptible Little Flying Corps* (London: London Stamp Company, 1991).

Merriam, Frederick Warren, *First Through The Clouds, Autobiography of a Box-Kite Pioneer* (Barnsley: Pen & Sword Books Ltd, 2018).

Morley, Robert M., *Earning Their Wings, British Pilot Training 1912–1918* (Canada: MA Thesis; University of Saskatchewan, 2006).

Napier, Michael, *Gloster Javelin; an Operational History* (Barnsley: Pen & Sword, 2015)

Onderwater, Hans, *Second To None; History of No. II (AC) Squadron* (London: Airlife, 1992).

Oxspring, Gp Capt Robert Wardlow, *Spitfire Command* (London: Kimber, 1984).

Scott, Gp Capt A. J. L., *Sixty Squadron RAF* (London: William Heinemann, 1920).

Sturtivant, Ray, *RAF Flying Training & Support Units since 1912* (Tonbridge: Air Britain, 2007).

Tan, Jon E. C., *Aces, Airmen and the Biggin Hill Wing; A Collective Memoir 1941–1942* (Barnsley: Pen & Sword, 2016).

US Department of the Interior, National Park Service: National Register of Historic Places: Darr School of Aeronautics, Kay County, Oklahoma, OMB No. 1024–0018.

The Times History of the War, (e.g.) Vol 5, page 319.

Central Flying School Association: www.centralflyingschool. org.uk.

Cross & Cockade Magazine: www.crossandcockade.com.

Dundee Courier.

Flight Magazine.

Lichfield Mercury.

London Gazette.

Tamworth Herald.

National Archives, AIR series documents: e.g. AIR1/29/60, CFS ORB. AIR1/204/4/153 List of RFC pilots. AIR 27/822; 104 Sqn ORB; AIR50/30/45 Combat Reports. AIR76/433/197 & 524/48; Officer's Service Records.

www.airhistory.org.uk

www.airwar19141918.wordpress.com

www.aviationpostcard.co.uk

www.projectgutenberg.com

www.thenorthernecho.co.uk

www.westfrontassoc.mtcdeserver.com

ACKNOWLEDGEMENTS

In the preparation of this book, I have received help from many people over the years and I am grateful to them all, but I would like to mention the following in particular.

John and Richard Barwell for information and access to and permission to use material from documents and photographs relating to their father, Group Captain Philip Reginald Barwell DFC; Mrs Freda Fern for allowing me access to and permission to use material in logbooks, personal documents and photos of her late husband, Sqn Ldr Brian Fern, and for her personal recollections and kind hospitality; Mike Charlton of www.aviationpostcard. co.uk for his help with pre-First World War images; John Chester, Western Front Association – Spalding Branch; Martyn Chorlton for providing advice, contacts and images; Michael Davis, editor of Cross & Cockade Magazine for permission to quote from various articles; Paula Denson (USA) for her help with images and information about No. 6 BFTS Ponca City USA; Aldon Ferguson, 611 Squadron historian, for his help with photographs; Flightglobal Archive; Norman Franks for his generous access to Biggin Hill-related photographs; Paul Gausden for personal recollections of his time with No. 214 Squadron; Mike Igglesden for his help with information about BFTS flying training schools in America during the Second World War; Helen Jordan for assistance with images from BAE SYSTEMS Heritage Dept, Farnborough; Victoria Northridge, Collections Access at IWM London; Jeremy Ransome, editor of *Lincolnshire Free Press* and *Spalding Guardian* newspapers (Iliffe Publishing Ltd) for access to and permission to use archive material; Vic Savage, for his recollections about his service as a former RAF Valiant crew chief; Marvin L. Skelton for information about No. 2 Squadron in its early days; Geoff Taylor of Heritage South Holland; www.heritagesouthholland.co.uk; Group Captain John Ward, former pilot with No. 101 Squadron, for his personal recollections of Vulcan flight-refuelling operations; Guy Warner, historian, for permission to quote from his articles about No. 2 Squadron; Montrose Air Station Heritage Centre: rafmontrose.org.uk; President and Council of Spalding Gentlemen's Society for access to archive material; Connor Stait; Shaun Barrington and the team at Amberley Publishing.

Relating to Crown copyright material, this book contains public sector information licensed under the Open Government Licence v.3.0 (www.nationalarchives.gov.uk/doc/open-government-licence.version/3/). Crown copyright is also acknowledged through MOD Consent Licence Version 3.0, April 2016 (www.gov.uk/government/publications/crown-copyright-mod-consent-licence).

Illustrations have come from many sources across the world and in view of the passage of up to one hundred years in some cases, the original ownership of some images remains obscure or has been unable to be established and/or verified and I apologise for any due credit omitted for this reason.

INDEX

Also available from Amberley Publishing

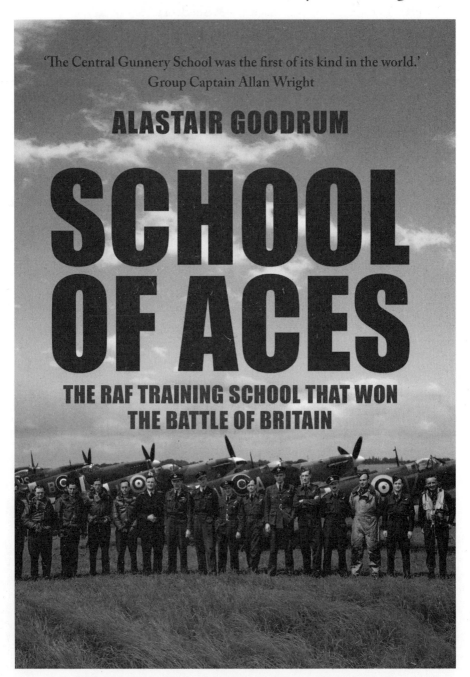

'The Central Gunnery School was the first of its kind in the world.'
Group Captain Allan Wright

ALASTAIR GOODRUM

SCHOOL
OF ACES

THE RAF TRAINING SCHOOL THAT WON
THE BATTLE OF BRITAIN